WI

WINE
BUYER'S
GUIDE

DORLING KINDERSLEY
London • New York • Stuttgart • Moscow

A DORLING KINDERSLEY BOOK

First published in Great Britain in 1996
by Dorling Kindersley Limited,
9 Henrietta Street, London WC2E 8PS
Visit us on the World Wide Web at http://www.dk.com

Copyright © 1996 Dorling Kindersley Ltd, London
Text and illustration copyright © 1996,
WINE Magazine.

A CIP catalogue second for this book is available
from the British Library.

ISBN 0 7513 0395 X

Printed and bound in Great Britain
by Bath Press Colourbooks, Glasgow

CONTENTS

INTRODUCTION

No sooner have you focused your attention on one bottle on the shelf than another barges its way into your line of vision, screaming 'Try me!' The merchant's shelf is indeed a bitter and confusing battleground, where wines from around the world jostle for position and favour. Some rely on fancy packaging and enticing label literature; others rely on reputation and word-of-mouth. The majority, however, are often an unknown quantity.

The citizens of many other nations, of course, never face quite such a dilemma. Their shelves are stocked mainly with national produce, providing little choice and even less scope for experimentation. Britain, on the other hand, profits from little national bias and an innovative market, in which wines from around the world can be bought in the local high street. What method, then, does one use to distinguish the good from the bad, the star performer from the pretender in the designer shirt but dirty vest?

THE WINES LAID BARE

WINE magazine's International WINE Challenge is precisely that method, laying bare thousands of wines of every style before several hundred of the world's most finely tuned palates. The following pages list the 1,600 medal winners from the 1996 International WINE Challenge, by nationality and price. Whether it's a zingy Sauvignon Blanc for a summer picnic, a plummy Burgundy for a winter feast or a fine fizz for sheer pleasure, you will find a great selection, together with tasting notes, guide prices and availability.

THE CHALLENGE

WINE magazine's International WINE Challenge was created in 1984 by Robert Joseph, WINE's publishing editor, and Charles Metcalfe, associate editor, as the basis of an article which examined how English wine-makers were doing compared to their counterparts in other countries. Neither had any idea at that stage that the Challenge would transform itself into the world's most international, most comprehensive and, increasingly, most respected wine competition.

During the past 12 years, the number of wines entered into the Challenge has grown from 38 to 6,500. The number of professional judges has risen from 20 to 350.

Broken down to a basic level, the Challenge's success lies in two essential factors. The first is the support it receives from both the wine trade in this country and the wine producers elsewhere in the world; the second is the ruthless impartiality and organisation with which it is run.

A taster putting wine into words

During the past ten years, wines appearing in this country have become increasingly diverse, due mainly to wine retailers looking to attract the consumer. Wines from the former Soviet republic of Moldova now sit alongside Australian Chardonnay and German Gewürztraminer.

However, the difficulty for retailers is that diversity is not enough; quality and value for money are the real

The infamous Super-Juror acted as an essential safety net

selling points, especially to discerning British consumers. The same is true within the wine trade itself, where restaurateurs buying from importers are justly looking to make money from the wines they put on their lists. Consequently, both retail and trade sectors quickly recognised the need for a fair method of evaluating the wines on the market and, more importantly, for an effective mechanism of putting the results across to the wine drinker.

Thus their support for the International WINE Challenge began, and so it continues. Companies ranging from such retail giants as Safeway, Tesco and Marks & Spencer, retail chains such as Thresher, Wine Cellar and Victoria Wine, to specialist merchants such as Justerini & Brooks and Morris & Verdin all submit wines to compete on level terms.

Equally important is the support of such companies in the evaluation of Challenge wines, for it is their representatives who judge each and every wine. Buyers from these companies, renowned for their experience and accuracy, together with winemakers from all over the world and

Britain's most respected wine writers make up the tasting team which works so hard for the two weeks of the Challenge. It is their involvement that generates the unique trust in the results, and reinforces the care with which every entrant to the Challenge is examined.

The process begins in January, when entry kits are distributed to thousands of companies worldwide, inviting them to submit their wines. Within a few weeks, the replies start pouring in, detailing information on every wine to be tasted, such as the principle grape varieties used and the regions in which the grapes were grown.

Once this information is logged in, the entire Challenge team descends to the venue to begin receiving the wines themselves. Some are delivered by local companies; others are New World samples brought in specially by courier. During the next two weeks, 28,000 individual bottles are unpacked, labelled and coded.

The team of international wine tasters in full flow

Next comes the 'flighting': placing entries into groups of 12-18 wines. All wines within a group are similar in origin, variety and retail price so that they can be evaluated fairly among equals. This process normally takes the team of 24 Challenge helpers several days. Bottles are then inserted into special 'co-extruded' wine bags, tagged with tamper-proof seals, and

The Challenge team checks and re-checks

boxed, ready for tasting. Sparkling wines are chilled, vintage ports decanted and wines with distinctive bottles transferred.

It is now that the tasters arrive in droves, only to be split into tasting teams of five or six to tackle the wines. Flights are tasted, removed and recorded. Corked bottles are replaced within four minutes, and corks pulled at an alarming rate. Over 1,500 wines are tasted each day.

Lurking beneath is the less glamorous process of control. All results are double-checked; discarded wines are tasted once again by a 'Super Juror', an experienced and respected trade member or Master of Wine whose task it is to ensure no worthy wine slips the net. Tasting sheets proceed to the computer 'nerve-centre', where every result is recorded and double-checked to ensure accuracy. This information is used to create the flights for the second-round tasting, where medals are awarded by a separate panel of judges. Attention to detail is meticulous: even the chlorine was removed from a nearby fountain to reduce the risk of contaminating smells!

After two weeks of frenetic activity, the medals are decided. This year, only 131 Gold Medals were awarded, indicating how harshly some of the best palates in the world judge some of the best wines in the world.

All of which helps to explain why, when you buy the winners listed in this book, you'll be drinking some of the tastiest, most interesting and best-value wines in the world.

THE TROPHIES

Having tasted the wines and chosen the Gold Medal winners, the final task is to select supreme champions in each category: the Trophy winners. At this stage, considerations such as price and volume of production are disregarded; wines compete against each other on their intrinsic qualities alone.

The judges in this year's trophy tasting were, for the most part, the Super-Jurors who had toiled so hard during the Challenge. Among them were David Peppercorn MW, Dr Caroline Gilby MW, Patrick McGrath MW, Maggie McNie MW, Charles Crawfurd MW, Robin Crameri MW, wine writers Charles Metcalfe, Oz Clarke and Tom Stevenson, Geraldine Jago of Victoria Wine and Hew Blair of Justerini & Brooks.

Unlike other events, the judges were not constrained by the obligation to award a single Trophy in every category. From the outset, they were told to make awards only where they thought they were deserved.

The first trophy to be awarded in the white wine section was for CHARDONNAY, and this brought one of the greatest-ever surprise victories. The winner was the **Nekeas Barrel-Fermented Chardonnay 1994** from

Navarra, in Spain. This wonderfully complex wine outclassed many more reputable Chardonnays, and was approved by one and all.

The Sauvignon Blanc category proved a great disappointment this year, with no trophy awarded. Last year's wash-out in New Zealand may well be the culprit, but it is worrying that no other region could step into its shoes. Fortunately, relief came in the form of a Viognier so exceptional that the judges decided to create a special VIOGNIER TROPHY. This went to **Les Ceps du Nébadon Condrieu 1993**, from the vineyards of Paret et Depardieu.

The AROMATIC TROPHY went to **Domaine Zind-Humbrecht's Heimbourg Gewurztraminer 1992**, making a hat-trick for this Alsace producer – a remarkable feat in the face of three years' stiff competition.

Moving onto the reds, California drew first blood in spectacular fashion: a single producer claimed two separate trophies, beating such heavyweights as Château Lynch-Bages 1990 in the process. The BORDEAUX-STYLE TROPHY went to **Ridge Monte Bello Cabernet Sauvignon 1991**, while the SPICY RED TROPHY was awarded, after a great deal of deliberation, to **Ridge Geyserville Zinfandel 1992**.

Bitterly fought contests took place in the red wine categories, the

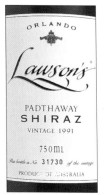

fiercest for the BURGUNDY-STYLE TROPHY, which resulted in the judges awarding a joint trophy to two outstanding wines, both from California: the **Rochioli Pinot Noir 1993**, from Russian River Valley, and **Au Bon Climat Pinot Noir 1994**, from the Santa Maria Valley.

The quality of finalists competing for the ITALIAN TROPHY was exceptional. The winner, **Terre Brune 1992**, by **Santadi** of Sardinia, was eventually preferred to the Barbaglio Rosso del Salento 1993 and the Cumaro Rosso Conero 1993.

Competition for the RHONE-STYLE TROPHY was equally lively, with a very close contest between New and Old Worlds. Eventually, a single winner emerged: the wonderful **Lawson's Shiraz 1991** from **Orlando Wines** in Padthaway, South Australia.

The judges declined to award a Spanish Red Trophy, but instead created a trophy for a wine they felt to be an exceptional example of its type. Hence, the special AUSTRIAN RED TROPHY was awarded to **Weingut Stiegelmar's Juris St-Laurent 1993**.

The final award in the red section was the PORTUGUESE RED TROPHY, which, after careful deliberation, was given to the **Duas Quintas Reserva 1992** by **Ramos-Pinto**.

The SPARKLING TROPHY became a three-horse race. **Champagne Louise Pommery Cuvée Speciale Brut 1987** emerged victorious, defeating Veuve Clicquot Rich Reserve 1988 and Dom Pérignon Cuvée Brut 1985.

The fortified categories yielded wonderful surprises. The PORT TROPHY went to **Taylor's Quinta de Vargellas 1984**: plummy, spicy and powerful. Superlatives also described **Henriques & Henriques' 10-Year-Old Malmsey**, which claimed the MADEIRA TROPHY.

The SHERRY category produced a surprise winner: **Osborne's Solera India Oloroso Rare Sherry**, with its rich Brazil nut and smoky clove tones. So outstanding was this wine that it was also awarded the overall FORTIFIED TROPHY. The overall DESSERT WINE TROPHY went to the superb **Schilfwein Tradition 1994** by Burgenland's **Nekowitsch**.

McWilliam's Liqueur Muscat Show Series Limited Release 1994 (New South Wales) claimed the FORTIFIED MUSCAT TROPHY.

The judges then had to decide which trophy winners would receive the overall white and red wine trophies. The WHITE WINE TROPHY went to **Zind-Humbrecht's Heimbourg Gewurztraminer 1992**, while the RED WINE TROPHY was claimed by the **Lawson's Shiraz 1991.**

WINES OF THE YEAR

While on the one hand, the International WINE Challenge seeks to recognise excellence irrespective of price, its other major role is that of introducing the consumer to readily available, great-value wines.

The Wines of the Year are either Gold or Silver Medal wines which fit two crucial criteria: price (under £5 and £8 for table wines and under £12 for sparkling) and widespread availability. Possible candidates were tasted by the Trophy Tasting panel and selected on their merits.

THE WHITES

The Languedoc-Roussillon region lays claim to two white Wines of the Year: the **Laroche Grande Cuvée Chardonnay 1995** and **Domaine de la Baume Philippe de Baudin Sauvignon Blanc 1995.** This proves that, even in these inflationary days, France can still cater for the wine enthusiast who has only a limited budget. Representing the New World, **Basedow Barossa Chardonnay 1995** is a perfect example of Aussie oak and fruit.

THE REDS

The reds are a wonderful mix of both nationality and grape. The **Barbaglio Rosso del Salento 1993** from Puglia blends the Primitivo and Negro Amaro grapes, while the **Bright Brothers Douro 1995** also uses a national favourite: the Touriga Nacional. Both are excellent examples of their particular style, as is the third winner – and the second Wine of the Year from the Barossa Valley – the **Yaldara Reserve Shiraz 1994**.

THE FIZZ

While the French may still excel in the production of 'quality-above-all-else' sparkling wines, the New World yields great fizz at affordable prices. For the second year running, the judges selected the **Scharffenberger Brut** from Mendocino County, California: an outstanding example of quality winemaking employing the traditional Champagne method. The **Seaview Pinot Noir/Chardonnay 1993** from Australia captured the final award, impressing everyone with its tropical-fruit tones and toasty finish.

HOW TO USE THIS BOOK

Every wine in this guide has been awarded a medal at the **1996 International Wine Challenge**. We have listed the winning wines by country and region, with up to seven wine headings: red, dry white, medium white, sweet white, rosé, sparkling and fortified.

Under each of these headings the wines are listed in price order, from the least to the most expensive. Every wine carries the same range of information: the wine name (and vintage where applicable), the tasting note, the average retail price, the code for stockists (*see* page 242), and the medal the wine was awarded. Below is an example of how wines are listed, showing the meaning of each column.

There is also a complete alphabetical index starting on page 251 and a listing of white and red wines under £5, and sparkling wines under £10 starting on page 233.

With all this information, we are sure you will make the best decisions about which wines best suit your palate and wallet.

The wine name, vintage and region	The average retail price	The Medals; **G** Gold, **S** Silver, **B** Bronze	
ANGOVE'S NANYA ESTATE MALBEC/RUBY CABERNET 1995 South Australia	*Initial sweet cherries, spicy white pepper, and a gameyness wrapped in a warming, rich and complex palate.*	£3.90	W BU WR TH	(S)

The description provided by Challenge tasters.	*Codes for stockists (see page 242)*

THE
WINES

AUSTRALIA

WIDELY KNOWN AS THE COUNTRY producing the best value up-front white wines, Australia is still a favourite for many. Winemakers are increasingly experimenting and varying the styles of wine to create a wider range which will augment, not replace, those wines which have already found success in the UK. Interestingly, regional characteristics and identities are becoming more apparent.

CABERNET SAUVIGNON

ANGOVE'S NANYA ESTATE MALBEC/RUBY CABERNET 1995 South Australia	*Initial sweet cherries, spicy white pepper, and a gameyness wrapped in a warming, rich and complex palate.*	**£3.90**	W BU WR TH	(S)
MARIENBERG COTTAGE CLASSIC CABERNET SAUVIGNON/ MOURVÈDRE 1994 South Australia	*A well-balanced wine with big, sweet, upfront, concentrated berry fruit, spice and pepper.*	**£4.00**	LAY	(B)
ORLANDO RF RUBY CABERNET/SHIRAZ 1995, South Australia	*Violety, blackcurrant fruits give good complexity. Soft tannins and hints of mint precede a good finish.*	**£4.20**	Widely available	(B)
CO-OP AUSTRALIAN CABERNET SAUVIGNON 1993, ANGOVE'S South Australia	*Shows a nice fruit content with a high acidic level on the palate and hints of mint.*	**£4.30**	CWS	(B)
SOMERFIELD AUSTRALIAN CABERNET/SHIRAZ 1991, PENFOLDS (SOUTHCORP) South Australia	*This deep-coloured wine has a fruity nose, followed by a palate showing a minty edge and refreshing acidity.*	**£4.50**	SMF	(B)

HARDY'S NOTTAGE HILL CABERNET SAUVIGNON/ SHIRAZ 1994, BRL HARDY WINE COMPANY South Australia	*A pleasant, deep-garnet wine mixes lovely, juicy fruit with good acidity and stalky tannins.*	£4.90	Widely available	**B**
RAWSON'S RETREAT BIN 35 CABERNET/SHIRAZ 1994, PENFOLDS (SOUTHCORP) South Australia	*Minty, eucalyptus nose. Soft, minty, spiced fruit; cassis edge. Good depth, smooth tannins and a lengthy finish.*	£5.00	Widely available	**B**
LINDEMANS BIN 45 CABERNET SAUVIGNON 1994 South Australia	*Mint and pungent fruits on nose and palate. Mature tannins and hints of oak in harmony.*	£5.40	Widely available	**S**
MARIENBERG CABERNET SAUVIGNON 1992 South Australia	*Red-fruit aromas and jammy fruits. Ripe tannins with a mature balance and length on the palate.*	£5.60	LAY DBY	**B**
REDCLIFF ESTATE CABERNET SAUVIGNON 1994, WINGARA WINE GROUP South Australia	*A rich, tempting, plummy nose, followed by a full palate of peppermints and smooth vanilla tones.*	£5.70	NRW WWG SHG CHF BI BU WR TH	**S**
TESCO COONAWARRA CABERNET SAUVIGNON 1994, RYMILL WINES South Australia	*The berry fruits and charred oak are well integrated. Shows good style and balance.*	£6.00	TO	**B**
WYNNS JOHN RIDDOCH CABERNET SAUVIGNON 1993, WYNNS COONAWARRA ESTATE South Australia	*A vibrant wine with a moist, minty nose. Hot, nutty fruit combines with plum and juicy blackcurrant flavours.*	£6.00	JS TO MWW VWC OD HOU	**S**
INGLEBURNE ESTATE CABERNET SAUVIGNON 1994, MAGLIERI WINERY South Australia	*Superb ruby colour; lovely, rich, ripe berries. Its spicy structure leads to a long smooth finish.*	£6.50	TO	**B**

AUSTRALIA • RED

BAROSSA VALLEY ESTATE MOCULTA CABERNET/ MERLOT 1994, BRL HARDY WINE COMPANY South Australia	*Deep red with raspberries and spices. Excellent quality, balanced tannins. Delicious wine, and ready now.*	**£6.70**	R DBY HOU	(G)
WYNNS COONAWARRA CABERNET/SHIRAZ 1990 South Australia	*This deep-garnet wine shows blackcurrants and oak notes as well as rich currants on the palate.*	**£6.80**	EP TAN BOO DBY HOU MHW WOC AMW	(S)
ROSEMOUNT ESTATE CABERNET SAUVIGNON 1994 South Australia	*Soft, blackcurrant tones dominate, but there are spicy hints in the smooth, rich tannins, and a juicy persistence on the finish.*	**£6.90**	Widely available	(S)
PETER LEHMANN CABERNET SAUVIGNON 1994 South Australia	*Wonderful blackcurrant fruits with hints of mint and tobacco. A well-balanced wine with a long, clean finish.*	**£7.00**	Widely available	(B)
WOLF BLASS YELLOW LABEL CABERNET SAUVIGNON 1994 South Australia	*Deep ruby-red. Hints of new oak with berry flavours are followed by balanced tannins and a nice finish.*	**£7.00**	Widely available	(S)
GOUNDREY CABERNET/ MERLOT 1993 Western Australia	*Berry-fruit character adds depth. Shows smooth tannins and good balance as well as a long finish.*	**£7.20**	Widely available	(B)
LEASINGHAM CLARE VALLEY CABERNET SAUVIGNON/MALBEC 1994, BRL HARDY WINE Co South Australia	*A nose of oak and fruit, precedes a fine, complex palate. Soft smooth tannins are rounded off by a long finish.*	**£7.20**	Widely available	(S)
CLANCY'S RED 1994, PETER LEHMANN WINES South Australia	*This ruby-coloured wine, with initial vegetal and cherry aromas, has excellent flavour and a strong finish.*	**£7.30**	Widely available	(B)

ROUGE HOMME COONAWARRA CABERNET SAUVIGNON 1992 South Australia	*Complex nose with delicate flavours. Full-fruit palate has good spicy flavours. Balanced tannins, minty finish.*	**£7.70**	Widely available	(B)
CHATEAU REYNELLA BASKET-PRESSED CABERNET SAUVIGNON 1993, BRL HARDY WINE Co South Australia	*Spicy vanilla oak on nose and palate. Full-fruit flavours with ripe tannins. Longish finish.*	**£8.00**	SAF OD SMF VDV HOU VLW IVY	(B)
HILL-SMITH ESTATE TERRA ROSSA BLOCK CABERNET SAUVIGNON/ SHIRAZ 1993, YALUMBA South Australia	*Deep, ripe-fruit aromas are complemented by a strawberry-and-cream palate.*	**£8.00**	TOU MAR	(B)
MAGLIERI CABERNET SAUVIGNON 1994 South Australia	*Sweet, new-oak aromas lead to sweet, ripe summer fruits and hints of herbs.*	**£8.00**	TO	(B)
ST HALLETT CABERNET SAUVIGNON/CABERNET FRANC/MERLOT 1993 South Australia	*Plummy/garnet colour with a lovely fruity nose. Lush, sweet fruits. Well-balanced with a medium finish.*	**£8.00**	Widely available	(B)
JAMIESON'S RUN RED 1994, MILDARA BLASS South Australia	*A rich, blackcurrant-coloured wine displaying a green, minty, curranty, jammy nose and soft, balanced tannins.*	**£8.00**	Widely available	(S)
YALUMBA THE MENZIES COONAWARRA CABERNET SAUVIGNON 1992 South Australia	*Robust but classy. Lots of fruits and strong oak. Rich palate with smooth tannins; well-balanced.*	**£8.00**	JN WSO F&M DBY	(S)
ANGOVE'S SARNIA FARM PADTHAWAY CABERNET SAUVIGNON 1994, South Australia	*Deep ruby-red with a classy, herbaceous, peppermint nose. A complex palate of vanilla and blackcurrants.*	**£8.00**	AUC	(S)

AUSTRALIA • RED

TWO RIVERS CABERNET SAUVIGNON 1993, INGLEWOOD VINEYARDS New South Wales	*Wonderfully balanced, full of red summer fruits. Rich, sweet oak gives aded depth. Rich, lasting finish.*	**£8.00**	HW	Ⓢ
ORLANDO ST HUGO CABERNET SAUVIGNON 1993 South Australia	*Heavyweight palate with lots of spice and good, dark fruits. Well-balanced, with smooth tannins.*	**£8.20**	U B&B PEA CEN CAP CAX VDV	Ⓑ
WYNNS COONAWARRA CABERNET SAUVIGNON 1993 South Australia	*Good, strong, fruity nose. Palate has some fine cassis flavours integrated with tannins and wood.*	**£8.20**	Widely available	Ⓢ
PENFOLDS BIN 407 CABERNET SAUVIGNON 1993, (SOUTHCORP) South Australia	*Forest fruits last from palate to finish; oak content is sweet. Long finish, great potential.*	**£8.40**	Widely available	Ⓢ
CUVÉE TWO SPARKLING CABERNET SAUVIGNON NV, YALUMBA South Australia	*Blackcurrant colour with hints of orange; plenty of Shiraz pepper on the nose, excellent acidity on finish; good fruit.*	**£8.50**	TO ADN OD	Ⓢ
ORLANDO ST HUGO CABERNET SAUVIGNON 1990 South Australia	*Palate is complemented by pepper and spices. Good fruit content leaves room for coffee-like tannins to finish.*	**£8.80**	Widely available	Ⓑ
THISTLE HILL CABERNET SAUVIGNON 1991 New South Wales	*Pungent fruit and sweet oak. Tannins are balanced and smooth. Great depth and length.*	**£8.80**	VR	Ⓑ
GRANT BURGE BAROSSA VALLEY CABERNET SAUVIGNON 1994 South Australia	*Good acidity balances the rich tannins. Smoky spice and oak lead to pungent berry flavours. Mouthwatering finish.*	**£8.80**	FUL DLA DBY LWE GGW COK VLW CNL	Ⓢ

MICHELTON RESERVE CABERNET SAUVIGNON 1994 Victoria	*Blackcurrant and sweet vanilla abound on the nose of this deep-ruby wine, which has jammy fruit on the palate.*	£9.20	ROD SHG COK MTL WMK	(S)
CHAPEL HILL CABERNET SAUVIGNON 1993 South Australia	*Spicy nose and palate. High fruit content. The tannins are robust, with great balance.*	£9.30	TO TH DBY NRW AUC BU WR	(S)
MOUNT LANGI GHIRAN CABERNET SAUVIGNON 1991 Victoria	*Good depth with plenty of upfront flavours. Fresh blackcurrant fruits, vanilla oak and balanced tannins.*	£9.40	ENO SEL DBY PIM	(B)
ST HUBERTS CABERNET SAUVIGNON 1993, Victoria	*A lovely vanilla-almond nose is followed by a mouthful of delicious, minty, ripe blackcurrants on the palate.*	£9.40	HOF DBY COK VLW GRT	(S)
ROSEMOUNT SHOW RESERVE CABERNET SAUVIGNON 1993 South Australia	*Cassis and tobacco nose. Elegant palate with sweet forest fruits, oak and big, rich tannins.*	£9.50	TO DBY BWC FEN WCR	(S)
PENFOLDS COONAWARRA CABERNET SAUVIGNON 1993, (SOUTHCORP) South Australia	*Deep purple in the glass, with touches of cinnamon on the nose. Plenty of delicious loganberry fruit.*	£9.60	Widely available	(B)
ST HUBERTS CABERNET/MERLOT 1994 Victoria	*Deep ruby-red, with a complex, cedary nose and sweet, juicy flavours. Soft fruits abound on the mid-palate.*	£9.60	DAV SAN VLW	(S)
THE SIGNATURE CABERNET SAUVIGNON/ SHIRAZ 1992, YALUMBA South Australia	*The nose is smoky with minty overtones. Wonderfully rich berry fruit dominates the palate.*	£9.70	JN BH F&M ADN OD BEN DBY	(B)

PENFOLDS BIN 389 CABERNET/SHIRAZ 1993, (SOUTHCORP) South Australia	*Black and enigmatic in the glass. Ripe blackcurrant flavours mingle with soft tannins. Drinking well now.*	£9.70	Widely available	(G)
EBENEZER CAB/MALBEC/ MERLOT/CABERNET FRANC 1992 BAROSSA VALLEY ESTATE (BERRI-RENMANO-HARDY's) South Australia	*On the palate, lots of oaky tones are backed up by an explosion of black berry fruits.*	£10.00	VWC OD ROD DBY VDV VW HOU MHW	(S)
INGLEWOOD SHOW RESERVE RANGE CABERNET 1993 New South Wales	*Berry-fruit nose. Intense, warm, woody character, with a plummy richness. Velvety structure. Fruity oak finish.*	£10.00	HW	(S)
WOLF BLASS SHOW RESERVE COONAWARRA CABERNET SAUVIGNON 1993, MILDARA BLASS South Australia	*Lovely herbal, fruity nose. On the palate, there is a touch of spiciness with a long enigmatic finish.*	£10.00	ODD OD WFB SEA	(S)
BETHANY CABERNET/ MERLOT 1992 South Australia	*Cedar, fruit, and coconut nose. Baked fruit and rich wood on palate. Fruity finish, firm tannins.*	£10.10	NI WSC SOM	(S)
WOLF BLASS PRESIDENT'S SELECTION CABERNET SAUVIGNON 1993, MILDARA BLASS South Australia	*Coconut and oak aromas precede rich Cabernet fruit and cinnamon touches. Fine balance and structure.*	£10.50	Widely available	(B)
MENTOR 1991, PETER LEHMANN WINES South Australia	*Young, bright, purple fruit with minty hints and lots of depth. Balanced and fine.*	£11.00	PLE OD	(B)
ZEMA ESTATE CABERNET SAUVIGNON 1993 South Australia	*Deep and dark, with touches of tar, oak and juicy fruit. Almost Italianate.*	£11.00	ENO NY	(B)

CULLENS CABERNET/MERLOT RESERVE 1993 Western Australia	*Cool, clean, deep and straightforward wine, with touches of cinnamon and a fresh, fruity finish.*	£11.10	LWE AD DBY NY P ADN	**B**
KATNOOK ESTATE CABERNET SAUVIGNON 1992 South Australia	*Soft, rich, fruitcake nose with a minty/peppery quality on the palate. This one shows excellent ageing potential.*	£11.20	VWC VW SHG BD GGW NRW BI	**S**
LINDEMANS LIMESTONE RIDGE VINEYARD SHIRAZ/CABERNET 1992 South Australia	*Lovely violet colour with fine, ripe, black fruit on the nose, and a rich, fruitcake palate.*	£11.30	Widely available	**B**
LEASINGHAM CLASSIC CLARE VALLEY CABERNET SAUVIGNON 1993, BRL HARDY WINE COMPANY South Australia	*Deep colour with a rich, plummy, minerally nose. Ripe sweet fruit. Ready for drinking now.*	£11.50	VWC FUL DBY ES OD VDV VW	**B**
LINDEMANS PYRUS 1992 South Australia	*A complex nose of chocolate, smoky berries. A sweet, oily start on the palate precedes robust, hedgerow fruit.*	£11.60	Widely available	**S**
ST GEORGE VINEYARD CABERNET SAUVIGNON 1992, LINDEMANS South Australia	*Shows a chocolatey colour in the glass with touches of mulberry and cassis flavours and well-balanced tannins.*	£11.90	Widely available	**B**
ST MICHAEL COONAWARRA CABERNET SAUVIGNON 1992, JAMES HALLIDAY South Australia	*Slightly meaty nose with chewy blackcurrant on the palate, soft tannins and a resonant finish.*	£12.00	M&S	**B**
EVANS VINEYARD COONAWARRA CABERNET SAUVIGNON 1992, PETALUMA South Australia	*Intense berry fruit with suggestions of pepper and tobacco; firm tannins with almost syrupy legs.*	£12.40	TH OD DBY RBS	**B**

HARDY'S THOMAS HARDY COONAWARRA CABERNET SAUVIGNON 1991, BRL HARDY WINE COMPANY South Australia	*Rich, mulberry oak on the nose; deep, blackcurrant fruit with well-integrated oak and light tannins.*	£12.60	OD WMK JHL DBY VDV HOU	(S)
HARDY'S THOMAS HARDY COONAWARRA CABERNET SAUVIGNON 1992, BRL HARDY WINE COMPANY South Australia	*Super colour with very concentrated, cedary oak. Sweet, ripe – and very attractive.*	£13.00	JHL VDV	(B)
McGUIGAN BROTHERS PERSONAL RESERVE CABERNET 1994 New South Wales	*Modern style with sweet vanilla oak and young tannins. Oodles of fruit and fine acidity.*	£13.00	GAL P&R WOC VNO	(B)
MOSS WOOD CABERNET SAUVIGNON 1994 Western Australia	*Damson red in colour. Blackcurrant with touches of forest fruits. Solid tannins and balanced acidity.*	£13.30	JOB PLA NI DBY LWE SOB COK	(S)
MOUNTADAM THE RED CABERNET/MERLOT 1992 South Australia	*Fresh berry fruit with touches of cedar; there are also walnuts on the palate, with a spice and coriander herbiness.*	£14.10	JAR PLA CHF HVW CWI P ADN MFS	(S)
PENLEY ESTATE CABERNET SAUVIGNON 1992 South Australia	*Green, herbaceous tones are underpinned by ripe fruit and young, fresh tannins, all wrapped up in a hot, spicy finish.*	£14.80	WTR HAR VDV DBY NY L&W VLW	(B)
RAVENSWOOD CABERNET SAUVIGNON 1992, HOLLICK WINES South Australia	*Rich, southern-hemisphere fruit with some sweetness. Round and soft, with enhancing structural tannins.*	£15.80	AUC JN VDV HVW NY L&W	(S)
HENSCHKE ABBOTT'S PRAYER LENSWOOD VINEYARD CABERNET/MERLOT 1993 South Australia	*Full Cabernet colour with smoked sesame seed on the nose and some very elegant tannins on the palate.*	£16.30	Widely available	(B)

AUSTRALIA • RED					
HENSCHKE CABERNET SAUVIGNON 1993 South Australia	*Dark ruby with an aromatic, spicy bouquet. Intense, black-fruit flavours. Will age well.*	**£17.00**	Widely available		**B**
ORLANDO JACARANDA RIDGE CABERNET SAUVIGNON 1988 South Australia	*Mint and leather on the nose. Fine cedary tannins mingle with ripe, fresh fruit. Drink now.*	**£17.20**	D MHW WTR CEN OD CAX VDV		**S**
ORLANDO JACARANDA RIDGE CABERNET SAUVIGNON 1989 South Australia	*Hints of tobacco and cinnamon as well as juicy, wild, forest fruit. Long finish.*	**£18.00**	Widely available		**G**
PENFOLDS BIN 707 CABERNET SAUVIGNON 1993 (SOUTHCORP) South Australia	*Cedary tones with hints of walnut and eucalyptus freshness. Splendid tannins balance beautifully with fresh, cherry fruit.*	**£18.30**	Widely available		**G**
SALLY'S PADDOCK CABERNET/SHIRAZ 1994, REDBANK Victoria	*Lovely, youthful red colour with soft mint and berry sweetness on the palate.*	**£20.00**	TOU WIN		**B**

🍇

SHIRAZ

ANGOVE'S RIDGEMOUNT BAY SHIRAZ/CABERNET 1995 South Australia	*Savoury, meaty notes leading to vanilla and berry-fruit palate. Dense and clean, this one will develop.*	**£3.70**	BES		**B**
HG BROWN SHIRAZ/RUBY CABERNET BIN 60 1995, BRL HARDY WINE COMPANY South Australia	*With rich oak, caramel and cinnamon tones, this wine finishes well with definite spice and fruit tones.*	**£4.00**	SAF		**B**

TESCO AUSTRALIAN SHIRAZ/CABERNET SAUVIGNON NV, BRL HARDY South Australia	*A sweetly warm, spicy bouquet, simply over-flowing with ripe black-currant and damsons.*	£4.00	TO	(S)
LINDEMANS CAWARRA SHIRAZ/CABERNET 1995 South Australia	*Lots of soft and plummy blackcurrant fruit. Weighty, rich and peppery wine with soft tannins.*	£4.60	Widely available	(B)
ROWLANDS BROOK SHIRAZ/CABERNET 1994, PENFOLDS (SOUTHCORP) South Australia	*Soft, ripe and peppery plum. Full of spicy fruit, balanced acidity and tannin.*	£4.70	Widely available	(B)
PETER LEHMANN VINE VALE SHIRAZ 1994 South Australia	*Pleasant, herbal and slightly tarry, toffeed wine with a smooth but weighty palate.*	£4.90	Widely available	(B)
LINDEMANS BIN 50 SHIRAZ South Australia	*Rich, sweet fruit mingles with hot spices, complementing the powerful menthol and plum nose.*	£5.20	Widely available	(S)
CANOE TREE SHIRAZ 1993 South Australia	*Shows plenty of spicy black pepper on the nose, with supple, black-cherry fruit on the palate.*	£5.70	JN CHF P ADN	(B)
PETER LEHMANN SHIRAZ 1994, South Australia	*An appetising amalgam of mint, spice and blackcurrants on the nose, followed by a crisp, elegant palate.*	£5.80	Widely available	(S)
YALDARA RESERVE SHIRAZ 1994 South Australia	*Strong and powerful with good complexity. Stylish oak, nutty and spicy fruit tones give this wonderful depth.*	£5.80	Widely available	(G) WINE OF THE YEAR

AUSTRALIA • RED

ROUGE HOMME SHIRAZ/CABERNET 1993 South Australia	*The tasters liked the medicinal, herbal and fruity style and the smooth, clean finish of this wine.*	£5.90	Widely available	(B)
TEMPLE BRUER SHIRAZ/MALBEC 1989 South Australia	*The peppery, fruity, rich, toffee nose expands to warm, ripe fruit flavours with a fine finish.*	£6.00	TO	(S)
HARDY'S BANKSIDE SHIRAZ 1993, BRL HARDY WINE COMPANY South Australia	*This clean, garnet-red wine boasts a crushed-pepper and blackberry nose with rich, spicy fruit.*	£6.10	Widely available	(B)
TYRRELLS OLD WINERY SHIRAZ 1994 New South Wales	*Strong oak on nose. Lots of spice, hints of earthy currants and a lovely finish.*	£6.30	AMP B&B VIL SHG G&M HOU COK MTL	(B)
HARDY'S BANKSIDE SHIRAZ 1994, BRL HARDY WINE COMPANY South Australia	*Nice blueberry fruit and peppery spice are set off by a streak of rich vanilla oak.*	£6.30	Widely available	(B)
MARIENBERG SHIRAZ 1993 South Australia	*An inviting, ripe-fruit nose is followed by a nice, sweet, chocolatey palate with delicious, peppery/ plummy characters.*	£6.30	CMI CPW	(B)
CANOE TREE SHIRAZ/MOURVÈDRE 1994 South Australia	*A pleasant, light, well-made wine. Tobacco on the nose preceding soft, jammy fruit on the palate.*	£6.50	ADN JN CHF P AMW	(B)
MOCULTA SHIRAZ 1994, BAROSSA VALLEY ESTATE (BERRI-RENMANO-HARDY'S) South Australia	*Refreshing berry-fruit on the nose, with ripe fruits and pepper notes on the palate. Well-balanced arming tannins.*	£6.50	FUL R DBY	(B)

AUSTRALIA • RED

INGLEBURNE ESTATE SHIRAZ 1994, MAGLIERI South Australia	*Pungent fruit with woody spice in good proportion. Firm tannins and long finish.*	£6.50	TO	**B**
D'ARRY'S ORIGINAL SHIRAZ/GRENACHE 1994, D'ARENBERG South Australia	*Big flavour: full of fruit gums, currants and orange peel, with a nice, gentle spice.*	£6.50	OD VDV WES	**S**
ANDREW GARRETT SHIRAZ 1994, MILDARA BLASS South Australia	*Bitter fruit on nose and palate, with plenty of ripe fruit and good spices. Good balance and finish, too.*	£6.60	LTW PHI HVW WFB MTL	**B**
STONYFELL METALA OAK-MATURED SHIRAZ/ CABERNET 1994 South Australia	*A deep, concentrated, jammy nose is followed by cherry and blackcurrant flavours. Full, juicy finish.*	£6.60	OD VDV VLW	**B**
LEASINGHAM CLARE VALLEY SHIRAZ 1994, BRL HARDY WINE COMPANY South Australia	*A jammy nose leads to a rich palate of damson and black pepper flavours.*	£6.70	Widely available	**B**
PAULETTS SHIRAZ 1993 South Australia	*Good, spicy, berry fruit with a eucalyptus twist. Subtle oak with good length.*	£6.70	J&B	**B**
BROWN BROTHERS SHIRAZ 1994 Victoria	*Spicy/toasty blackcurrants. Full-bodied and showing good, firm, oaky tannins. Long, rich, fruity finish.*	£6.80	Widely available	**S**
HAMILTON RIDGE SHIRAZ 1994, PETER LEHMANN South Australia	*A subtle style with good complexity, lots of berry fruits and spices with sweet oak and smooth, rounded tannins.*	£7.00	BD	**S**

AUSTRALIA • RED				
PENFOLDS CLARE VALLEY ORGANIC SHIRAZ/ CABERNET 1994, (SOUTHCORP) South Australia	*A full and complete wine with dense, tarry fruit, currants, mint and peppery, stalky, tannic finish.*	**£7.10**	Widely available	(S)
ROSEMOUNT ESTATE SHIRAZ 1994 South Australia	*Spicy oak bouquet. Good Shiraz fruits and rich tannins. Good depth and great fruity finish.*	**£7.10**	Widely available	(B)
ST MICHAEL ROSEMOUNT ESTATE SHIRAZ 1994 South Australia	*Ripe sweet, American oak. Hot, attractive fruits and earthy spiciness to it. Very appealing.*	**£7.30**	M&S	(B)
BASEDOWS SHIRAZ 1994 South Australia	*Fruity flavours with sweet new oak and hints of vanilla. Rounded tannins, long length.*	**£7.50**	Widely available	(S)
LINDEMANS PADTHAWAY SHIRAZ 1994 South Australia	*Spicy, sweet, fruity nose. Peppery palate leads to good, ripe fruits and a long, tannic finish.*	**£7.60**	TO OD VDV HOU	(B)
MITCHELTON III SHIRAZ/MOURVÈDRE/ GRENACHE 1993 Victoria	*Spicy, succulent fruits add depth to good, hot oak and warming tannins. Long finish.*	**£7.80**	Widely available	(B)
TOLLEY'S SHIRAZ 1992, TOLLEY PEDARE (MILDARA BLASS) South Australia	*Warm, spicy aromas with herbal, fruity flavours well-balanced by the hot tannins. Long finish.*	**£7.80**	EP	(B)
PENFOLDS BIN 28 KALIMNA SHIRAZ 1993, (SOUTHCORP) South Australia	*Tangy acidity on the nose. Concentrated, plummy fruits and spicy tannins on the finish.*	**£7.90**	Widely available	(B)

AUSTRALIA • RED

PENFOLDS BIN 128 COONAWARRA SHIRAZ 1993, (SOUTHCORP) South Australia	*Spicy, green-pepper nose with blackberry flavours. Good balance of acidity and tannins.*	£7.90	Widely available	**B**
KINGSTON ESTATE RESERVE SHIRAZ 1992 South Australia	*Full, fruity nose and soft fruits on palate. Good structure and great length.*	£8.00	VNO TO	**S**
CHATEAU REYNELLA SHIRAZ 1994, BRL HARDY WINE COMPANY South Australia	*Lovely, concentrated nose and intense, fruit flavours. Upfront, fruity palate with smooth, juicy finish. Wow!*	£8.10	Widely available	**G**
ROTHBURY ESTATE HUNTER VALLEY RESERVE SHIRAZ 1994 New South Wales	*Good, hot, summer fruits and sweet oak; good tannins and good length.*	£8.30	Widely available	**B**
THE IRONSTONE PRESSINGS GRENACHE/ SHIRAZ 1994, D'ARENBERG WINES South Australia	*A full, spicy flavour precedes firm, ripe fruits on the nose. Strong finish and good length.*	£8.50	OD VDV VDV	**B**
CHAPEL HILL SHIRAZ 1994 South Australia	*Very well-balanced wine with good acidity and rich, ripe fruits, smooth tannins and a long finish.*	£8.50	TO SOM AUC BU WR TH	**S**
PETER DENNIS SHIRAZ 1993 South Australia	*An impression of oak, baked fruit and vanilla leads to a spicy and nicely tannic wine.*	£8.50	THP	**S**
MAGLIERI SHIRAZ 1994 South Australia	*Intense, spicy nose and lots of new oak lead to masses of berry-fruit flavours and good tannins.*	£8.50	TO U	**G**

AUSTRALIA • RED

Wine	Description	Price	Stockists	
YALUMBA FAMILY RESERVE SHIRAZ 1994 South Australia	*Lots of berry-fruit flavours and sweet oak. Well-balanced tannins add to a long finish.*	£9.00	ADN JN HAR SEL MM	**S**
GRANT BURGE BAROSSA VALLEY OLD VINE SHIRAZ 1994 South Australia	*Deep-purple colour; warm, fruity nose. Soft and fresh, rich, plummy flavours make up a palate with good length.*	£9.10	Widely available	**B**
BAILEYS 1920s BLOCK SHIRAZ 1994 Victoria	*Lovely, spicy fruits, ripe pepper and smooth tannins on the palate with good complexity and structure.*	£9.40	POR HAL HOF CLA OD DBY COK MFS	**S**
BEST'S GREAT WESTERN SHIRAZ 1993 Victoria	*Wonderful fruity nose. Vanilla oak, peppery spice, fresh fruits, creamy depth. Faultless balance and persistent length.*	£9.50	Widely available	**G**
BAROSSA VALLEY ESTATE EBENEZER SHIRAZ 1992, BRL HARDY WINE COMPANY South Australia	*Strong vanilla and mint aromas are matched with sweet oak and chocolate on the palate.*	£9.70	OD PEA COR DBY VDV HOU WCR	**B**
PENLEY ESTATE SHIRAZ/CABERNET 1993 South Australia	*Chocolate, caramel and grass enfold spice and berry fruit to give a very enjoyable wine.*	£10.00	PON HAR WTR NY L&W VLW	**B**
ROSEMOUNT ESTATE ROSE LABEL McLAREN VALE SHIRAZ 1993 South Australia	*Ripe fruit and alcohol on the nose. Broad fruit content gives depth. Good oak, long finish – great wine.*	£10.00	M&S FTH	**G**
LEASINGHAM CLASSIC CLARE VALLEY SHIRAZ 1993, BRL HARDY WINE COMPANY South Australia	*Warm cassis fruits, mint and pepper on the palate. Subtly oaked, nice tannins, good length.*	£10.20	FUL AWS TO OD DBY VDV COK VLW	**B**

AUSTRALIA • RED

WOLF BLASS PRESIDENT'S SELECTION SHIRAZ 1993, MILDARA BLASS South Australia	*Sweet and intense eucalyptus and new oak notes are followed by good, smooth, slightly cooked, spicy fruit.*	£10.20	Widely available	(G)
ST HALLETT BLOCK SHIRAZ 1993 South Australia	*Full, fruity, leathery wine with a sweet, almost vanilla, character enhancing a long, pleasing finish.*	£10.40	Widely available	(S)
TIM ADAMS SHIRAZ 1994 South Australia	*Rich, soft, fruity nose. Smooth, plummy character with hints of mint and eucalyptus. Firm tannins.*	£10.50	TO DBY MM AUC	(B)
PENLEY ESTATE SHIRAZ/CABERNET 1992 South Australia	*A ruby wine with a minerally, complex nose of oak and berries. Full and spicy.*	£10.50	PON WTR HAR SEL DBY NY L&W VLW	(S)
HANGING ROCK SHIRAZ 1994 Victoria	*A smooth and silky texture delivers leafy notes with ripe fruit and chocolate. Good acid balance.*	£10.80	THP	(B)
BETHANY SHIRAZ 1994, BETHANY WINES South Australia	*Sweet fruit, orange peel and spicy oak seamlessly integrated. Smooth tannins, good length.*	£10.80	NI DBY WSC MHW SOM	(G)
LAWSON'S SHIRAZ 1989, ORLANDO WINES South Australia	*A powerful wine packed with liquorice, spice, lovely fruit and even a hint of cedar.*	£10.90	PEA CEN JCK WTR OD CAX VDV NRW	(B)
INGLEWOOD SHOW RESERVE RANGE SHIRAZ 1994 New South Wales	*Sweet fruit and dusty American oak. Firm tannins, good character and green fruits on the finish.*	£11.00	HW	(B)

AUSTRALIA • RED

Wine	Description	Price	Availability	
LAWSON'S SHIRAZ 1988, ORLANDO WINES South Australia	*A firm, balanced and well rounded wine, with plenty of attractive fruit and spice.*	£11.20	Widely available	(S)
PLANTAGENET MOUNT BARKER SHIRAZ 1994, Western Australia	*Oaky fruit aromas, full and spicy palate of rich, ripe fruits. Great length. Wonderful!*	£11.20	CRM GI COK	(G)
THE DEAD ARM 1994, D'ARENBERG South Australia	*A really attractive wine, despite its name: massively concentrated, deep, meaty fruit and superb vanilla oak.*	£11.30	OD CHF VDV	(G)
LEASINGHAM CLASSIC CLARE VALLEY SHIRAZ 1994, BRL HARDY WINE COMPANY South Australia	*Forest fruits on the nose and sweet fruits on the palate. Good oak, fine tannins and a long finish.*	£11.40	FUL AWS TO OD VDV COK MHW	(S)
LAWSON'S SHIRAZ 1991, ORLANDO WINES South Australia	*This deliciously complex wine is packed with rich fruit, gentle spice and sweet new oak.*	£11.40	Widely available	(G)
PENFOLDS ST HENRI SHIRAZ CABERNET 1992, (SOUTHCORP) South Australia	*Soft, forward bouquet. Elegant style and well-blended grapes give a good depth. Long finish.*	£11.90	Widely available	(B)
HARDY'S EILEEN HARDY SHIRAZ 1993, BRL HARDY WINE CO South Australia	*A fruity theme with good complexity. Lots of oak, good balance and a peppery finish.*	£12.10	Widely available	(B)
TYRRELLS VAT 9 SHIRAZ 1990 New South Wales	*This giant of a wine is a melting pot of rich flavours, all of which complement each other.*	£12.90	VHW NIC PWY VIL SHG CEB RD HOU	(G)

AUSTRALIA • RED

McGuigan Brothers Personal Reserve Shiraz 1994 South Australia	Superb, rich nose packed with ripe plums and cherries along with nuts, violet tones and hints of smoky bacon.	£13.00	GAL P&R WOC VNO	(G)
Georgia's Paddock Shiraz 1993, Jasper Hill Vineyard Victoria	A huge, peppercorn aroma, very, very powerful - big, gutsy violet, clove and black-fruit flavours.	£13.70	H&H YAP AUS ADN	(G)
E&E Black Pepper Shiraz 1993, Barossa Valley Estates (Berri-Renmano-Hardy's) South Australia	Deep red colour with some brown, indicating maturity. This shows a generous, evolved, cedary nose and palate.	£13.90	Widely available	(B)
Peter Lehmann Stonewell Shiraz 1991 South Australia	Subtle flavour, full of juicy, spiced plums and damsons with a hint of blackcurrant.	£13.90	FUL G&M BOO PLE OD VDV G&M	(S)
Tim Adams Aberfeldy Shiraz 1994 South Australia	A richly appealing nose precedes a palate stacked full of juicy berry fruit and rich spice.	£14.00	AUC	(G)
Magpie Estate 'Malcom' Shiraz 1994 South Australia	This has a beautiful nose with a hint of wood. Spicy, soft, velvety, long and smooth.	£16.00	NY	(S)
Henschke Mount Edelstone Shiraz 1993 South Australia	Lively nose of violets and jammy fruits, especially plums and mulberries. The palate shows masses of fruit concentration.	£16.20	Widely available	(S)
Grant Burge Meshach Shiraz 1992 South Australia	A soft, ripe and fleshy wine with lashings of plums, plenty of liquorice and spicy fruit.	£16.60	FUL PLA DBY LWE GGW HOU COK VLW	(S)

THE OCTAVIUS 1992, YALUMBA South Australia	*With its tightly packed fruit and spice, this is a rich and well-structured wine showing good blackberry fruit.*	**£16.90**	OD DBY	**B**
ROSEMOUNT ESTATE BALMORAL SYRAH 1993 South Australia	*Superlatives abound. Rich and powerful, with excellent balance and length. Complex and beautifully balanced.*	**£17.40**	TO CEB DBY ALD BWC FTH WES	**G**
WYNNS COONAWARRA ESTATE MICHAEL SHIRAZ 1993 South Australia	*A wonderful, spicy, creamy nose, masses of jammy fruit, sweet, green spices and a great finish.*	**£18.40**	EP BOO OD VDV MWW DBY HOU POR	**S**

OTHER RED

BREAKAWAY GRENACHE SHIRAZ 1994, STRATMER VINEYARDS South Australia	*Sweet and light with blackcurrant and bramble aromas and flavours. Unusual, white-pepper finish.*	**£5.00**	SAF PLE VDV	**B**
BROWN BROTHERS TARRANGO 1995 Victoria	*A bright, clean, purple wine with ripe, jammy, berry undertones.*	**£5.30**	Widely available	**B**
SALISBURY ESTATE GRENACHE 1995, ALAMBIE WINE COMPANY Victoria	*This vibrant, complex wine combines fresh raspberries and violets with a dash of spicy white pepper*	**£5.60**	ENO RTW HAW VW NY	**S**
TESCO BAROSSA MERLOT 1993, GRANT BURGE South Australia	*Ripe berry fruits mingle with a rich, smooth texture, adding complexity. Sweet oak and long, juicy tannins.*	**£6.00**	TO	**S**

AUSTRALIA • RED

WHITMORE OLD VINEYARD GRENACHE RESERVE 1995, YALDARA South Australia	*This raspberry wine has a lovely, fleshy, fruity nose complemented by a touch of pepper and spice.*	£6.30	Widely available	(B)
YALDARA RESERVE CABERNET/MERLOT 1993 South Australia	*Sweet berry fruits and a touch of dusty wood give good depth. Rich, smooth, juicy finish*	£6.70	SHG SWS VDV HVW HOU COK WOI	(B)
ANDREW GARRETT CABERNET/MERLOT 1994, MILDARA BLASS South Australia	*Deep ruby colouring, showing maturity. Rich blueberries and plums. Clean and balanced with smooth tannins.*	£7.40	LTW PHI WFB MTL	(B)
BUSH VINE GRENACHE 1994, YALUMBA South Australia	*Spicy, leafy nose with chewy fruit on the mid-palate and warm, spicy tannins. Well-balanced.*	£8.00	TO JN OD BEN MWW	(B)
ROTHBURY RESERVE MUDGEE MERLOT 1994 New South Wales	*Plummy red colour. Earthy damsons on the nose are followed by a sweet, soft palate.*	£8.50	OD VLW	(B)
THE IRONSTONES PRESSINGS 1994, D'ARENBERG South Australia	*Packed with violety, fruity and sweetly spicy flavours, this is a rich and firmly structured wine; robust and tannic.*	£8.60	OD VDV	(B)
DAVID WYNN PATRIARCH SHIRAZ 1994 South Australia	*Fruity, peppery nose. Sweet oak and creamy vanilla. Wonderful ripe, rich fruits. Good balance and length.*	£9.40	Widely available	(S)
ROBERTSON'S WELL CABERNET SAUVIGNON 1993, MILDARA BLASS South Australia	*Hints of vanilla pod and tobacco on the nose. Flavours of summer fruit and soft tannins.*	£9.70	PHI CVR CEB WFB SEA GRT	(S)

AUSTRALIA • RED				
SCOTCHMANS HILL PINOT NOIR 1994 Victoria	*Good, raspberry nose; good, dry oakiness; well-balanced, fruity and spicy bite on the finish.*	£10.00	J & B J&B	(S)
CULLENS PINOT NOIR 1995 Western Australia	*Deep cherry colour. Raspberry/strawberry nose; new oak. Very good tannins, full-bodied and excellent.*	£10.20	HW PAV NI CPW DBY P ADN AMW	(S)
MORRIS DURIF 1993 Victoria	*There is a minty, chocolate nose with charred wood married to ripe, dark, juicy fruit.*	£10.40	Widely available	(S)
MORRIS DURIF 1991 Victoria	*A big wine with a dense, dark appearance and complex, gamey fruit on nose and palate.*	£10.50	Widely available	(G)
YALDARA FARMS MERLOT/ CABERNET 1992 South Australia	*There's a smoky creaminess on the nose with rich blackcurrants and wild forest fruit on the palate.*	£11.40	BOO SHG SWS VDV G&M	(S)
BANNOCKBURN PINOT NOIR 1993 Victoria	*Tawny red colour, vegetal farmyard nose; old oak, good tannins, balanced acidity. Spicy with good potential.*	£12.40	JN BEN DBY RBS HOU ADN	(B)
MOSS WOOD PINOT NOIR 1994 Western Australia	*Youthful nose with mint and plums. The palate shows herbaceous tones with fresh raspberry fruit, well-balanced.*	£12.70	JOB PLA CEB DBY LWE SOB COK	(S)
HARDY'S BASTARD HILLS PINOT NOIR 1994, BRL HARDY WINE COMPANY Victoria	*Good, deep colour, reasonable, complex nose. Herbaceous, leather/saddle soap tones. Balanced, needs ageing.*	£20.00	R MHW	(B)

ROSE

MOUNT HURTLE GRENACHE 1995 South Australia	*Full of ripe strawberry and sweet cherry fruit; great on its own or with food.*	**£5.40**	JS PLE OD VDV DBY WMK	(S)

CHARDONNAY

MONTY'S HILL VICTORIA CHARDONNAY/ COLOMBARD 1995 Victoria	*Musky lemon and gentle oak nose, intense and well-balanced fruity palate with good length.*	**£4.00**	SAF	(B)
ANGOVE'S CHARDONNAY CLASSIC RESERVE 1995, South Australia	*Soft, spicy, creamy well-used oak. A full-bodied, rich and complex mouthful.*	**£4.70**	KWI CHF MWW HOU	(B)
TOLLANA OAK MATURED CHARDONNAY 1993 South Australia	*Rich, heavy oak. A wine with full, ripe, fruity flavour, good acidity and a medium finish.*	**£5.00**	BU CLA WR TH	(B)
PENFOLDS KOONUNGA HILL CHARDONNAY 1995 (SOUTHCORP) South Australia	*Richly buttered flavour, lots of oak and good acidity, with great fruit awareness.*	**£5.10**	Widely available	(S)
TYRRELLS LONG FLAT CHARDONNAY/ SEMILLON 1995 New South Wales	*Clean and fresh with a ripe complexity of succulent fruits, some oak and a good, lengthy finish.*	**£5.30**	Widely available	(B)

AUSTRALIA • WHITE				
ANGOVE'S SARNIA FARM PADTHAWAY CHARDONNAY 1994, South Australia	*Big, ripe, papaya nose and an attractive over-ripe, full-blown palate with a dry length.*	**£5.30**	SOM	**B**
CANOE TREE CHARDONNAY 1994 South Australia	*Bright yellow wine with a toasty style. Oily, tropical palate, nice complex flavours.*	**£5.60**	JN CHF P ADN	**B**
MARIENBERG CHARDONNAY 1994, South Australia	*A well-structured wine, tasting of passion-fruit and ripe banana. Oakiness complemented by good acidity.*	**£5.60**	RVA DBY	**S**
LEASINGHAM CLARE VALLEY CHARDONNAY 1994, BRL HARDY WINE COMPANY South Australia	*Asparagus/lime nose, rich bitter/sweet and slightly vegetal mouthful. A citrus twist on finish.*	**£6.00**	OD BLS JHL WMK VLW	**B**
RENMANO CHARDONNAY RESERVE 1995 South Australia	*Intense, new French oak and a creamy, coconut nose. The palate is a rich, buttery vanilla and exotic, fruity mouthful.*	**£6.10**	U VIL DBY NY POR	**S**
WAKEFIELD CHARDONNAY 1994 South Australia	*A well-balanced youthful wine full of smooth butterscotch and lemon tones with an attractive dry finish.*	**£6.40**	HOU RW CNL RAE IVY	**B**
HARDY'S COLLECTION CHARDONNAY 1995, BRL HARDY WINE COMPANY South Australia	*A big mouthful with hints of tropical fruits and asparagus. A hefty, oaked Chardonnay.*	**£6.70**	LTW BLS VDV WMK	**B**
PENFOLDS BARREL-FERMENTED CHARDONNAY 1994 (SOUTHCORP) South Australia	*A wine with good acidity which tastes of pineapple and butterscotch. It is really mouthfilling and big.*	**£6.80**	Widely available	**S**

AUSTRALIA • WHITE				
GOUNDREY UNWOODED CHARDONNAY 1995 Western Australia	*Cool, herbaceous nose with light, tropical fruit and racy acidity elegantly balanced on the palate.*	£6.90	Widely available	(S)
WEST END NO 1 CHARDONNAY 1995 New South Wales	*A crisp middleweight with a ripe nose and palate of medium intensity and a reasonable length.*	£7.00	BD	(B)
RIDDOCH CHARDONNAY 1994, WINGARA WINE GROUP South Australia	*A creamy, rich mouthful that tastes of softly oaked fruit gums, but is slightly short on finish.*	£7.10	NRW WWG HOT BI BU WR TH	(B)
WYNDHAM ESTATE OAK CASK CHARDONNAY 1994, ORLANDO WYNDHAM New South Wales	*A heavily oaked wine with a full, ripe, pineapple nose and toasted-honey taste.*	£7.10	MRN MWW CVR AMA	(B)
YALDARA RESERVE CHARDONNAY 1994 South Australia	*Straw-yellow colour with a slightly green edge. This wine is a fruity mouthful.*	£7.10	TP SHG SWS RBS HOU WOI	(B)
WYNNS COONAWARRA ESTATE CHARDONNAY 1995 South Australia	*Mild peaches and cream on the nose and tasting of apple peel and butterscotch.*	£7.10	Widely available	(S)
YALLUM RIDGE PROPRIETOR'S RESERVE CHARDONNAY 1995, COOPER COUNTY WINES South Australia	*A little closed on the nose, but delicate and fruity to taste. A simple, enjoyable wine.*	£7.20	BD	(B)
WOLF BLASS SOUTH AUSTRALIAN BARREL-FERMENTED CHARDONNAY 1995, MILDARA BLASS South Australia	*A pale, straw-green wine with vanilla passion fruit and lime undertones. Great balance.*	£7.20	Widely available	(B)

CHATEAU REYNELLA CHARDONNAY 1995, BRL HARDY WINE COMPANY South Australia	*A slightly lean but clean, well-made wine, which offers a stalky, lemony mouthful.*	£7.40	Widely available	B
BASEDOW BAROSSA CHARDONNAY 1995 South Australia	*A delicious, intense yet delicate Chardonnay tasting of caramelised fruit. Great structure.*	£7.50	Widely available	G WINE OF THE YEAR
JAMIESON'S RUN CHARDONNAY 1995, MILDARA BLASS South Australia	*Perfumed, apple-blossom nose, light oaky fruit flavour, and a long finish make up this well-balanced wine.*	£7.70	Widely available	B
McGUIGAN BROTHERS SHAREHOLDERS RESERVE CHARDONNAY 1995 New South Wales	*Toasty, nutty oak on the nose is followed by a palate displaying rich, juicy, lychee and melon flavours.*	£7.70	GLY P&R JAG SNO VNO WAC	G
CHAPEL HILL UNWOODED CHARDONNAY 1994 South Australia	*Vanilla and pineapple on the nose; a clean, balanced palate with hints of melon and a crisp finish.*	£7.80	TO NRW SOM AUC	S
SEPPELT CORELLA RIDGE CHARDONNAY 1994 Victoria	*Attractive honeyed almond nose, marshmallow and zesty palate. A wine which needs time; good potential.*	£7.90	WSG BOO SHG LWE HOU COK	B
TWO RIVERS UNWOODED CHARDONNAY 1995, INGLEWOOD VINEYARDS New South Wales	*Marshmallow nose. A light pineapple palate; fine viscous body, excellent acid balance and short, limey finish.*	£8.00	SV HW	B
GREEN POINT VINEYARDS CHARDONNAY 1994, DOMAINE CHANDON Victoria	*Hefty oaked Chardonnay mellowed by a palate of peaches and cream. A friendly wine.*	£8.50	Widely available	B

AUSTRALIA • WHITE

PETER DENNIS CHARDONNAY 1995 South Australia	*Well-made, classy Burgundy type with a delicate, elegant flowery nose, great length and complexity.*	**£8.50**	THP	(S)
MOUNT HURTLE CHARDONNAY 1995 (STRATMER VINEYARDS) South Australia	*A pale, green-edged wine with a slightly restrained nose, but with a good bite of acidity.*	**£8.50**	PLE OD WMK WCR	(S)
PLANTAGENET WESTERN AUSTRALIA OMRAH CHARDONNAY 1995 Western Australia	*Fresh, varietal nose and a palate of ripe peach tones with excellent intensity, balance and a long finish.*	**£8.60**	GI COK	(B)
PIPERS BROOK VINEYARD NINTH ISLAND CHARDONNAY 1995 Tasmania	*Clean, young, citrus nose and a high-acid lime palate.*	**£8.80**	Widely available	(B)
HEGGIES VINEYARD EDEN VALLEY CHARDONNAY 1994 South Australia	*Subtle, smooth, integrated oak character with a big toasty palate which has good length.*	**£8.80**	JN	(B)
INGLEWOOD SHOW RESERVE RANGE CHARDONNAY 1995 New South Wales	*The nose consists of hints of asparagus, the palate is of medium length and shows floral tones.*	**£9.00**	HW	(B)
BETHANY CHARDONNAY 1995 South Australia	*A cocktail of tropical fruits on the nose follow through with a slight spritz on the palate.*	**£9.10**	DBY WSC	(B)
ROSEMOUNT ESTATE SHOW RESERVE CHARDONNAY 1994 New South Wales	*Attractive, woody nose. On the palate, strong, mellow, vanilla toast, but slightly falls away.*	**£9.20**	Widely available	(B)

AUSTRALIA • WHITE

SHAW & SMITH UNOAKED CHARDONNAY 1995 South Australia	*Long, balanced palate with medium acidity, dominant oak and a tropical fruit nose.*	£9.30	ENO CWI NY HOU	(S)
BAROSSA VALLEY ESTATE EBENEZER CHARDONNAY 1994 (BERRI-RENMANO-HARDY'S) South Australia	*Fragrant, buttery nose and rich, pineapple palate. A well balanced, easy-drinking, full-bodied Chardonnay.*	£9.60	MHW ROD COR PEA DBY VDV HOU	(S)
BAROSSA VALLEY ESTATE EBENEZER CHARDONNAY 1995 (BERRI-RENMANO-HARDY'S) South Australia	*A tropical-fruit nose, judicious use of oak creating a well balanced, modern, commercial wine.*	£9.90	MHW ROD COR PEA VDV	(B)
WOLF BLASS PRESIDENT'S SELECTION CHARDONNAY 1995, MILDARA BLASS South Australia	*Fresh, appley nose follows through in the mouth with nice old oak tone. Slightly short.*	£9.90	Widely available	(B)
GEOFF MERRILL CHARDONNAY 1994 (STRATMER VINEYARDS) South Australia	*Golden colour and seductive vanilla nose, light toasty oak, well-integrated fruit and acidity.*	£10.00	PLE	(B)
ST HUBERTS CHARDONNAY 1995 Victoria	*A nose that exudes spring blossom aromas gives way to a rich, grapefruit/lychee mouthful.*	£10.00	OD WNS FUL U COK VLW GRT	(S)
ROSEMOUNT ROSE LABEL ORANGE CHARDONNAY 1994 New South Wales	*Attractive, smoky, burnt-butter nose, plenty of savoury wood and great, concentrated length.*	£10.00	M&S FTH	(S)
SCOTCHMANS HILL GEELONG CHARDONNAY 1994 Victoria	*Oatmeally, strangely clinical nose which then presents lots of ripe pineapple and melon on the palate.*	£10.00	J&B	(S)

AUSTRALIA • WHITE				
GREEN POINT RESERVE CHARDONNAY 1995, DOMAINE CHANDON Victoria	*Light, chocolate nose, a delicate palate of pink grapefruit and melon, subtle oak and a long finish.*	**£10.00**	AV WCE L&W VW FUL OD	(S)
BEST'S GREAT WESTERN CHARDONNAY 1995 Victoria	*Well-integrated fruit and oak have created an elegant lingering peaches-and-cream taste.*	**£10.30**	Widely available	(S)
PLANTAGENET MOUNT BARKER CHARDONNAY 1994 Western Australia	*Great lemony, exotic, fruity nose, oaky on the palate. Will mature.*	**£10.80**	CRM GI	(S)
ST MICHAEL CAPEL VALE CHARDONNAY SPECIAL RESERVE 1993 Western Australia	*Rich, buttery palate enhanced by lots of ripe fruit, peaches in particular.*	**£11.00**	M&S	(B)
PETALUMA PICCADILLY VALLEY CHARDONNAY 1992 South Australia	*Very attractive, concentrated wine. Pronounced roasted fruit aromas on the palate, with a strong toffee character.*	**£11.20**	TH OD DBY	(S)
PETALUMA PICCADILLY VALLEY CHARDONNAY 1994 South Australia	*An aromatic nose and a complex palate of mango, apple, hints of melon and spicy lemon.*	**£11.50**	OD BEN AMA BU WR	(G)
STONIER'S RESERVE CHARDONNAY 1994 Victoria	*Deep, golden colour. The palate offers nicely integrated wood and a full, buttery taste.*	**£11.60**	DIR PV HOL RES OD MRF WAW	(S)
VOYAGER ESTATE CHARDONNAY 1994 Western Australia	*An interesting, waxy slightly oily nose followed by full-bodied, fleshy mango and banana flavours.*	**£12.00**	GGW	(S)

AUSTRALIA • WHITE

SHAW & SMITH RESERVE CHARDONNAY 1994 South Australia	*Delicately fruity nose, a palate of creamy peaches and light smoky oak. Well-made.*	£12.20	ENO CWI NY	(B)
TYRRELLS VAT 47 PINOT CHARDONNAY 1994 New South Wales	*Tangy, lively, fruity nose; fun, fresh, zingy style enriched by light oak. Still young.*	£12.40	Widely available	(B)
PETALUMA PICCADILLY VALLEY CHARDONNAY 1993 South Australia	*Light gold colour, lovely creamy, lemony nose. Oak dominance with good fruit behind. Will mature.*	£12.50	TH OD BEN MRF RBS WMK AMA	(B)
McGUIGAN BROTHERS PERSONAL RESERVE CHARDONNAY 1995 New South Wales	*Fragrant, sweet, pineapple aromas, a citric/sherbetty palate which is mellowed by a subtle creaminess.*	£13.00	P&R WON GAL VNO	(B)
ROXBURGH CHARDONNAY 1993, ROSEMOUNT ESTATE WINES New South Wales	*On the palate, tasters enthused about the rich, lemony fruit laced with toast and nuts.*	£17.30	Widely available	(G)

🍇 RIESLING

TIM KNAPPSTEIN RIESLING 1995 (PETALUMA) South Australia	*'An excellent nose' thought John Worontschak, 'with a powerful, lifted palate'.*	£6.20	OD WMK AMA	(B)
MITCHELL WATERVALE RIESLING 1994 South Australia	*Creamy and simple, with bags of lemony citrus fruit. The finish is long and well-balanced.*	£7.10	Widely available	(B)

AUSTRALIA • WHITE

Mount Langi Ghiran Riesling 1995 Victoria	*A lovely, gentle nose doesn't prepare you for the huge, rich, dense palate of this wine.*	**£7.30**	ENO SEL VDV CWI NY VLW SOM **(B)**
Georgia's Paddock Riesling 1994, Jasper Hill Vineyard Victoria	*Good balance and length with a lemon-zesty flavour and more than a hint of oak.*	**£10.00**	ADN AUS **(B)**

SEMILLON

Malt House Vintners Australian Semillon NV, Redello Wines New South Wales	*Long, melony fruit and hints of ripe bananas with a touch of subtle, well-integrated oak.*	**£3.90**	MHV **(B)**
Hardy's Stamps of Australia Semillon/ Chardonnay 1995, BRL Hardy Wine Co South Australia	*A pleasant and soft, gently perfumed nose broadening out to soft, fleshy fruit on the palate.*	**£4.30**	Widely available **(B)**
Marienberg Semillon/ Chardonnay 1994 South Australia	*Bright, lemon-and-lime nose with ripe, balanced smoke and a buttery palate. Excellent length.*	**£5.20**	LAY DBY **(B)**
McWilliams Inheritance Fruit Wood NV South Australia	*Pale straw in colour with a lovely nose of apple blossom, followed by refreshing, zesty palate.*	**£5.50**	SHG WAV **(B)**
Eastwood Semillon/Chardonnay 1995, Miranda Wines New South Wales	*An attractive, gentle floral style, full of refreshingly attractive citrus and pineapple flavours.*	**£5.90**	BD **(B)**

AUSTRALIA • WHITE				
IRONSTONE SEMILLON/CHARDONNAY 1995, CAPE MENTELLE VINEYARDS Western Australia	*A heady and vibrant nose bursting with grassy aromas and asparagus, mistaken by many as Sauvignon Blanc.*	**£6.10**	Widely available	(S)
PENFOLDS BARREL-FERMENTED SEMILLON 1994, (SOUTHCORP) South Australia	*A fresh, lemon nose precedes a ripe, fruity palate balanced with oak and butter. Raspberries make up the finish.*	**£6.30**	W VWC CLA VDV VW MWW NRW SOM	(B)
LEASINGHAM CLARE VALLEY SEMILLON 1993, BRL HARDY WINE COMPANY South Australia	*Creamy, slightly botrytized nose, faintly metallic with buttery, ripe fruit and a pleasant length and finish.*	**£6.50**	WSO CWS JHL VDV FEN VLW DVY	(S)
BASEDOW SEMILLON 1994 South Australia	*Full, rich and creamy with ripe fruits, honey mint and vanilla. A clean finish.*	**£6.60**	Widely available	(B)
BROWN BROTHERS VICTORIAN SEMILLON 1992 New South Wales	*Subtle, citrus aroma, waxy, lemony palate with some oak and sweetened by melon and barley sugar.*	**£7.40**	Widely available	(B)
ST HALLETT SEMILLON/SAUVIGNON BLANC 1995 South Australia	*A clean, fresh and open bouquet with tones of grass, spicy apples and pineapple.*	**£7.50**	TO AUC	(B)
MCWILLIAMS MOUNT PLEASANT ELIZABETH SEMILLON 1989 New South Wales	*Deeply coloured wine with a pronounced, developed nose and soft, evolved fruit.*	**£7.80**	TO DBY WAV ADN	(B)

Pinpoint who sells the wine you wish to buy by turning to the stockist codes. If you know the name of the wine you want to buy, use the alphabetical index. If the price is your motivation, refer to the invaluable price guide index; red and white wines under £5, sparkling wines under £10 and champagne under £15. Happy hunting!

AUSTRALIA • WHITE

LONG GULLY SEMILLION 1992, REINER KLAPP Victoria	*Light and zesty with a citrus nose and palate and a hint of Muscat and spice.*	£8.00	HAR SAN NY	B
TIM ADAMS SEMILLON 1994 South Australia	*Crisp and well-balanced, with tangy, passion-fruit nose, ripe, citrus palate, slight oak with a clean finish.*	£9.10	TO DBY RD MM AUC BU WR TH	S

OTHER WHITE

DALWOOD MEDIUM DRY WHITE 1995, SOUTHCORP South Australia	*Sweet, dessert, grapey aromas. Rich fruit balanced by some zesty citrus acidity. Good complexity.*	£3.70	MGN ABY CLA CPW HOU COK POR	B
ANGOVE'S RIDGEMOUNT BAY COLOMBARD/ CHARDONNAY 1995 South Australia	*Pleasant aromas of boiled sweets and guavas. Lovely round, creamy character offset by lemony acidity.*	£3.70	BES	B
FOREST FLOWER FRUITY DRY WHITE 1995, MAISON VIN Western Australia	*A balanced and elegant wine with excellent and distinctive flavours of nettle and fresh, crisp apple.*	£4.00	CWS	S
HOUGHTON WILDFLOWER RIDGE CHENIN BLANC 1995 Western Australia	*Well-balanced flavour of lemon and lime develops on the palate before a clean finish.*	£5.30	Widely available	B
ST HALLETT POACHERS BLEND 1995 South Australia	*Lovely, fragrant, zesty fruit-salad aroma and a palate full of gentle, attractive, floral fruit.*	£5.40	TH AUC RD POR NRW SOM BU WR	B

AUSTRALIA • WHITE				
BEST'S COLOMBARD 1995 Victoria	*A very fruity wine with a pleasant, flowery nose and a crisp, lemon-sherbet flavour.*	**£5.70**	Widely available	B
MOONDAH BROOK CHENIN BLANC 1994, BRL HARDY WINE COMPANY Western Australia	*Soft richness with a complexity of apples, quinces, lemons and limes. Well-balanced acidity.*	**£5.90**	Widely available	B
CHATEAU TAHBILK MARSANNE 1994 Victoria	*Lemon nose and a powerful mint, sweet-pea and honey palate with a limey, marmalade finish.*	**£6.10**	PLE OD SHG VDV G&M WMK IVY	B
ROSEMOUNT ESTATE SAUVIGNON BLANC 1995 New South Wales	*Fresh, ripe and stylish, this wine has abundant, zingy acid with a clean, sharp finish.*	**£6.90**	Widely available	B
GOUNDREY SAUVIGNON BLANC 1995 Western Australia	*A green and fragrant wine with an open nose. Tangy, soft fruit with a gripping finish.*	**£7.00**	Widely available	B
BROWN BROTHERS VINTAGE FAMILY SELECTION SAUVIGNON BLANC 1994 Victoria	*Greengage and asparagus make up a sweet, complex nose and follow through on palate and finish.*	**£7.20**	DIR TAN CPW NAD VIL OD BRB DBY	B
McGUIGAN BROTHERS SHAREHOLDERS RESERVE SAUVIGNON BLANC 1996 New South Wales	*This has a calming greenish tinge to it with a vegetal, citrusy aroma.*	**£8.00**	VNO GLY	S
JAMIESON'S RUN SAUVIGNON BLANC 1995, MILDARA BLASS South Australia	*A fresh, ripe, fruity nose leads into a medium-bodied style with balance and acidity.*	**£8.10**	BTH BKW OD VDV WFB MTL SEA WCR	B

AUSTRALIA • WHITE

STAFFORD RIDGE LENSWOOD SAUVIGNON BLANC 1995 South Australia	*Ripe fruit, a smoky savoury nose with crisp, lively acid in an appealing Sauvignon style.*	**£8.30**	ADN ADN MFS	(B)
KATNOOK ESTATE SAUVIGNON BLANC 1995, WINGARA WINE GROUP South Australia	*A full, rich, smoky Sauvignon style offers pungency, astringency and a racy, fresh, acidic finish.*	**£8.60**	Widely available	(B)
YALUMBA SHOW RESERVE VIOGNIER 1994 South Australia	*Bright, soft and intense apricot fruit with tones of banana, peach and marshmallow. Great length.*	**£9.00**	OD	(S)

SWEET WHITE

BEST'S VICTORIA LATE HARVEST MUSCAT 1995 Victoria	*A delightful wine. Toffee and spice on the nose with hints of almonds.*	**£6.50**	BOO TP SHG BUT HOT SWS VDV COK	(B)
FAMILY RESERVE BOTRYTIS SEMILLON/SAUVIGNON BLANC 1995, YALUMBA South Australia	*Lovely and full-bodied wine. Complex nose, comprising peach, pineapple and honey aromas.*	**£8.10**	OD ADN RBS HAL BH DBY	(S)
CRANSWICK ESTATE BOTRYTIS SEMILLON 1994 New South Wales	*Honey and rich toffee aromas. Gentle yet full, with creamy fruit and a long finish.*	**£10.60**	GAR NY	(B)

Pinpoint who sells the wine you wish to buy by turning to the stockist codes. If you know the name of the wine you want to buy, use the alphabetical index. If the price is your motivation, refer to the invaluable price guide index; red and white wines under £5, sparkling wines under £10 and champagne under £15. Happy hunting!

SPARKLING

SEAVIEW BRUT NV South Australia	*Rich, burnt caramel on the nose; effervescent mousse; tart, raspberry palate; sweet finish.*	£6.00	Widely available	**B**
SEAVIEW PINOT NOIR/CHARDONNAY 1993 South Australia	*Lasting fizz of ripe, tropical palate with toasty edge, good balance and long, creamy finish.*	£7.90	Widely available	**S** WINE OF THE YEAR
HARDY'S SPARKLING NV, BRL HARDY WINE COMPANY South Australia	*Fat, upfront nose with good mousse; rich, long, lasting, balanced length and a polished finish.*	£8.00	R VLW	**B**
REDBANK CUVÉE EMILY BRUT NV Victoria	*Golden straw colour; full, rich flavours with a vanilla edge and long, dry fruity aftertaste.*	£8.00	TOU WIN	**B**
CUVÉE TWO SPARKLING CABERNET SAUVIGNON NV, YALUMBA South Australia	*Blackcurrant colour with hints of orange; plenty of Shiraz pepper on the nose, excellent acidity on finish; good fruit.*	£8.50	TO ADN OD	**S**
CUVÉE ONE PINOT NOIR/CHARDONNAY NV, YALUMBA South Australia	*Lovely, tropical flavours with a biscuity edge. Fresh and mouthfilling with a pleasant, dry aftertaste.*	£8.70	Widely available	**B**
SEPPELT SPARKLING SHIRAZ 1992 South Australia	*Wonderfully subtle Shiraz undertones shadow summer fruit and spice aromas. Good balance; crisp finish.*	£8.80	Widely available	**S**

AUSTRALIA • FORTIFIED				
GREEN POINT BRUT VINTAGE 1993, DOMAINE CHANDON Victoria	*Light, green nose; soft, moussy fruit on palate with creamy acidity and a good finish.*	£10.70	Widely available	B
CROSER BRUT 1992, PETALUMA South Australia	*Fresh nose and classy, creamy fruit with good length, elegant complexity and a dry finish.*	£11.20	OD BEN SOM BU WR	B
CROSER BRUT 1993, PETALUMA South Australia	*Apple and biscuit nose; light, clean and crisp citrus palate, toasted finish. Young and improving.*	£11.30	OD BEN NEI BU WR TH	S
E&E SPARKLING BLACK PEPPER SHIRAZ 1991, BAROSSA VALLEY ESTATES (BERRI-RENMANO-HARDY's) South Australia	*Purple-red, lively mousse. Bright, fresh and fruity with spice and wonderful, balancing acidity.*	£13.00	OD DBY VDV HOU VLW	S

FORTIFIED

SEPPELT SHOW FINO DP 117 NV South Australia	*Pale green-gold. Suggestions of spice and salt with herbaceous undertones. Firm and dry.*	£6.00	OD VDV LWE NY HOU AMW	B
ROTHBURY MUSEUM RESERVE LIQUEUR MUSCAT New South Wales	*Refreshing, citrus-fruit nose. Richer palate of chopped nuts, sweet raisins and caramel.*	£6.10	Widely available	B
MICK MORRIS LIQUEUR MUSCAT NV, ORLANDO WINES Victoria	*Attractive, floral aromas with hints of coffee. Clean, citrus-fruit character. Rich, sweet finish.*	£7.00	Widely available	B

AUSTRALIA • FORTIFIED				
MUSEUM SHOW RESERVE RUTHERGLEN MUSCAT NV, YALUMBA Victoria	*Christmas-pudding and coffee aromas lead on to a mellow palate of caramel and golden syrup.*	£7.50	JN NI BEN CVR VW SOM WOC	(B)
SEPPELT RUTHERGLEN SHOW MUSCAT DP63 NV Victoria	*Classic, mature Muscat with complex palate, showing abundant flavours of dried fruits, ginger and orange peel.*	£7.80	Widely available	(G)
STANTON & KILLEEN RUTHERGLEN MUSCAT NV Victoria	*Sweet and rich, with toffee and chewy raisin flavours. Fresh coffee and marmalade finish.*	£8.10	Widely available	(S)
STANTON & KILLEEN SPECIAL OLD RUTHERGLEN MUSCAT NV Victoria	*Burnt toffee, sweet raisin and toasted-nut flavours. Rich and luscious with delightfully tangy acidity.*	£10.30	SEL NI LWE NY AMW	(B)
CAMPBELLS OLD RUTHERGLEN MUSCAT NV Victoria	*Rich nose of coffee and smooth caramel with a sprinkling of spice. Very rich and sweet.*	£11.30	Widely available	(S)
BROWN BROTHERS LIQUEUR MUSCAT NV Victoria	*Coffee and orange marmalade aromas. Rich palate of spicy raisins and burnt marmalade.*	£11.70	Widely available	(G)
SEPPELT PARA TAWNY 116 NV, SEPPELT South Australia	*Brown amber, aromatic and concentrated caramel, almond and butter balanced by alcohol and acid.*	£15.80	CTH BOO VDV LWE HOU COK AMW	(G)
MCWILLIAM'S LIQUEUR MUSCAT SHOW SERIES LIMITED RELEASE 1994 New South Wales	*Rich coffee, chocolate and chopped-nut aromas. Sweet, rich, raisiny palate with great concentration and complexity.*	£23.00	WAV	(G)

AUSTRIA

INCREASINGLY OUTSTANDING LATE-HARVEST wines are the backbone of Austria's wine production. They have certainly generated respect throughout the world, despite the relatively small market for this particular style. A range of good white and red wines are also produced, and these are being seen more frequently on the shelves of supermarkets and specialist retailers in the UK. Definitely a country to watch for the future.

RED

BLAUFRÄNKISCH TROCKEN 1992, WINZERHOF KAISER Burgenland	*Deep purple; lots of dusty, leafy plum and damson flavours, young and nicely concentrated; high in tannin.*	**£11.40**	NUM RBS	**B**
PAUL ACHS PANNOBILE 1993 Burgenland	*Blackberry fruit and the smokiness of oak, very intense and tannic with excellent length.*	**£15.50**	NUM	**B**
FRAUENKIRCHER ST-LAURENT 1993, UMATHUM Burgenland	*Deep colour; complex nose with ripe, rich fruits – morello, damson – and spices on the big, fruity palate.*	**£21.60**	T&W	**S**

SWEET WINE

WEINKELLEREI BURGENLAND RUSTER BEERENAUSLESE 1981 Burgenland	*Sweet, botrytised nose. Rich, honeyed apple and apricot fruit. Gentle, raisiny finish.*	**£6.60**	PEA WTR CAX SEL TAN AMW AMA	**B**

AUSTRIA • SWEET WINE				
WEINKELLEREI BURGENLAND EISWEIN 1992 Burgenland	*Delicately scented nose with a sweet, honeyed palate showing attractive, tropical fruit.*	£8.10	PEA U WTR CAX MHW AMW AMA	B
WEINKELLEREI BURGENLAND TROCKENBEERENAUSLESE 1991 Burgenland	*Honeysuckle aromas with hints of citrus fruits. Luscious apricot/peach fruit. Creamy with a honeyed finish.*	£8.40	PEA U WTR CEN CAX AMA CWS	S
WEINKELLEREI BURGENLAND RUSTER AUSBRUCH 1992, WEINKELLEREI Burgenland	*Sweet tangy orange fruit with fresh limey acidity. Supple, fruity palate of peaches and melons.*	£9.50	PEA WTR JCK CDE CEN CAX	B
RUSTER AUSBRUCH PINOT CUVÉE 1994, WEINGUT FEILER-ARTINGER Burgenland	*Masses of ripe apricot and peach fruit with orange marmalade flavours cut by fine, citrus acidity.*	£13.50	L&W	B
PAUL ACHS WELSCHRIESLING EISWEIN 1992 Burgenland	*Ripe peach/apricot fruit, delightful honeyed character. Fabulous balance of sweet richness and lively, limey acidity.*	£17.00	NUM	S
SCHEUREBE BEERENAUSLESE 1994, ALOIS KRACHER Burgenland	*Ripe, flowery botrytis character; sweet rhubarb and fresh grapefruit. Ripe and fat in the mouth.*	£18.00	NY	B
ZWISCHEN DEN SEEN BEERENAUSLESE 1993, ALOIS KRACHER Burgenland	*Restrained nose, slightly floral with gentle lime aspects. Richer palate of barley sugar, baked oranges and marmalade.*	£18.00	RD H & D NY	S
NOUVELLE VAGUE BEERENAUSLESE 1994, ALOIS KRACHER Burgenland	*Zesty citrus fruit and pronounced botrytis character combine with warm, spicy vanilla. Rich and concentrated.*	£20.00	NY	S

AUSTRIA • SWEET WINE				
SCHILFWEIN TRADITION 1993, NEKOWITSCH Burgenland	*Classic botrytis nose, very honeyed with perfumed aromas. Elegant apricot and pineapple. Excellent richness and concentration.*	£20.00	NY	(G)
SCHILFWEIN TRADITION 1994, NEKOWITSCH Burgenland	*Excellent, super-ripe apricot and honeyed, peachy fruit. Incredibly rich and sweet with luscious tropical fruits.*	£20.00	NY	(G)
OPITZ ZWEIGELT BEERENAUSLESE 1994, WILLI OPITZ Burgenland	*Unusual with delicate rose-petal aromas. Sweet red cherry and perfumed, peachy fruit. Soft, ripe and honeyed.*	£22.00	T&W	(S)
KRACHER GRANDE CUVÉE BEERENAUSLESE 1994, ALOIS KRACHER Burgenland	*Captivating orange sweetie showing tremendous botrytis. Wonderful complexity; rich apricot/raisin fruit; creamy.*	£22.50	RD NY HW	(S)
NOUVELLE VAGUE BEERENAUSLESE CHARDONNAY/WELSCHRIESLING 1991, ALOIS KRACHER Burgenland	*Ripe bananas and intense, tropical fruits mingled with a warming spiciness. Elegant with plenty of complexity.*	£23.40	RD NY	(B)
ZWISCHEN DEN SEEN TROCKENBEERENAUSLESE 1994, ALOIS KRACHER Burgenland	*Rich botrytis; very sweet with gentle spiciness. Ripe peach and apricot fruit balanced by fresh acidity.*	£26.00	RD NY	(S)
NOUVELLE VAGUE TROCKENBEERENAUSLESE 1994, ALOIS KRACHER Burgenland	*Incredibly rich botrytis on the nose, with attractive aromas of ripe, perfumed, fresh apricots.*	£26.40	RD NY	(S)
ZWISCHEN DEN SEEN SCHEUREBE TROCKENBEERENAUSLESE 1995, ALOIS KRACHER Burgenland	*Freshly peeled oranges with plenty of botrytis character. Rich palate of creamy pineapples and ripe melons.*	£26.90	RD NY	(B)

AUSTRIA • SWEET WINE

WELSCHRIESLING TROCKENBEERENAUSLESE 1994, ALOIS KRACHER Burgenland	*Rich barley sugar-and-lime nose. Sweet and creamy palate with soft toffee and orange marmalade flavours.*	**£28.00**	RD NY	**B**
ZWISCHEN DEN SEEN WELSCHRIESLING TROCKENBEERENAUSLESE 1995, ALOIS KRACHER Burgenland	*Delightful, clean, fresh tropical-fruit character; ripe with wonderful, zingy fresh acidity. Concentrated, creamy texture.*	**£28.50**	RD NY	**G**
SCHILFMANDL 1994, MCLAREN/WILLI OPITZ Burgenland	*Lovely complexity with beeswax and soft caramel aromas. Honeyed concentration balanced by fresh acidity.*	**£36.00**	ADN	**G**
ROTER SCHILFMANDL 1994, WILLI OPITZ Burgenland	*Luscious and rich, it has sweet marmalade and caramel flavours cut by some fresh acidity.*	**£39.30**	T&W	**S**
OPITZ PINOT BLANC TROCKENBEERENAUSLESE 1995, WILLI OPITZ Burgenland	*Intense, exotic, peach and pineapple fruit, very ripe, with a smooth, golden-syrup flavour.*	**£41.30**	ADN T&W	**S**
WEISSER SCHILFMANDL 1994, WILLI OPITZ Burgenland	*Complex flavours of toasted nuts, peaches and pear-drops. A sweet, honeyed palate cut by some fresh acidity.*	**£41.30**	T&W	**S**
WELSCHRIESLING SCHEUREBE BEERENAUSLESE 1994, WILLI OPITZ Burgenland	*Rich, honeyed nose with a slight spiciness. Elegant and clean. Refreshing with good balance.*	**£44.00**	T&W ADN	**B**
WILLI OPITZ SCHEUREBE 1994 Burgenland	*Delicate floral aromas with hints of pink grape-fruit. Aromatic, peachy fruit with a smooth, creamy coconut.*	**£44.00**	T&W	**B**

AUSTRIA • SWEET WINE				
OPITZ ONE RED DESSERT BLAUBURGUNDER TROCKENBEERENAUSLESE 1994, WILLI OPITZ Burgenland	*Great nose of rose petals, marshmallows and coconut. Soft, raspberry and marmalade fruit, gentle acidity.*	**£46.50**	RBS ADN	**B**

EASTERN EUROPE

POSSIBLY THE AREA OF GREATEST change in the world. Through policies of privatisation, the arrival of Western winemakers and the influx of capital investment, the quality of wines is improving and beginning to make headlines in the wine trade. However, despite these advantages some regions have still not benefited, resulting in their wines reaching the UK only if they specifically suit the 'Western' palate.

BULGARIA • RED

BULGARIAN MERLOT/GAMAY 1993, VINPROM Russe	*Lovely ruby red colour with cherry and soft plummy fruit flavours. Very ripe and jammy.*	**£3.40**	SPR	(B)
DOMAINE BOYAR SUHINDOL CABERNET SAUVIGNON SPECIAL RESERVE 1990, LOVICO SUHINDOL Iambol	*Plum and summer fruit flavours coupled with a mouth watering toffee and rich smooth tannin.*	**£3.90**	DBO VW AMA BU WR TH	(S)
DOMAINE BOYAR IAMBOL SPECIAL RESERVE CABERNET SAUVIGNON 1990, VINIS IAMBOL Iambol	*Robust but smooth, ripe fruits and sweet oak; great complexity with a juicy finish.*	**£4.00**	Widely available	(S)

BULGARIA • WHITE

POMORIE REGION CHARDONNAY 1995, BLACK SEA GOLD POMORIE Pomorie	*Fresh and simple with a lemony nose and a dry, fruit salad palate. A tart, grapefruity finish.*	**£3.00**	DBO WRT	(B)

DOMAINE BOYAR BULGARIAN COUNTRY WHITE NV, VINEX SLAVIANTZI Slaviantzi	*Intriguing nose of lychees, rose petals and spice. Generous, grapey palate with hints of warming ginger.*	**£3.00**	OD DBO MHW WMK SPR BU WR	**B**
DOMAINE BOYAR TARGOVISCHTE CHARDONNAY 1995, LVK TARGOVISCHTE Targovischte	*Lemons and limes on the nose are followed by a crisp, acidic citrus-fruit palate with a firm finish.*	**£3.20**	DBO BU WR TH	**B**

HUNGARY • RED

GATSBERG CABERNET SAUVIGNON 1994, EGERVIN Eger	*There's a deep colour to this full bodied red. Earthy blackcurrant and vanilla tones abound.*	**£2.80**	WRT	**B**

HUNGARY • WHITE/SWEET WHITE

CHAPEL HILL BARRIQUE FERMENTED CHARDONNAY 1994, BALATONBOGLÁR WINERY South Balaton	*Lean, young complexity. Toasty aroma with a crisp, ripe, lemony flavour and clean finish.*	**£5.00**	SAF	**B**
CHATEAU MEGYER FURMINT 1995 Tokáji	*A pronounced, honeyed, floral aroma. Elegant, crisp, melon and lychee fruit – lovely.*	**£5.30**	Widely available	**S**
DISZNOKO TOKÁJI ASZÚ 5 PUTTONYOS 1992, DOMAINE DISZNOKO Tokáji	*Fresh peaches, marmalade and botrytis on the nose. Smooth, rich, caramel and sweet-raisin flavours.*	**£12.00**	PF OD MWW POR	**G**

TOKÁJI ASZÚ 5 PUTTONYOS 1988, BODEGAS OREMUS Tokáji	*Mature marmalade and candied orange-peel nose. Baked-orange flavour on the palate.*	£12.50	U DBY NY RAV	(B)
TOKÁJI ASZÚ 5 PUTTONYOS 1988, CHATEAU MEGYER Tokáji	*Apricot jam and baked-apple aromas. Rich, caramel and raisin flavours with ripe fruit.*	£12.70	ENO BEN DBY NIC MFS AMA	(B)
ROYAL TOKÁJI ASZÚ 5 PUTTONYOS 1991, ROYAL TOKÁJI WINE COMPANY Tokáji	*Fabulous apricot/peach fruit. Quite honeyed, with attractive botrytis. Smooth palate of soft caramel.*	£15.10	Widely available	(S)
BIRSALMANS Tokáji ASZÚ 5 PUTTONYOS, ROYAL Tokáji WINE COMPANY Tokáji	*A pleasantly botrytised nose of nectarine and marmalade with smooth raisiny fudge flavours on the palate.*	£22.60	HN LEA H&D RD SV HAY HW	(B)
NYULASZO Tokáji ASZÚ 5 PUTTONYOS, ROYAL Tokáji WINE COMPANY Tokáji	*Baked bramley and mincemeat on the nose and a fine palate of plums and honey.*	£33.60	LEA TAN RD ALD HAY	(B)

ROMANIA • RED

VALEA MIEILOR VINEYARDS SPECIAL RESERVE PINOT NOIR 1990, CEPTURA Sub-Carpathian Mountains	*Lovely nose with a good colour. Rich and stylish with enjoyable depth and macerated character.*	£3.50	MRN HAE	(B)

ENGLAND

IMPROVING EACH YEAR, today's English wines can no longer be pushed to one side and categorised as 'mock-German'; they now have more in common with the dry wines of the Loire and the aromatic wines of the north of Italy. Creating individual styles from lesser-known grape varieties is the thrust of English wine-making, resulting in interesting yet unusual wines.

RED

CHAPEL DOWN EPOCH RESERVE 1994 Isle of Wight	*Lots of lovely, soft and spicy cherry flavours – a lean, dry palate, woody and smoky.*	**£7.70**	CDO TV	**B**

WHITE

CO-OP ENGLISH TABLE WINE 1993, THREE CHOIRS VINEYARDS Gloucestershire	*Good, intense colour; concentrated, jammy nose; soft fruits; mature, slightly rotted finish with great fruit concentration.*	**£4.00**	CWS	**B**
VALLEY VINEYARDS STANLAKE 1994, THAMES VALLEY VINEYARDS (HARVEST WINE GROUP) Berkshire	*Very spritzy, with a tangy, green-fruit pastille character – a crisp and fruity wine of good length.*	**£4.00**	HWM SAF	**B**
NUTBOURNE VINEYARD SUSSEX RESERVE 1995, NUTBOURNE MANOR Sussex	*A rich, grassy and spicy wine with hints of sweet fruit on a lively, fresh palate.*	**£4.00**	SAF NBV	**B**

ENGLAND • WHITE

BRUISYARD ST PETER MEDIUM DRY 1994 Suffolk	*An intense and sweetly aromatic nose, with superb fruit balance and a lingering finish.*	£4.60	DBY BRU	(B)
BRUISYARD ST PETER MEDIUM SWEET 1994 Suffolk	*Distinctive, fresh and fragrant, slightly honeyed, ripe-lime fruit with a backbone of clean acidity.*	£4.60	DBY BRU	(B)
CARR TAYLOR SCHÖNBURGER DRY NV East Sussex	*A discreet but appealing aroma, fragrant and fruity. A soft, gentle wine with pleasing Muscat-style fruit.*	£4.90	CTV	(B)
TENTERDEN ESTATE DRY NV Kent	*A ripe, developed gooseberry fruit, very herbaceous, clean and crisp with hints of capsicum.*	£5.00	TV	(B)
SHAWSGATE MÜLLER THURGAU/SEYVAL BLANC MEDIUM DRY 1993 Suffolk	*Lightly spritzy - a good intensity of fresh clean fruit. Subtle with elegance and class.*	£5.00	SHA	(B)
VALLEY VINEYARDS REGATTA 1995, THAMES VALLEY VINEYARDS (HARVEST WINE GROUP) Berkshire	*Subtle, Sauvignon-style greenness. Crisp and appley with hints of citrus and sherbet.*	£5.30	TVV TH HWM OD BU WR	(B)
DENBIES RIESLING 1995 Surrey	*A lovely, floral nose with hints of spice, lemon and grass. Crisp, balanced and fresh.*	£6.00	DBS VIL OD	(B)
CHAPEL DOWN BACCHUS 1994 Kent	*A wonderful gooseberry nose. This is a slightly off-dry wine full of attractive grass and melon flavours.*	£6.20	BKW CEL WCR TV	(B)

ENGLAND • WHITE/SWEET WHITE

NORTHBROOK SPRINGS OBM 1993, HARVEST WINE GROUP Hampshire	*Lovely grassy fruit; full of fresh, sherbety, citrus characters and lovely zingy, mouthwatering acidity. Nice wine.*	£6.50	BV HWM NI NSV BU WR	(S)
BREAKY BOTTOM SEYVAL BLANC 1992 Southern Counties	*Delicate, with a strong, vegetal, wet-straw aroma and plenty of warm, honeyed-apple flavours.*	£7.00	WSO HAR BBV	(S)
WYKEN BACCHUS 1993 East Anglia	*Lean, appley aromas and a slightly earthy, mineral quality. Good, broad fruit with a slight spritz.*	£8.20	ADN WKV	(B)
SHAWSGATE BACCHUS 1994 Suffolk	*A grassily fruity bouquet with flinty, gunpowder hints. A fresh wine with a long, crisp finish.*	£8.50	SHA	(B)
CHANCTONBURY CLASSIC 1992 West Sussex	*A rush of smoky nettles combined with grape-fruit, wet wool and a touch of sweetness.*	£9.50	CVY NI	(B)
BARKHAM MANOR BACCHUS 1994 East Sussex	*A lovely big, fat, tropical nose bursting with grapefruit, spice and honey. This screams class.*	£10.50	BAK EWC	(S)

SWEET WHITE

DENBIES LATE HARVEST 1995 Surrey	*Light botrytis with fresh grapefruit, pineapple and heather honey. Elegant, floral style.*	£6.20	DBS OD GHL	(B)

SPARKLING

OLDACRES SAUVIGNON SPRITZER NV, OLDACRES & THREE CHOIRS VINEYARD Gloucestershire	*Lovely and pleasant; fruity with a flowery aroma. Excellent for a garden party*	**£2.00**	JS MRS A W CWS	**B**
CHAPEL DOWN CENTURY EXTRA DRY NV Kent	*A pungently smoky, kiwi fruit nose with a fruity, floral palate of medium length and a fruity aftertaste.*	**£6.50**	CDO W	**B**

FRANCE

STILL THOUGHT OF BY MANY as the heartland of the wine world, despite the dramatically increased competition from around the globe. This year's results show how varied the standard of French wines can be. In terms of sheer quality, there is no serious contender to Champagne's throne. The top houses still hold their own, but the red and white table wines are under threat from the fruity, up-front, New World rivals.

BORDEAUX • RED

CHÂTEAU LA COMMANDERIE DE QUEYRET 1994, POMEROL Bordeaux	*Elegant blackcurrant-leaf aromas lead to juicy fruits. Clean, fresh, zippy acidity to finish.*	**£4.80**	NEI GI DBY	B
CHÂTEAU DE LAGE 1994, ENTRE-DEUX-MERS, J CALVET Bordeaux	*Displays a clean, fresh nose. Medium-bodied fruit and violets with flavour and length.*	**£5.00**	WCR	B
CHÂTEAU LÉON PREMIÈRE CÔTES DE BORDEAUX 1993, PHILLIPPE PIERAERTS Bordeaux	*Open nose. With its berry fruits and mellow tannins this wine does not disappoint. Juicy.*	**£5.00**	TO	B
SOMERFIELD MÉDOC NV, LES CHAIS DU PRÉ LA REINE Bordeaux	*Peppers and full, rich fruits dominate, with balanced tannins. The long, smooth finish is mouthwatering.*	**£5.00**	SMF	B
SOMERFIELD OAK AGED CLARET NV, PETER SICHEL Bordeaux	*Luscious, well-balanced palate, good body with fruit and violet flavours. Satisfying, long finish.*	**£5.00**	SMF SIP	B

YVECOURT PREMIUM 1993, YVON MAU Bordeaux	*An array of good flavours come through in fruitful quantities. Some tannins make for a dryish finish.*	**£5.00**	MAR	**B**
CLARET ANDRÉ LURTON 1992 Bordeaux	*Interesting aromas of spice and hints of rubber. Old-fashioned style with soft tannins.*	**£5.30**	TDS BU WR TH	**B**
SPECIAL RESERVE CLARET BORDEAUX SUPÉRIEUR 1993, YVON MAU Bordeaux	*Light fruit, woody flavours. A good but rather dry wine. Will soften in time.*	**£5.30**	U	**B**
CHÂTEAU SAINT-ROBERT 1993, GRAVES Bordeaux	*Good Cabernet nose followed by a ripe and fruity mouthful. Lots of good oak.*	**£6.00**	SMF	**B**
CHÂTEAU HAUT-VEYRAC 1993, M CLAVERIE Bordeaux	*Robust with some rich fruit flavours. Good character packed with smooth tannins, giving a long finish.*	**£6.20**	MHV	**B**
CHÂTEAU DE BELCIER 1993, CÔTES DE CASTILLON Bordeaux	*Mid-palate fruit adds depth, while good spice leads to tannins and a lengthy finish.*	**£6.90**	CNL SCU HTD WER AMW DBY COK	**B**
CHÂTEAU CAMAIL 1993, FRANÇOIS MASSON REGNAULT Bordeaux	*Mint and smoked wood nose. Palate has fruit and hints of cinnamon. Good tannic finish.*	**£7.50**	BD	**B**
BARON PHILIPPE DE ROTHSCHILD SAINT-EMILION 1992 Bordeaux	*Ripe, cherry flavours and good acidity. Alcohol is well-balanced with ripe tannins. Good length.*	**£8.10**	PEA SHG GHL MTL MHW FEN	**B**

CHÂTEAU CHARMAIL CRU BOURGEOIS 1992, HAUT-MÉDOC Bordeaux	*Toasty oak on the nose. Dominant fruit and unrestricted, smooth tannins on the finish.*	£8.50	HRV U	**B**
CHÂTEAU PALOUMEY CRU BOURGEOIS 1993, HAUT-MÉDOC Bordeaux	*Elegant with a green fruit nose and hints of tobacco. Palate equally elegant with depth.*	£8.70	OD CVR NY	**B**
CHÂTEAU LES HAUTS DE PONTET 1991, PAUILLAC (CHÂTEAU PONTET-CANET) Bordeaux	*Good, clean nose with fruit and peppermint tones. The berries on the mid-palate have well-balanced acidity.*	£9.30	CWS	**B**
BARON PHILIPPE DE ROTHSCHILD PAUILLAC 1994 Bordeaux	*Perfume character on the nose. Cherry fruits with high acidity; mineral hints and soft tannins.*	£9.70	MWW SHG GDS MTL MHW MM IVY	**B**
SÉGLA DE RAUSAN 1993, MARGAUX, CHÂTEAU RAUSAN-SÉGLA Bordeaux	*Smoked cheese, oaky, slightly vegetal nose. Good balance and lovely smooth finish.*	£10.00	BKW WCR	**B**
CHÂTEAU LA CLARIÈRE LAITHWAITE 1994, CÔTES DE CASTILLON Bordeaux	*Plummy in the glass with tobacco and berry fruit on the nose. The firm, young tannins are developing well.*	£10.00	BD	**S**
CHÂTEAU LA GARRICQ MOULIS 1993, HAUT-MÉDOC, CANTEGRAVES Bordeaux	*Grenadine and spicy oak on the nose. Firm, structured tannins with light almost Gamay-like fruit on the mid-palate.*	£10.50	RAV	**B**
CHÂTEAU FOMBRAUGE GRAND CRU 1993, SAINT-EMILION Bordeaux	*Soft, easy-going personality with lots of obvious Merlot fruit backed by subtle, smooth tannins. Very drinkable.*	£11.00	CWL PAT	**B**

FRANCE • BORDEAUX RED

CHÂTEAU BEAU-SITE CRU BOURGEOIS 1991, SAINT-ESTÈPHE Bordeaux	*Coffee and green leafiness on the nose. Liquorice and berry fruit on the palate. Will mature superbly.*	£11.00	WAV	(S)
BERRY'S POMEROL NV, ALEXANDER THIENPONT Bordeaux	*Merlot-based wine with lots of ripe, plummy fruit. Slightly vegetal nose. Ready for drinking now.*	£11.30	BBR	(B)
CHÂTEAU HAUT-BAGES-AVEROUS 1992, PAUILLAC, (CHÂTEAU LYNCH-BAGES) Bordeaux	*Cherry-red with a cooked fruit nose. Light to medium-bodied with good berry-fruit flavours.*	£12.00	MWW	(B)
CHÂTEAU LA BESSANE 1993, MARGAUX, CANTEGRAVES Bordeaux	*Open, expressive and herbaceous. Complex personality with a sweet finish. Will evolve well.*	£12.00	SNW	(B)
ST-MICHAEL MOULIN DE DUHART 1990, PAUILLAC, DOMAINES BARONS DE ROTHSCHILD Bordeaux	*Ripe, cedary tones and roasted earthiness. Classic claret with fine tannin-fruit balance.*	£13.00	M&S	(B)
CHÂTEAU DE CLAIREFONT 1993, MARGAUX, (CHÂTEAU PRIEURÉ-LICHINE) Bordeaux	*Deep garnet colourings. A stalky nose with smoky, complex fruit and firm tannins giving grip to the lengthy finish.*	£13.50	NIC	(B)
CHÂTEAU BATAILLEY 1993, PAUILLAC Bordeaux	*Earthy, minerally nose. Well-integrated oak with a long, liquorice character to the fruit.*	£13.60	BBR OD DBY MM WAV	(B)
LA RÉSERVE DE LÉOVILLE-BARTON 1989, SAINT-JULIEN, CHÂTEAU LÉOVILLE-BARTON Bordeaux	*Voluptuous and velvety with a deep style and good grip. Great purity, elegance and balance.*	£13.80	Widely available	(B)

FRANCE • BORDEAUX RED

CHÂTEAU CLERC-MILON GRAND CRU CLASSÉ 1992, PAUILLAC, BARON PHILIPPE DE ROTHSCHILD Bordeaux	*Well-structured Cabernet with a balanced backbone and fleshy Merlot fruit. Fine grippy tannins.*	**£14.70**	JS TH SHG DBY MTL AMA BU WR	**B**
CHÂTEAU LABÉGORCE 1989, MARGAUX Bordeaux	*A mellow, cassis-flavoured wine which has aged well and shows all the attributes of a good claret.*	**£15.00**	THP	**B**
CHÂTEAU HAUT-MARBUZET CRU BOURGEOIS 1993, SAINT-ESTEPHE Bordeaux	*Chocolate and coffee flavours precede ripe cassis fruit mingled with vanilla pod hints.*	**£17.10**	AP BEC WON DBY HVW NIC AMW MFS	**B**
CHÂTEAU CANTEMERLE GRAND CRU CLASSÉ 1993, HAUT-MÉDOC Bordeaux	*Elegant, with good use of oak and hints of chocolate on the palate. Almost Margaux-like.*	**£18.50**	SHG	**B**
CHÂTEAU MONBOUSQUET GRAND CRU 1993, SAINT-EMILION Bordeaux	*Fine, cedary oak with a classy, figgy middle palate. Firm tannins and balanced fruit.*	**£18.70**	NIC	**S**
CHÂTEAU LASCOMBES MARGAUX 1989 Bordeaux	*Complex, tobacco nose with good intensity and a touch of green leafiness. Very elegant.*	**£20.80**	THP ALD CHL BU WR TH	**B**
CHÂTEAU CANTEMERLE GRAND CRU CLASSÉ 1990, HAUT-MÉDOC Bordeaux	*Wonderfully fruity and tremendously ripe. Rich with some berry sweetness. Excellent length. Will age well.*	**£20.90**	MWW SHG BEN TAN	**G**

Pinpoint who sells the wine you wish to buy by turning to the stockist codes. If you know the name of the wine you want to buy, use the alphabetical index. If the price is your motivation, refer to the invaluable price guide index; red and white wines under £5, sparkling wines under £10 and champagne under £15. Happy hunting!

FRANCE • BORDEAUX RED

CHÂTEAU LES ORMES-DE-PEZ 1990, SAINT-ESTÈPHE Bordeaux	*Vegetal nose with ripe juicy fruit on the palate. Hints of chocolate and oak. Peppery finish.*	**£22.20**	NIC SEB	**B**
CHÂTEAU D'ARMAILHAC GRAND CRU CLASSÉ 1990, PAUILLAC (BARON PHILIPPE DE ROTHSCHILD) Bordeaux	*Aromas of blackcurrant, cassis and nutmeg. Leather, strawberry and nutmeg also abound on the palate.*	**£22.40**	Widely available	**G**
CHÂTEAU TROPLONG-MONDOT GRAND CRU CLASSÉ 1992, SAINT-EMILION Bordeaux	*Plum and asparagus on the nose. Bordeaux-style grassy blackcurrant on the palate. Excellent ageing potential.*	**£25.00**	WCR	**S**
CHÂTEAU L'ANGÉLUS GRAND CRU CLASSÉ 1992, SAINT-EMILION Bordeaux	*Burnt-rubber nose with blackcurrant and liquorice. notes Creamy vanilla mingles with berry fruit and spice.*	**£28.40**	NIC	**G**
CHÂTEAU BEAUSÉJOUR-DUFFAU-LAGARROSSE GRAND CRU CLASSÉ 1989, SAINT-EMILION Bordeaux	*Warm and ripe with a baked, jammy nose. Medium intensity with good tannins.*	**£32.00**	J&B	**B**
CHÂTEAU PICHON-LALANDE 1989, PAUILLAC Bordeaux	*Bashful, raspberry nose contrasted by bold, cherry firmness. Leathery tannins with solid blackcurrant fruit.*	**£34.50**	CRM OD THP J&B RD DBY ALD	**S**
CHÂTEAU PETIT-VILLAGE 1990, POMEROL Bordeaux	*Classic, old-blood colour with signs of ageing at the rim. Baked fruit on the palate with plenty of tannins.*	**£40.50**	NIC WCR	**S**
CHÂTEAU LYNCH-BAGES 1990, PAUILLAC Bordeaux	*An excellent blend with a pencil-like character. An abundance of rich fruit and hints of the farmyard.*	**£46.70**	Widely available	**G**

CHÂTEAU HAUT-BRION 1990, PESSAC-LÉOGNAN Bordeaux	*Complex, herby nose with hints of liquorice and tobacco. Ripe berry fruit and balanced oak.*	**£79.10**	Widely available	**S**

BORDEAUX • WHITE

L'ESPÉRANCE MAUREGARD 1995, CHÂTEAU DE BEL AIR, LALANDE-DE-POMEROL Bordeaux	*A fresh, minerally nose with hints of asparagus, citrus and guava fruit. Richly fruity.*	**£4.00**	U	**B**
SAFEWAY BORDEAUX BLANC (SEC) OAK AGED 1995, CAVES UNION PRODIFFIN LAN DERROUAT Bordeaux	*A well-crafted, fresh and aromatic wine with a grapefruit nose and a lemony finish.*	**£4.00**	SAF	**B**
CHÂTEAU LA PERRIÈRE 1995, FRANÇOIS FARGUEYRET Bordeaux	*Gorgeous, aromatic, grassy limey fruit, reminiscent of Sauvignon; a complex, well-balanced wine.*	**£4.30**	MWW	**B**

BORDEAUX • SWEET WHITE

BARON PHILIPPE DE ROTHSCHILD SAUTERNES 1991 Bordeaux	*Soft and peachy, it has a gentle, nutty aspect which adds interest. Subtle, apricot fruit.*	**£12.50**	Widely available	**B**
FORTNUM & MASON SAUTERNES 1992, BRIATTE Bordeaux	*Rich, developed botrytis character. A creamy, honeyed palate with lively, citrussy acidity.*	**£15.00**	F&M	**S**

CHÂTEAU LA RAME RÉSERVE SAINT-CROIX-DU-MONT 1990 Bordeaux	*Plenty of rich botrytis, peachy/pineapple fruit and hints of candied peel and coconut.*	**£16.60**	CRM NI OD	(G)
CHÂTEAU DE CÉRONS 1989 Bordeaux	*Elegant, honeyed fruit; quite creamy with good botrytis. Soft, tropical fruit on the palate.*	**£17.80**	NIC	(B)
CHÂTEAU SUDUIRAUT SAUTERNES 1ER CRU 1989 Bordeaux	*Youthful, ripe pineapple and mango fruit. Hints of coconut and nutmeg adorn its richly textured palate.*	**£29.90**	OD BEN CPW ALD NIC TAN	(B)
CHÂTEAU RIEUSSEC SAUTERNES 1989 Bordeaux	*Rich and honeyed botrytis. Ripe peach and pineapple fruit; quite honeyed with clean, limey acidity.*	**£29.90**	JN OD RD ALD ADN SEB	(S)
CRU BARREJATS BARSAC 1991 Bordeaux	*Complex dessert wine with stewed-apricot fruit and ripe tangerines balanced by attractive citrus acidity.*	**£35.00**	J&B	(B)

BURGUNDY • RED

BOURGOGNE ROUGE PINOT NOIR 1994, VAUCHER PÈRE ET FILS Burgundy	*Light red with a good nose. Initially delicate, it strengthens in the mouth to give a complex finish.*	**£5.50**	BES	(B)
BOURGOGNE HAUTES CÔTES DE BEAUNE TÊTE DE CUVÉE 1992 Burgundy	*Attractive and developed; soft, well-balanced, clean nose. Complex fruit. A dry finish.*	**£7.00**	W	(B)

BOURGOGNE HAUTES CÔTES DE NUITS 1993, DOMAINE BERTAGNA Burgundy	*Rich nose and palate. A substantial and classy wine with some depth; needs some more time.*	**£7.50**	WEP	(B)
MAISON LOUIS JADOT PINOT NOIR 1994 Burgundy	*Good, young colour with attractive, burnt-cherry fruits. A firm, tannic backbone adds balance.*	**£7.90**	VW DBY HOU FEN MM BU WR TH	(B)
CHÂTEAU PHILIPPE LE HARDI MERCUREY LES PUILLETS 1993 Burgundy	*Deep cherry colour and complex nose. Full-bodied, racy fruit and gripping tannins.*	**£9.00**	ABY	(B)
CHOREY-LÈS-BEAUNE MAISON LOUIS JADOT 1993 Burgundy	*Good cherry colour. A palate of cherry and strawberry fruit with a dry, tannic finish.*	**£9.50**	VW	(B)
CHOREY-LÈS-BEAUNE DOMAINE ARNOUX 1991, DOMAINE ARNOUX PÈRE ET FILS Burgundy	*Bright cherry-red wine with complex fruit and burnt hints; soft finish. Good fruit.*	**£10.20**	ABY	(B)
MONTHÉLIE 1ER CRU MAISON LOUIS JADOT 1989 Burgundy	*Brick-red. Oaky aromas precede soft, plummy fruit flavours, good acidity, and a fine, tannic finish.*	**£10.50**	VW	(B)
SANTENAY 1ER CRU CLOS DES GRAVIÈRES 1992, ADRIEN BELLAND Burgundy	*Bright-red colour; light, fragrant nose and a palate full of raspberry and ripe-cherry flavours. Balanced with good length.*	**£11.00**	CAR TW UNC MK HVW	(S)
CÔTE DE BEAUNE JOSEPH DROUHIN 1993 Burgundy	*Light cherry-red; jammy nose and soft, velvety fruits. Lightweight style but firm, tannic finish.*	**£11.80**	OD RTW MM GRT	(B)

FIXIN CHÂTEAU DE MARSANNAY 1993 Burgundy	*Soft Pinot nose; complex middle flavours with peppery tannins, good balance and length.*	**£11.80**	GI NIC	(S)
CHOREY-LÈS-BEAUNE DOMAINE MAILLARD 1993, DOMAINE MAILLARD PÈRE & FILS Burgundy	*Deep red. Rich nose of violets and strawberries. Lean fruit with high acidity though softening tannins. Good potential.*	**£12.10**	NIC W	(B)
ALOXE-CORTON CHÂTEAU PHILIPPE LE HARDI 1993, Burgundy	*Aromas of strawberries and raspberries. Cherry and red-berry flavours dominate through to a good finish*	**£12.80**	ABY	(B)
BEAUNE 1ER CRU CLOS DU ROI 1992, CHÂTEAU PHILIPPE LE HARDI Burgundy	*A raspberry nose and lovely, rich, burnt-cherry palate. A complex wine, ready to be appreciated.*	**£13.00**	ABY	(G)
CHAMBOLLE-MUSIGNY ROPITEAU 1992 Burgundy	*Very light in colour; subdued nose. A palate of soft fruit. Good use of oak and tannin.*	**£15.00**	WAV	(B)
SAVIGNY-LÈS-BEAUNE 1ER CRU LES DOMINODES DE CÔTE D'OR 1992, BRUNO CLAIR Burgundy	*Complex, earthy nose with farmyard and tobacco notes. A slightly astringent finish.*	**£15.50**	J&B	(B)
BEAUNE CENT VIGNES 1ER CRU 1992, DOMAINE DU CHÂTEAU DE MEURSAULT Burgundy	*Elegant, fragrant style. Soft, raspberry fruit with enticing use of subtle oak. Good length on finish.*	**£16.60**	WON PTR MHW PAT	(B)
GEVREY-CHAMBERTIN VIEILLES VIGNES 1992, VINCENT GEANTET PANSIOT Burgundy	*Young colour, well-integrated fruit. Firm acidity and oak produce a lingering finish.*	**£17.00**	WCR	(B)

FRANCE • BURGUNDY RED

ST MICHAEL BEAUNE 1ER CRU CLOS DES COUCHEREAUX 1992, LOUIS JADOT Burgundy	*An enjoyable wine with all the traditional flavours; good balance and nice oak on finish.*	£17.00	M&S	Ⓑ
VOSNE-ROMANÉE 1991, DANIEL RION Burgundy	*Vegetal aromas, hints of mint; good fruit and length, needs ageing. Harsh tannins mask underlying fruit .*	£17.40	JVS HN SOM CWS	Ⓑ
BEAUNE 1ER CRU 'LES TEURONS' 1993, DOMAINE ROSSIGNOL TRAPET Burgundy	*Very youthful colour; complex, damp wool and spice on the nose. Ripe cherry and good acidity.*	£18.30	ABY MTR	Ⓑ
NUITS-SAINT-GEORGES LES VIGNES RONDES 1989, DANIEL RION Burgundy	*Pinot Noir showing more maturity; farmyard smell; vegetal with lovely damson fruit. Long, fragrant finish.*	£18.60	JVS SOM	Ⓑ
BEAUNE 1ER CRU BOUCHEROTTES 1992, MAISON LOUIS JADOT Burgundy	*A lovely wine with lightness and intensity. Pinot character on nose, gamey flesh, good balance – excellent.*	£19.10	NIC	Ⓑ
NUITS-SAINT-GEORGES 1ER CRU LES BOUDOTS 1993, MAISON NAIGEON-CHAUVEAU Burgundy	*Pale colour, good fruit beneath gentle tannins. Good acidity and a fine lingering finish.*	£19.90	PIM PWW HAW	Ⓑ
GEVREY-CHAMBERTIN CLOS DU MEIX DES OUCHES 1993, DOMAINE DES VAROILLES Burgundy	*Pale colour, good underlying fruit beneath soft tannins, sweet cherries and gamey flavours. Complex structure.*	£20.00	PIM PWW HAW	Ⓖ
CHASSAGNE-MONTRACHET LES CHAMPS DE MORGEOT 1992, DOMAINE LAMY-PILLOT Burgundy	*Good fresh nose, slightly peppery palate with lean, tight fruit; high acidity hard tannins.*	£20.80	ABY JAR	Ⓟ

VOLNAY-FREMIETS 1ER CRU DOMAINES DU CHÂTEAU BEAUNE 1986, BOUCHARD PÈRE ET FILS Burgundy	*Aged colour with a soft fruit nose, gentle strawberry and marmite palate; some acidity in the dry finish.*	**£20.90**	NIC MHW	B
BEAUNE 1ER CRU LOUIS JADOT 1990 Burgundy	*Full, rich, chocolatey Pinot fruit; palate dominated by rich, ripe, red-berry flavours. Elegant finish.*	**£21.20**	TO DBY HOU	S
POMMARD 1ER CRU JEAN-MARC BOILLOT 1991 Burgundy	*Deep ruby with pungent, concentrated red fruits, a complex palate and a long finish.*	**£21.60**	BI GRI BLS RW RAE	S
NUITS-SAINT-GEORGES CLOS DE L'ARLOT 1993, DOMAINE DE L'ARLOT Burgundy	*A young Burgundy showing promise. Abundance of lively fruit and creamy vanilla oak.*	**£22.30**	HOT ABY L&W	B
NUITS-SAINT-GEORGES 1ER CRU LES CAILLES 1992, ROBERT CHEVILLON Burgundy	*Ripe strawberry and cherry fruit; creamy, new oak. A very intense, vegetal nose, rich and full-flavoured.*	**£22.50**	J&B	S
NUITS-SAINT-GEORGES 1ER CRU LES BOUSSELOTS 1992, JEAN CHAUVENET Burgundy	*Pale ruby with a subtle, closed nose and a developed, complex palate. Good fruit. Ready to drink now.*	**£23.00**	BEL C&B TW UNC RW BI	B
CHARMES-CHAMBERTIN GRAND CRU DOMAINE DES VAROILLES 1993 Burgundy	*Elegant, fresh, strawberry nose. Berry fruits and oak make up the complex palate, sweet fruit, fine tannins, dry finish.*	**£23.00**	PIM PWW	S
GEVREY-CHAMBERTIN 1ER CRU LA ROMANÉE 1993, DOMAINE DES VAROILLES Burgundy	*Young, raspberry nose and good, red-berry fruit palate. An attractive length; raspberry and cream flavours.*	**£23.20**	PIM PWW HAW	B

NUITS-SAINT-GEORGES 1ER CRU DOMAINE DE L'ARLOT 1993 Burgundy	*Light cherry colour, sweet, ripe Pinot aromas with new oak. Good length; very elegant.*	**£23.60**	HOT ABY L&W JAR	(S)
VOLNAY 1ER CRU LES PITURES 1990, BITOUZET PRIEUR Burgundy	*Medium-garnet; complex, spicy beetroot, vegetal nose. Good weight of fragrant cherry fruit on palate.*	**£24.00**	CAR TW CB UNC MK POR	(S)
VOLNAY 1ER CRU CLOS D'AUDIGNAC 1993, DOMAINE DE LA POUSSE D'OR Burgundy	*Deep, sweet black cherry with an oaky, peppery nose. Complex, developed palate of creamy fruit and chunky tannins.*	**£26.30**	ABY RBS	(B)
CHAMBOLLE-MUSIGNY LES CRAS 1992, PATRICE & MICHELE RION Burgundy	*Complex, slightly vegetal, minty nose; tea-leaf palate with high acids and soft tannins. Excellent.*	**£27.00**	JVS R ACH RBS	(S)
CLOS DE VOUGEOT 1ER CRU CLOS DE LA PERRIÈRE 1993, DOMAINE BERTAGNA Burgundy	*Pale red, good Pinot Noir fruit. Rich plums and herbaceous, complex developed oak. A fine, lengthy finish.*	**£27.70**	WEP	(B)
NUITS-SAINT-GEORGES 1ER CRU CLOS DES FORETS 1993, DOMAINE DE L'ARLOT Burgundy	*Medium-garnet, complex, red-fruit nose; oak; cherries and damsons on the palate with chocolate hints. A long finish.*	**£28.10**	HOT ABY CEB L&W JAR	(G)
CORTON BRESSANDES 1992, DOMAINE CHANDON DE BRIAILLES Burgundy	*Bright colour, plummy nose, soft fruit on palate. A good, balanced finish of fruit, tannins and acidity.*	**£29.50**	WCR AMA	(G)
VOSNE ROMANÉE 1ER CRU DOMAINE DE L'ARLOT 1993 Burgundy	*Complex nose of cranberry, strawberry and earthy aromas. Creamy oak, fruity palate. Lasting finish.*	**£30.00**	ABY L&W	(B)

VOLNAY 1ER CRU DOMAINE DE LA POUSSE D'OR 1991 Burgundy	*Good colour; gamey Pinot nose. Lovely jammy middle palate with a fruity, balanced finish.*	**£30.50**	BEN ABY L&W CNL	(G)
CLOS SAINT-DENIS GRAND CRU DOMAINE BERTAGNA 1993 Burgundy	*Lively, purple colour; good blackcurrant, brambley nose; soft fruits on palate. Good balance and finish.*	**£31.70**	WEP	(S)
CHARMES-CHAMBERTIN DOMAINE DUJAC 1994 Burgundy	*Slightly subdued nose. Bitter cherry with new oak and young fruit. Tight yet easy-drinking.*	**£41.20**	ABY	(B)
CLOS DE LA ROCHE GRAND CRU 1992, DOMAINE DUJAC Burgundy	*Good colour, nice, lively Pinot fruit on nose. Well-balanced with soft, strawberry fruits. Good, firm tannins.*	**£42.70**	ABY L&W	(B)
LE CORTON GRAND CRU 1989, DOMAINES DU CHÂTEAU DE BEAUNE, BOUCHARD PÈRE & FILS Burgundy	*Mature colour; a ripe, fruity nose with herbal notes. Good length.*	**£43.50**	HV MM	(B)

BURGUNDY • WHITE

HENRI LA FONTAINE BOURGOGNE CHARDONNAY 1995, JEAN CLAUDE BOISSET Burgundy	*Clean, fruity nose, simple balanced palate with a hint of bubblegum and a tight, young finish.*	**£5.30**	MHV	(B)
ANDRÉ SIMON WHITE 1994, MAISON ALBERT BICHOT Burgundy	*Slightly burnt nose opens into complex, balanced palate of light fruit with a pleasant finish.*	**£5.90**	HOU WRT	(B)

HAUTES-CÔTES DE BEAUNE BLANC 1994, VAUCHER PÈRE ET FILS Burgundy	*Light aromas with full, crisp, soft, citrussy palate and medium-soft finish.*	**£6.00**	SMF	**B**
ASDA CHABLIS 1994, GUY MOTHE Burgundy	*Closed, creamy, green-fruit and honey nose. A long, balanced, tropical-fruit palate and pleasing finish.*	**£7.00**	A	**S**
MÂCON UCHIZY DOMAINE TALMARD 1994, Burgundy	*Complex and intense nose of spicy tropical fruit; full, balanced palate with an enjoyable, intense finish.*	**£7.00**	J&B GRT ADN	**G**
SOMERFIELD CHABLIS 1995, CAVE DES VIGNERONS DE CHABLIS Burgundy	*Cool and chalky, herbaceous nose with a crisp, clean palate. Good intensity, subtle finish.*	**£7.50**	SMF	**B**
HENRY DE VEZELAY BOURGOGNE CHARDONNAY 1994, Burgundy	*Cool, complex and finely balanced with a wispy nose and a clean, delicate melon palate.*	**£7.50**	TH WW TTG TCW DBY COK POR NRW	**S**
LA COLOMBE CHABLIS 1995, PAUL BOUTINOT Burgundy	*Crisp and clean melon and tropical-fruit nose with a lively acid zing on the palate.*	**£7.70**	Widely available	**B**
MONTAGNY 1ER CRU LE VIEUX CHÂTEAU 1994, DOMAINE DES MOIRATS Burgundy	*Creamy, dark fruit, biscuit nose with well-balanced kiwi and passion fruit palate. A long, creamy finish.*	**£8.70**	ABY	**S**
CHABLIS DOMAINE SAINT-CLAIRE 1994, JEAN-MARC BROCARD Burgundy	*Toasty biscuit and lemon nose; less toasty, more lemony palate. Good balance and finish.*	**£8.70**	J&B FTH ADN AMA	**S**

CHABLIS CHÂTEAU DE MALIGNY 1994, JEAN DURUP Burgundy	*Creamy, melon and tropical-fruit nose balanced by a clean, ripe palate with lasting fresh finish.*	£9.00	ABY P BU WR TH	**B**
CHABLIS DOMAINE DES MANANTS 1994, JEAN-MARC BROCARD Burgundy	*Fresh, citrus aroma and full, dry palate. Subtle fruit and delicate length.*	£9.20	BLS SHJ HOT G&M POR TAN ADN	**B**
CHABLIS DOMAINE DES MALANDES 1995 Burgundy	*Peach and melon nose with tart, apple-skin tones intruding on the palate. A crisp finish.*	£9.30	ES GRT MTR	**B**
CHABLIS SAINT-MARTIN 1994, DOMAINE LAROCHE Burgundy	*Fresh, creamy, citrus aroma; crisp, clean, lemony palate and a good, long-lasting, fresh finish.*	£9.70	MWW TP HOU MTL WOC	**B**
CHABLIS 1ER CRU CHÂTEAU DE MALIGNY L'HOMME MORT 1994, JEAN DURUP Burgundy	*Clean and pleasant with fresh aromas and good acidity. Ripe fruit and a medium-long finish.*	£10.40	ABY	**B**
CHABLIS 1ER CRU MONTÉE DE TONNERRE CHÂTEAU DE MALIGNY 1994, JEAN DURUP Burgundy	*Peach nose. Well-balanced, tangy marmalade fruit on the palate with good length and strong finish.*	£10.40	ABY	**B**
CHABLIS 1ER CRU BEAUROY 1993, LA CHABLISIENNE Burgundy	*Rich, pineapple nose and dry, fruity palate in harmony. A firm finish.*	£11.00	BKW VLW WCR W	**B**
CHABLIS 1ER CRU FOURCHAUME, LA CHABLISIENNE 1992 Burgundy	*Soft, slightly oaked varietal nose with citrus and toasty, sweet fruit on a long palate.*	£11.00	GI VLW	**B**

ST MICHAEL SAINT-AUBIN CHARDONNAY 1990, LOUIS JADOT Burgundy	*Champagne-like, biscuity nose. A complex mouthful of toasty oak flavours, buttery, tropical fruits and lime zest.*	£11.00	M&S	(B)
CHABLIS 1ER CRU SELECTION 1990, CAVE DES VIGNERONS DE CHABLIS Burgundy	*Refined nose, reminiscent of grassy gun-flint. The palate offers elegant lemon peel and delicate vanilla flavours.*	£11.00	SMF	(S)
POUILLY FUISSÉ FÛT DE CHÊNE GEORGES DUBOEUF 1994 Burgundy	*Wonderful and rich with real fruity character. Good oaky aromas balance this fine, classy Pouilly Fuissé.*	£11.40	LNR JN BWC	(B)
CHABLIS 1ER CRU MONT DE MILIEU LES DOMAINE 1992, LA CHABLISIENNE Burgundy	*Some lemon fruit; a well-structured body and a decent length. Long, flinty finish that lasts well.*	£11.50	GI VLW	(B)
MONTAGNY 1ER CRU CHÂTEAU DE LA SAULE 1994 Burgundy	*Oaky nose, with a rich, strong fruit palate; good acid balance and a sharp twist to finish.*	£12.00	CAR TW UNC MK BD	(B)
CHABLIS 1ER CRU FOURCHAUME CHÂTEAU DE MALIGNY 1994, JEAN DURUP Burgundy	*Varietal nose, full, ripe, tangy, fruity palate with length, depth and a long, lemony finish.*	£12.90	ABY CWI P	(S)
MEURSAULT DE ROPITEAU 1992, ROPITEAU FRÈRES Burgundy	*Musty, floral aromas; on the palate, good fruit and gentle oak. A great introduction to the joys of Meursault.*	£13.00	WAV	(B)
ST MICHAEL CHABLIS 1ER CRU 1990 GRANDE CUVÉE, LA CHABLISIENNE Burgundy	*Subtle and interesting. Pale-lemon colouring, medium depth with a delicate, flinty palate.*	£13.00	M&S	(B)

FRANCE • BURGUNDY WHITE			
POUILLY FUISSÉ CUVÉE VIEILLES VIGNES 1994, CLAUDE DENOGENT Burgundy	Smoky and lemony palate with rounded, soft, marzipan flavours. Well-balanced fruit and acid, and a good finish.	£16.00	BI	(B)
PULIGNY-MONTRACHET JOSEPH DROUHIN 1993 Burgundy	Complex chalky nose followed by peach and melon palate. Enhanced by well-balanced oak.	£18.00	WCR	(B)
PULIGNY-MONTRACHET LOUIS CARILLON 1993 Burgundy	Complex, full-flavoured melony taste. An elegant yet intense Burgundy.	£18.10	OD L&W POR BWC GRT MTR	(B)
CHABLIS BOUGROS GRAND CRU 1991, DOMAINE DE LA MALADIÈRE Burgundy	Softly rounded and buttery, complemented by good citrus acidity. Simple and well-made.	£19.00	HBJ RTW RD	(B)
NUITS-SAINT-GEORGES 1ER CRU DOMAINE DE L'ARLOT 1993 Burgundy	A really big Burgundy with yeasty, peachy fruit aromas. Good balance between fruit and acidity.	£20.60	HOT ABY L&W JAR BU WR	(S)
MEURSAULT DOMAINE DU CHÂTEAU DE MEURSAULT 1992 Burgundy	Peach, cream, subtle oak; intrinsic complexity and a long, mouth-watering finish. A delicious, elegant wine.	£21.00	WON PTR PAT	(G)
CHABLIS GRAND CRU VAUDÉSIR 1992, ALBERT BICHOT Burgundy	A delicious, fat palate composed of peach and grapefruit flavours combining well with creamy vanilla tones.	£22.00	U NIC ETV	(S)
MOREY-SAINT-DENIS BLANC DOMAINE DUJAC 1992 Burgundy	Golden yellow with sawdust and pine on the nose. Buttery, raisiny palate. Unusual but enjoyable.	£22.50	ABY DBY L&W	(B)

MEURSAULT 1ER CRU MAISON LOUIS JADOT 1994 Burgundy	*Mineral, flinty nose; rounded woody palate with good depth and a long, grapefruity finish.*	**£23.50**	M&S DBY	**B**
MEURSAULT BLAGNY 1ER CRU MAISON LOUIS JADOT 1990 Burgundy	*Soft, fruity, toasty nose with lots of lemon and orange flavours on the palate.*	**£26.80**	TH WR BU DBY HOU	**S**
MEURSAULT 1ER CRU DOMAINE ALBERT GRIVAULT 1992 Burgundy	*Lemon gold with masses of oak on the nose. Full, creamy, citrus and peach palate.*	**£27.00**	J&B	**B**
MEURSAULT 1ER CRU GENEVRIÈRES CHÂTEAU DE BEAUNE 1994, BOUCHARD PERE & FILS Burgundy	*On the palate, sweet oak with melon and mature, malolactic flavours. A long, smooth finish.*	**£27.90**	BEN JEH SHG	**S**
BÂTARD MONTRACHET GRAND CRU 1993, DOMAINE JEAN NOËL GAGNARD Burgundy	*A vanilla, citrus nose and lemony, nutty palate. High acidity on the finish.*	**£55.00**	J&B	**B**
CHEVALIER MONTRACHET GRAND CRU LES DEMOISELLE 1991, LOUIS JADOT Burgundy	*A very soft, melon palate with fresh melon bouquet and long, creamy finish.*	**£63.50**	NIC HOU	**S**

BEAUJOLAIS • RED

ANDRÉ SIMON BEAUJOLAIS VILLAGES 1995, JEAN PAUL SELLÈS Beaujolais	*Youthful, light plum with an elegant, spicy, strawberry nose hinting at its well balanced character.*	**£5.20**	GDS HOU MTL WRT	**B**

FRANCE • BEAUJOLAIS				
MORGON GEORGES BADRIOU 1995 Beaujolais	*Well-structured and full of ripe fruit; deep and rich, yet beautifully clean.*	£6.00	NUR	(S)
MORGON DOMAINE DE LA VOUTE SAINT VINCENT 1995, CELLIER DES SAMSONS Beaujolais	*A delightful, light wine with a sweet nose and soft fruit. Balanced, clean berry finish.*	£7.20	ABY	(B)
MORGON DOMAINE JEAN DESCOMBES 1995, LES VINS GEORGES DUBOEUF Beaujolais	*Bitter cherry nose leads onto plenty of ripe fruit. Gutsy with good acidity. Will develop.*	£7.80	LNR THR MHW AMA	(B)
ST. MICHAEL FLEURIE CRU DU BEAUJOLAIS 1995, ROGER DUMAS Beaujolais	*Clean purple, balanced wine. Warm fruity nose; on the palate hints of round, ripe cherries.*	£8.00	M&S	(B)
FLEURIE GEORGES DUBOEUF 1995 Beaujolais	*Clear violet with nettles and brambles on the nose. Boiled sweet raspberry and chocolate.*	£8.40	Widely available	(B)
BROUILLY DOMAINE BENOIT TRICHARD CRU DE BEAUJOLAIS 1994 Beaujolais	*Juicy gamay nose and light, fresh fruit. Good crisp acidity. Lovely wine.*	£8.50	NY NRW	(B)
MOULIN À VENT FÛT DE CHÊNE 1994, LES VINS GEORGES DUBOEUF Beaujolais	*Hints of new oak and vanilla. Plenty of spice and fruit. Lovely, full body and good length.*	£9.00	LNR JN AMA	(B)
FLEURIE DOMAINE DU VISSOUX 1994 Beaujolais	*Subtle pear-drop aromas followed by an elegant mouthful of ripe cherries and good, firm, acidity.*	£10.50	ENO	(B)

CHAMPAGNE

CHAMPAGNE BRUT RICHARD LOURMEL NV, CENTRE VINICOLE DE LA CHAMPAGNE Champagne	*Clean and aromatic with fresh apple and lemon on the nose and palate. Good finish.*	£9.00	A	B
LAYTONS CHAMPAGNE BRUT NV, F BONNET Champagne	*Peach/pineapple nose and a complex apple palate with an excellent, balanced finish.*	£11.50	LAY AS	B
TESCO BLANC DE NOIRS CHAMPAGNE BRUT NV, J C INTERNATIONAL Champagne	*Malty nose and clean apple fruit palate with balanced composition and a long finish.*	£11.80	TO	B
ASDA CHAMPAGNE BRUT NV, CENTRE VINICOLE DE LA CHAMPAGNE Champagne	*Flowery aroma and firm, straight-forward lemony palate with strong acid and a short, fresh finish.*	£12.00	A	B
CHAMPAGNE BROSSAULT BRUT NV, FERDINAND BONNET Champagne	*Toasted, malty nose; a long flavour-packed apple palate with a crisp and juicy finish.*	£12.70	BUD D FUL WIL DBY MTR	B
CHAMPAGNE H BLIN CUVÉE TRADITION BRUT NV Champagne	*Toasted biscuit with oak, peach and yeast; complex ,balanced, vanilla palate with delicious creamy length.*	£14.00	OD	B
CHAMPAGNE F BONNET BRUT HERITAGE NV, FERDINAND BONNET Champagne	*Well-balanced with lovely mousse, biscuity nose, balanced acidity and citrus fruit with good length.*	£14.00	OD KWI DBY P	B

FRANCE • CHAMPAGNE				
WAITROSE BLANC DE BLANCS CHAMPAGNE BRUT NV, F BONNET Champagne	*Well-settled with a distinct biscuity nose, rounded palate and an impressive, dry finish.*	£14.00	W	(S)
CHAMPAGNE BROSSAULT NV, FERDINAND BONNET Champagne	*Yeasty, mature nose; lemony, appley aftertaste. Medium-intense flavour with good length*	£14.10	BUD D FUL MTR	(B)
CHAMPAGNE LE MESNIL BLANC DE BANCS BRUT NV, L'UNION DES PROPRIÉTAIRES RÉCOLTANTS Champagne	*Individual, cheesy nose; an explosive mouth with a large vocabulary and a poker-faced finish.*	£14.20	ADN BU WR TH	(B)
CHAMPAGNE LOUIS BOYIER & CIE BRUT NV, EL VINO Champagne	*Fruit-bread nose and a ripe fruit palate with almond and sherbet overtones. Finishes well.*	£14.90	ELV	(B)
CHAMPAGNE DE NAUROY BLACK LABEL BRUT NV Champagne	*Delicate nose with a full, well-constructed palate of tropical ripe fruits.*	£15.00	TW	(B)
CHAMPAGNE LE BRUN DE NEUVILLE BLANC DE BLANCS BRUT Champagne	*Biscuit aromas; a concentrated mouthful of mixed fruits with low acidity. Elegant finish.*	£15.00	PV WAW	(S)
CHAMPAGNE ARISTON BRUT NV Champagne	*Savoury nose with toast and Marmite, strong, biscuity palate. Will develop further.*	£15.00	BKW WCR	(S)
CHAMPAGNE PRINCESSE DE FRANCE GRANDE RÉSERVE BRUT NV, FERDINAND BONNET Champagne	*Goat's cheese nose and a superb palate. Good length and depth. Will develop further.*	£15.00	ROI	(S)

CHAMPAGNE PATRICK ARNOULD GRAND CRU RÉSERVE NV Champagne	*Meaty style with a yeasty nose and a complex, nutty palate. Good finish.*	**£15.00**	TO	**S**
CHAMPAGNE DE NAUROY CUVÉE SPECIALE MILLENNIUM NV Champagne	*Full, mature, yeasty nose with smokiness which moves through to the pleasantly fruity palate. Shows some age.*	**£15.00**	TW	**S**
CHAMPAGNE ALBERT ETIENNE VINTAGE BRUT 1990, MARNE & CHAMPAGNE DIFFUSION Champagne	*A lemon marmalade nose and a simple, agreeable palate with abundant character.*	**£15.10**	CLA SAF	**B**
CHAMPAGNE CANARD-DUCHÊNE BRUT NV Champagne	*Mineral nose and bone-dry, melon and apple palate; well concentrated with a short length.*	**£15.10**	Widely available	**B**
CHAMPAGNE MERCIER DEMI-SEC NV, MERCIER Champagne	*Good, toasty nose; clean fruit flavours – very well balanced; good length.*	**£15.40**	Widely available	**S**
CHAMPAGNE NICOLAS FEUILLATTE DEMI-SEC NV Champagne	*Fine mousse, delicate flowery nose, firm structure. Good mid-palate, nicely developed fruit and acidity; refreshing.*	**£16.00**	A	**S**
DEUTZ BRUT CLASSIC NV Champagne	*A real bargain and a good introduction to champagne. Fruity, rich yet refreshing.*	**£16.10**	NIC MTL MHW FTH	**B**
CHAMPAGNE NICOLAS FEUILLATTE RÉSERVE PARTICULIÈRE 1ER CRU NV Champagne	*High, youthful concentrated biscuit nose, good mousse bead and citrus length. Needs time to mature.*	**£16.10**	HCK U VW RBS WCR	**S**

CHAMPAGNE CANARD-DUCHÊNE DEMI SEC NV Champagne	Yeasty, biscuit aromas; lovely toasty, nutty, full, rich flavours – very good length.	£16.20	AMP VIL SHG COK	(S)
CHAMPAGNE CHARTOGNE-TAILLET BRUT NV Champagne	Zesty and expansive apple and honeydew melon nose; softly concentrated apple palate; good overall balance.	£16.30	SAF CDE WTR PEA CEN CRM CAX AMW	(G)
CHAMPAGNE CUVÉE PRESTIGE BRUT 'PRINCESSE DES THUNES' GRAND CRU NV, PAUL DETHUNE Champagne	Persistent fruit nose; a light Muscat palate hinting at oak with a long, satisfying finish.	£16.50	B&B TRV	(B)
CHAMPAGNE PIPER HEIDSIECK DEMI-SEC GRANDE MARQUE NV Champagne	Good complex nose with toast, biscuits and fruit. Good mousse; creamy style with an attractive final finish.	£16.80	TO WSC FEN DVY	(S)
CHAMPAGNE HENRIOT BRUT BLANC DE BLANCS DE CHARDONNAY NV Champagne	Wonderful, rich, toasty nose balanced by a fruity, delicate palate. Excellent length.	£17.00	BKW CEL ABY WCR	(B)
CHAMPAGNE FERDINAND BONNET BRUT 1989 Champagne	Wonderful apple and lemon bouquet with yeasty overtones. Long with a honey character.	£17.00	OD	(B)
CHAMPAGNE DRAPPIER BLANC DE BLANCS NV Champagne	Almond and apple nose with vanilla highlights, long, ripe lemon palate with chocolatey richness.	£17.00	ABY AMA	(S)
CHAMPAGNE PHILLPPONNAT ROYAL RÉSERVE NV Champagne	Vibrant, toasty, yeasty nose; lean, light, citrus fruit with good acidity, length and a crisp finish.	£17.20	HAR HN SEL SHG FEN WAV	(B)

CHAMPAGNE HENRIOT SOUVERAIN BRUT NV Champagne	*A real pleasure to taste and drink. Light, delicate with outstanding balance between fruit and acidity.*	**£17.90**	BKW CEL ABY NIC WCR	**B**
CHAMPAGNE POMMERY BRUT ROYAL NV Champagne	*Young but looking good for the future with citrus nose and palate; good balance, clean finish.*	**£18.00**	Widely available	**B**
CHAMPAGNE JACQUART BRUT SELECTION NV Champagne	*Delicate, grapey nose with medium depth and concentration of dry fruit through to the end.*	**£18.50**	MYS SEL CFT BEN PAT	**B**
CHAMPAGNE CANARD-DUCHÊNE VINTAGE BRUT 1990 Champagne	*Pineapple, biscuit and nuts on the nose; a clean, balanced palate with a persistent finish.*	**£18.70**	JUS MFW HAR B&B VIL SHG CEB RBS	**S**
VICTORIA WINE VINTAGE CHAMPAGNE 1989, MARNE ET CHAMPAGNE Champagne	*Light, toasted, yeasty nose; rich well-integrated palate of ripe apples and a trim finish.*	**£19.00**	VWC CLA VW	**S**
CHAMPAGNE DE VENOGE DEMI SEC NV Champagne	*Slightly marzipan nose, good mousse; fine bubbles. Sweet with a good finish.*	**£19.00**	Widely available	**S**
CHAMPAGNE CHARTOGNE-TAILLET BRUT VINTAGE 1989 Champagne	*Lovely, honeyed style; creamy with a toasty edge and full fruit flavours.*	**£19.50**	DIO CDE WTR PEA CEN CRM CAX	**B**
CHAMPAGNE MOËT & CHANDON BRUT IMPÉRIAL NV Champagne	*Lively, fruity character with well-defined citrus palate; dry style and a clean, brisk finish.*	**£19.80**	Widely available	**B**

FRANCE • CHAMPAGNE				
FORTNUM & MASON CHAMPAGNE BLANC DE BLANCS GRAND CRU NV, HORSTOMME & CHAULLY Champagne	*Pleasant, biscuit nose with a balanced, aggressive fruit palate leading to a firm finish.*	**£20.00**	F&M	**B**
CHAMPAGNE FLEUR DE L'EUROPE BRUT 1989, FLEURY PERE ET FILS Champagne	*Malty nose with chocolate coating, a rich, soft middle palate and a long fresh finish.*	**£20.00**	VR RW	**B**
CHAMPAGNE PHILIPPE GUIDON GRAND CRU CHARDONNAY 1988 Champagne	*Pleasant and secretive aroma and a palate of soft apple. A strong, lemony finish.*	**£20.00**	HRV	**B**
CHAMPAGNE CHARLES HEIDSIECK BRUT RÉSERVE GRANDE MARQUE NV Champagne	*Floral, biscuit nose; creamy mousse and a complex, balanced fruit palate with a persistent, honeyed finish.*	**£20.10**	Widely available	**S**
CHAMPAGNE POL ROGER WHITE FOIL EXTRA DRY NV Champagne	*Fresh, apple and biscuit nose and competent balance of citrus fruit with a sound finish.*	**£21.50**	Widely available	**B**
CHAMPAGNE HENRIOT BRUT MILLESIME 1988 Champagne	*Excellent aroma of fruity biscuit and good, dry, fruit flavours on an impressively long palate.*	**£21.60**	BKW CEL ABY NIC WCR	**B**
CHAMPAGNE VEUVE CLICQUOT-PONSARDIN YELLOW LABEL BRUT NV Champagne	*Nutty, sweet nose and full, gutsy palate showing more character than finesse, but fair length.*	**£21.60**	Widely available	**B**
CHAMPAGNE VEUVE CLICQUOT-PONSARDIN WHITE LABEL DEMI SEC NV Champagne	*Big, powerful, mature nose with biscuit notes, good small bubbles; fruit well balanced, toasty finish.*	**£21.70**	Widely available	**S**

CHAMPAGNE DRAPPIER GRANDE SENDRÉE 1983 Champagne	*Absolutely wonderful with exquisite honey-biscuit nose, tropical fruit, hints of yeast and an excellent finish.*	£21.80	ABY	S
CHAMPAGNE MILLENNIUM CUVÉE CHAMPAGNE BRUT GRAND CRU 1990, LE MESNIL Champagne	*Rich, heavy, honey nose and creamy, nutty flavour showing bottle-age. Lovely complex length of tropical fruits and biscuity character.*	£22.00	VWC VW RW	B
CHAMPAGNE TAITTINGER BRUT-RÉSERVE NV Champagne	*Big, gutsy wine which fills the mouth with creamy, toasty tones and has a robust finish.*	£22.10	Widely available	S
CHAMPAGNE PIPER HEIDSIECK SAUVAGE GRANDE MARQUE 1985 Champagne	*Timid fruit aroma with biscuity length and a bone-dry palate with a nutty finish.*	£22.80	F&M CLA WSC VLW DVY BU WR	B
CHAMPAGNE POMMERY BRUT VINTAGE 1989 Champagne	*As dry as expected with a toasty nose, buttery fruit and a delicate balance.*	£23.30	MWW CLA TEL OD HOT NIC FEN BI	B
CHAMPAGNE BOLLINGER SPECIAL CUVÉE NV Champagne	*Sweet, perfumed nose; clean, long Pinot palate with citrus and a pleasant apple peel finish.*	£23.70	Widely available	B
CHAMPAGNE DE VENOGE BRUT VINTAGE 1988 Champagne	*New World style with toasty notes on the nose; richer toasty fruit and balanced acid palate.*	£23.70	NET WTL PIM NY BOO CHV PIM AMA	B
CHAMPAGNE MOËT & CHANDON BRUT IMPÉRIAL VINTAGE 1988 Champagne	*Light, lemon nose; balanced palate swells from subtle beginnings to a full fruit finish.*	£24.70	Widely available	B

CHAMPAGNE CATTIER VINTAGE CHIGNY-LES-ROSES 1ER CRU 1989 Champagne	Pale white gold with a mild bouquet and some melon fruit. Delicate in every way	£25.00	TO	**B**
CHAMPAGNE MUMM DE CREMANT BRUT NV Champagne	Grape and almond nose; a good, concentrated palate of apples and yeast. Wonderful length.	£25.00	Widely available	**S**
ORPALE BLANC DE BLANCS 1985, UNION CHAMPAGNE Champagne	A grapey, yeasty nose and a well-balanced, concentrated palate of lemon with hints of apple.	£25.00	J&B	**S**
CHAMPAGNE CHARLES HEIDSIECK VINTAGE GRANDE MARQUE 1989 Champagne	Aggressive mousse, yeast-extract nose; full of flavour and very drinkable. Good acid/fruit balance.	£25.70	Widely available	**B**
CHAMPAGNE GOSSET GRANDE RÉSERVE NV Champagne	Apple nose with biscuit and taut fruit on the palate; a crisp, long finish	£26.40	Widely available	**S**
CHAMPAGNE POL ROGER VINTAGE 1988 Champagne	Fresh-baked biscuits on the nose – rich, crunchy fruit flavours, good length and lovely finish.	£27.40	Widely available	**G**
CHAMPAGNE VEUVE CLICQUOT-PONSARDIN VINTAGE RÉSERVE 1989 Champagne	Bronze hue and oatmeal nose with well-defined Pinot grapiness and a good finish. Needs time.	£27.50	Widely available	**B**

Pinpoint who sells the wine you wish to buy by turning to the stockist codes. If you know the name of the wine you want to buy, use the alphabetical index. If the price is your motivation, refer to the invaluable price guide index; red and white wines under £5, sparkling wines under £10 and champagne under £15. Happy hunting!

CHAMPAGNE POL ROGER BLANC DE BLANCS 1988 Champagne	*Cox Orange Pippin apple nose; long, sweet fruit palate with vanilla hints and a pleasant finish.*	£28.30	Widely available	(S)
CHAMPAGNE VEUVE CLICQUOT-PONSARDIN RICH RÉSERVE 1988 Champagne	*Fleshy nose; big, weighty, toasty style with fine mousse. Great length with up-front rich fruit.*	£29.10	Widely available	(G)
CHAMPAGNE GRAND MILLÉSIME 1983, GOSSET Champagne	*Citrus nose and a palate of gutsy cherry and toasted kernel finish. Rich and bold.*	£29.30	Widely available	(S)
CHAMPAGNE NICOLAS FEUILLATTE CUVÉE SPECIALE 1986 Champagne	*Soft, boneyed nose; well-balanced crisp lemon fruit with hint of wet wool and some length.*	£30.00	HCK	(B)
CHAMPAGNE CUVÉE WILLIAM 1988, DEUT Champagne	*Toasty, savoury nose successfully matched with a fresh and fruity palate and a long aftertaste.*	£31.20	FTH	(B)
CHAMPAGNE BOLLINGER GRANDE ANNÉE 1988 Champagne	*Soft, boneyed nose; weighty fruit on the mid-palate and a long, fresh finish. Shows age.*	£33.50	Widely available	(B)
CHAMPAGNE BOLLINGER GRANDE ANNÉE 1989 Champagne	*Mature fruit nose; broad, ripe palate with a hint of mint. A long, smooth finish.*	£35.00	Widely available	(S)
CHAMPAGNE GRAND MILLÉSIME BRUT GOSSET 1985 Champagne	*Complex and well-defined. Yeasty apple nose, ripe fruit palate, cognac over-tones and a long finish.*	£35.00	Widely available	(S)

FRANCE • CHAMPAGNE

CHAMPAGNE DE VENOGE DES PRINCES 1989 Champagne	*Simple and sweetish. Coffee bean nose, yeast and apple palate with a hint of marshmallow.*	**£39.20**	AMA NET WTL BOO NY NIC CHV	**B**
CHAMPAGNE CUVÉE SPECIALE LOUISE POMMERY BRUT 1987 Champagne	*Up-front biscuity nose, complex depth of clean, ripe fruit and a perky, acidic finish.*	**£42.40**	CLA TEL OD RBS NIC MTL BI	**G**
CHAMPAGNE LA GRANDE DAME BRUT 1989, VEUVE CLICQUOT-PONSARDIN Champagne	*Clean, delicate scent of liquorice; rich nutty, biscuity fruit, reasonable depth and a tart finish.*	**£53.60**	Widely available	**B**
CHAMPAGNE PHILLIPPONNAT CLOS DES GOISSES 1986 Champagne	*Fruit and nut on the nose and finish with a yeasty fruit palate. Fine and exceedingly long.*	**£53.70**	HAR SHG WAV	**S**
CHAMPAGNE PIPER HEIDSIECK RARE GRANDE MARQUE 1985 Champagne	*Honeyed biscuit nose; thin, appley palate and a long dry sherbet finish. Needs drinking now .*	**£54.10**	REM WSC DVY	**S**
CHAMPAGNE POL ROGER PR 1988 Champagne	*Honey nose; full palate with yeasty melon fruit and a dry finish. A massive, lasting length.*	**£55.00**	CWW	**S**
CHAMPAGNE CUVÉE DOM PÉRIGNON BRUT 1985, MOËT & CHANDON Champagne	*Biscuit nose; sweet, ripe apples and lemons with honey and sherbet. Good now, better later.*	**£60.20**	Widely available	**G**

Pinpoint who sells the wine you wish to buy by turning to the stockist codes. If you know the name of the wine you want to buy, use the alphabetical index. If the price is your motivation, refer to the invaluable price guide index; red and white wines under £5, sparkling wines under £10 and champagne under £15. Happy hunting!

ROSE

CHAMPAGNE ANDRÉ SIMON CHAMPAGNE ROSÉ NV, CO-OP DE BETHON Champagne	*Pale pink; lovely complex nose with yeasty characteristics. Soft mousse with warm, ripe flavours.*	£14.00	CLA MTL POR WRT	Ⓢ
PRINCE WILLIAM CHAMPAGNE ROSÉ NV, HENRI MANDOIS Champagne	*Onion-skin colour; very yeasty nose, fine mousse. Intense flavours and good length.*	£15.00	SMF	Ⓑ
CHAMPAGNE DRAPPIER ROSÉ BRUT NV Champagne	*Pale pink; mature, fine nose with toasty, intense, developed flavours. Good mousse and lasting fruit.*	£16.00	ABY COK AMA BU WR TH	Ⓖ
CHAMPAGNE PAUL DETHUNE ROSÉ GRAND CRU NV, HENRI DETHUNE Champagne	*Pale rose colour; lemony, yeasty nose and fresh strawberry palate. Fine mousse, elegant long finish.*	£17.00	B&B TRV	Ⓑ
CHAMPAGNE CANARD-DUCHÊNE ROSÉ NV Champagne	*Maturity on the nose; yeasty, crusty bread and some sweet fruit; fine, delicate length.*	£17.90	Widely available	Ⓑ
CHAMPAGNE CHARTOGNE-TAILLET BRUT ROSÉ NV Champagne	*Very pale onion-skin and acidic, lemony nose; excellent mousse – refined, long finish.*	£18.50	DIO CDE WTR PEA CEN CAX	Ⓑ
CHAMPAGNE JOSEPH PERRIER ROSÉ NV Champagne	*Very pale lipstick colour with small, tight bubbles; slightly sweet with a rich, toasty, nutty flavour.*	£19.40	FS JFR EVI CVR LWE GRT TAN	Ⓑ

FRANCE • ALSACE WHITE

CHAMPAGNE HENRIOT VINTAGE ROSÉ 1988 Champagne	*Transparent, orange onion-skin colour; floral nose with rich fruit giving length and complexity.*	£20.00	BKW CEL ABY WCR	(B)
CHAMPAGNE POMMERY BRUT ROSÉ NV Champagne	*Very fresh, peachy nose; good mousse leading to a well-balanced, complex finish. Rich.*	£21.00	CLA TEL HOT SEL MWW RBS FEN BI	(B)
CHAMPAGNE DEVAUX CUVÉE DISTINCTION ROSÉ 1988 Champagne	*Clean and delicate with fine mousse; well-balanced, full, rich and nutty. A real must.*	£24.50	WIM CWL VEX	(B)
CHAMPAGNE MOËT & CHANDON BRUT IMPÉRIAL VINTAGE ROSÉ 1988 Champagne	*Lipstick pink; heavy mousse, ripe fruits and vanilla on palate; well-balanced, good length.*	£24.70	Widely available	(S)

ALSACE • RED

DOMAINE ZIND-HUMBRECHT PINOT NOIR HERRENWEG TURCKHEIM 1992 Alsace	*Good, intense colour; jammy nose, lovely soft fruits. A mature, slightly over-ripe finish with great fruit concentration.*	£7.70	ABY CWS	(B)

ALSACE • WHITE

WAITROSE GEWURZTRAMINER VIN D'ALSACE 1993, C V B Alsace	*A deep and spicy nose. Finely judged, well-structured and balanced; complex smoke and spice.*	£5.80	W	(B)

FRANCE • ALSACE WHITE

GEWURZTRAMINER BÉBLENHEIM 1995, CAVE VINICOLE DE BÉBLENHEIM Alsace	*A nutty and peppery style; light-weight and very well-balanced with some length.*	£6.00	MWW NUR	**B**
J HORSTEIN GEWURZTRAMINER 1993, HORSTEIN CAVE VINICOLE DE PFAFFENHEIM Alsace	*Beautifully soft and alluring fresh cream, strawberries and rasp-berries and a honeyed, oily texture.*	£6.30	L&W SHJ PEY AV TAN	**B**
CHASSELAS VIELLES VIGNES RESERVE PIERRE SPARR 1993 Alsace	*Highly attractive wine full of gently-spiced apple fruit and herbaceous flavours.*	£7.00	NIC	**S**
BOTT-GEYL MUSCAT 1993, JEAN-CHRISTOPHE BOTT-GEYL Alsace	*An intense muscat nose with delicious hints of spice and rosewater. Fresh, clean and grapey.*	£7.70	MWW	**B**
BARON DE SCHIELE RIESLING PARTICULIÈRE 1995, KUEHN Alsace	*Youthful and delicate; a flowery nose with well-weighted, attractive, mineral fruit.*	£8.00	EVI	**B**
DOMAINE ZIND-HUMBRECHT PINOT D'ALSACE 1994 Alsace	*Big, fat nose full of peach-es, spice and honey with lovely soft, smoky fruit.*	£8.40	ABY DBY	**B**
DOMAINE ZIND-HUMBRECHT GEWURZTRAMINER WINTZENHEIM 1994 Alsace	*A lovely rich, spicy nose; fragrant lemon and lime with really delicious full fruit flavours.*	£9.00	ABY DBY	**B**
GEWURZTRAMINER HEIMBOURG 1993, CAVE DE TURCKHEIM Alsace	*Gentle lanolin aroma and a great balance of spicy fruit and soft fresh acidity.*	£9.20	DBY MHW WCR	**B**

FRANCE • ALSACE WHITE				
DOMAINE ZIND-HUMBRECHT GEWURZTRAMINER HERRENWEG 1994 Alsace	*Fresh, aromatic and typically Gewürztraminer - rich and honeyed, yet with refreshing acidity.*	**£9.50**	ABY DBY	**B**
DOMAINE ZIND-HUMBRECHT GEWURZTRAMINER HERRENWEG 1992 Alsace	*Clean, fresh, resiny and aromatic - there is a lovely prickle of acidity on the tongue – well-rounded.*	**£9.60**	ABY DBY	**B**
TURCKHEIM TOKAY/PINOT GRIS GRAND CRU 1993, CAVE DE VINICOLE DE TURCKHEIM Alsace	*Pronounced banana bouquet; hints of talcum powder, lovely apricot and spice on the palate.*	**£9.60**	GNW GRT JUS DBY HOU	**B**
GEWURZTRAMINER ALTENBERG DE BERGHEIM GRAND CRU 1992, DOMAINE CHARLES KOEHLY ET FILS Alsace	*Subtle and delicious lychee fruit - big and rich with great potential throughout.*	**£10.00**	SV HW	**B**
SCHOENENBOURG RIESLING GRAND CRU 1992, BÉBLENHEIM Alsace	*This wine displays plenty of zesty fruit salad with some vegetal undertones.*	**£10.00**	WCR	**B**
DOMAINE ZIND-HUMBRECHT RIESLING TURCKHEIM 1994 Alsace	*Very attractive, delicate, peach and honeysuckle aromas; slightly off-dry, with great concentration.*	**£10.30**	ABY DBY	**B**
DOMAINE ZIND-HUMBRECHT RIESLING CLOS HAUSERER 1992 Alsace	*A very complex, earthy wine full of such aromas as wet wool, grapefruit and orange fruits.*	**£11.20**	ABY	**B**
DOMAINE ZIND-HUMBRECHT GEWURZTRAMINER HERRENWEG 1993 Alsace	*Rich gold in colour, the style is slightly off-dry; very elegant, well-balanced and long.*	**£11.40**	ABY	**B**

FRANCE • ALSACE WHITE				
DOMAINE ZIND-HUMBRECHT GEWURZTRAMINER TURCKHEIM 1993 Alsace	*A deep yellow colour - the bouquet contains an intriguing blend of mineral and floral tones.*	£11.40	ABY	(B)
CÔTE DE ROUFFACH GEWURZTRAMINER 1994, DOMAINE JOSEPH RIEFLÉ ET FILS Alsace	*Lots of lovely lychee, pineapple and orange blossom flavours - a wine of great balance and length.*	£11.50	WTR	(B)
DOMAINE ZIND-HUMBRECHT GEWURZTRAMINER HEIMBOURG 1992 Alsace	*A huge, earthy fruit palate with highly concentrated, hot, spices – promising for the future.*	£12.40	ABY CEB DBY AMA	(G)
DOMAINE ZIND-HUMBRECHT MUSCAT GRAND CRU GOLDERT 1994, OLIVIER HUMBRECHT Alsace	*Immensely appealing with its excellent Muscat fruit character; fresh grapiness and citrus acidity.*	£12.70	ABY	(B)
DOMAINE ZIND-HUMBRECHT GEWURZTRAMINER GRAND CRU GOLDERT 1992 Alsace	*Young and tight - a lean, racy wine with well-balanced yellow plum and greengage flavours.*	£13.40	ABY	(S)
GEWURZTRAMINER MAMBOURG GRAND CRU 1993, PIERRE SPARR Alsace	*Bagfuls of exotic, spicy, perfumed fruit and an evolved palate leading to a honeyed, nutty finish.*	£13.60	HBJ CVR	(B)
DOMAINE ZIND-HUMBRECHT GEWURZTRAMINER HEIMBOURG 1993 Alsace	*Round, ripe spiciness with a hint of crisp fruit and green stalkiness.*	£14.50	ABY	(B)
DOMAINE ZIND-HUMBRECHT GEWURZTRAMINER CLOS WINDSBUHL 1991 Alsace	*A tight, toasty nose and some ripe, complex wood characters dominating over strong, green fig flavours.*	£16.10	ABY	(S)

DOMAINES SCHLUMBERGER GEWURZTRAMINER KESSLER GRAND CRU 1991 Alsace	*A fine, honeyed, lemon nose with some real liquorice richness and spice. Beautiful!*	£16.20	Widely available	**B**
CUVÉE SEIGNEURS DE RIBEAUPIERRE TRIMBACH GEWURZTRAMINER GRAND CRU 1990 Alsace	*A complex background of greengages and subdued, flinty fruit alongside muted spice.*	£16.50	GON T&W LV U TP DBY	**B**
DOMAINE ZIND-HUMBRECHT CLOS WINDSBUHL GEWURZTRAMINER 1992, Alsace	*Well-balanced and very stylish; cinnamon, green-gage and fig flavours compete for attention.*	£16.90	ABY DBY	**S**
DOMAINE ZIND-HUMBRECHT PINOT GRIS VIEILLES VIGNES 1994 Alsace	*Wonderfully aromatic lychee and rose petal along with honeyed, smoky fruit and hints of dry honey.*	£16.90	TH BU WR ABY AMA	**S**
DOMAINES SCHLUMBERGER RIESLING KITTERLE GRAND CRU 1991 Alsace	*Wonderfully fruity with herbaceous overtones. A definite must to try on a summer day.*	£17.30	L&W HV	**B**
DOMAINE ZIND-HUMBRECHT RIESLING CLOS WINDSBUHL 1994 Alsace	*Very nice peachy fruit; fragrant wine with citrus tones and a balanced, crisp finish.*	£18.30	ABY	**B**
DOMAINE ZIND-HUMBRECHT GEWURZTRAMINER CLOS WINDSBUHL 1990 Alsace	*An open, ripe nose invit-ing further exploration of a richly honeyed, guava and tropical fruit palate.*	£18.30	ABY DBY	**S**
DOMAINE ZIND-HUMBRECHT GEWURZTRAMINER CLOS WINDSBUHL 1994 Alsace	*Tasters praised the flavours of 'honey and sul-tanas' and the 'full, rich nose'.*	£18.30	ABY	**G**

FRANCE • ALSACE SWEET WHITE

KIENTZHEIM KAYSERSBERG TOKAY/PINOT GRIS GRAND CRU 1994, PETIT DEMANGE Alsace	*Leafy, with gentle sweetness and definite personality - a broad and spicy wine of character.*	**£18.60**	ABY	(B)
DOMAINE ZIND-HUMBRECHT RIESLING GRAND CRU BRAND 1994 Alsace	*Peach syrup; loads of acidity and decent, ripe fruit give a firm, full, rounded palate.*	**£18.70**	ABY	(B)
KIENTZHEIM KAYSERSBERG GEWURZTRAMINER VENDAGES TARDIVES 1990 Alsace	*Full of creamy fruit with hints of rich, orangey botrytis. An outstanding, heavy-weight wine.*	**£19.80**	ABY	(B)
DOMAINE ZIND-HUMBRECHT GEWURZTRAMINER GRAND CRU HENGST 1989 Alsace	*Intriguing, vegetal melon aromas and lots of lush, sweet, late-picked fruit with hints of lanolin.*	**£32.20**	ABY	(S)
DOMAINE ZIND-HUMBRECHT TOKAY GRIS CLOS JEBSAL 1992 Alsace	*Delicate spice and sweet, gentle, Muscat-like aromas; a big honeyed palate with a little residual sweetness.*	**£50.50**	ABY	(B)

ALSACE • SWEET WHITE

ANDRÉ SENNER MUSCAT RESERVE PARTICULIÈRE 1993, CAVE DU GALTZ Alsace	*Delicate floral/muscat nose with gentle spice. Clean, dry, grapey fruit; quite rich but zesty acidity adds balance.*	**£7.20**	NIC	(B)
GEWURZTRAMINER ALTENBERG DE BERGHEIM VENDAGES TARDIVES 1989, DOMAINE CHARLES KOEHLY ET FILS Alsace	*Fresh citrus fruit aromas. Grapefruit and orange peel with a slight spiciness. Intense and hedonistic.*	**£18.70**	SV HW	(B)

FRANCE • LOIRE WHITE				
TRIMBACH GEWURZTRAMINER VENDAGES TARDIVES GRAND CRU 1990 Alsace	*Ripe tropical fruit and zesty mandarin aromas. Richly textured with luscious guava and lychee fruit.*	£20.00	GON U T&W LV SEL	(B)
DOMAINE ZIND-HUMBRECHT GEWURZTRAMINER VENDAGE TARDIVE GRAND CRU GOLDERT 1994 Alsace	*Rich, honeyed elder-flower and grapey aromas. Sweet with plenty of botrytis-enriched tropical fruit.*	£33.40	ABY	(S)
DOMAINE ZIND-HUMBRECHT CLOS JEBSAL 1993 Alsace	*Incredibly rich and luscious, this has wonderfully ripe and sweet tropical fruit. Powerful finish.*	£61.90	ABY	(B)

LOIRE • RED

CHÂTEAU DE LA GRILLE 1990, LAURENT GOSSET Loire	*Spicy, sweet bell peppers; quite concentrated cassis and berry fruit with warm vanilla and gentle acidity.*	£11.30	BRP PLA MK JBR PAV SEL	(B)

LOIRE • WHITE

ASDA MUSCADET 1995, DOMAINE BAUD Loire	*A sweet and spicy, easy drinking, muscadelle-style nose; delicate yet flavourful and full of fruit.*	£3.00	A	(B)
VIN DE PAYS DU JARDIN DE LA FRANCE SAUVIGNON BLANC 1995, DOMAINE BAUD Loire	*A light gooseberry and leafy nose; a little closed now but has medium-weight fruit with a high acid finish.*	£3.30	BES SAF	(B)

FRANCE • LOIRE WHITE

MALT HOUSE VINTNERS MUSCADET SÈVRE ET MAINE 1995, EDGARD DEBREUIL Loire	*Soft and fruity – almost melony; a clean acid balance and some nice citrus fruit flavours.*	£3.60	MHV	(B)
CHENIN JARDIN DE LA FRANCE 1995, ACKERMAN Loire	*Grassy, zippy aroma – very youthful and some-what stalky with lovely lychee fruit.*	£3.60	JS MWW	(B)
MUSCADET DE SÈVRE ET MAINE SUR LIE CELLIERS DU PRIEURÉ 1995 Loire	*A classy food wine with strong, fresh, lemony flavours; lively acidity and a rich, peachy palate.*	£4.00	BES	(B)
MUSCADET DE SÈVRE ET MAINE SUR LIE CHÂTEAU DE LA BOTINIÈRE 1995, JEAN BEAUQUIN Loire	*An exciting aroma of fresh leaves and ripe melon fruit; spritzy and full of interest.*	£4.50	NUR	(B)
MUSCADET SUR LIE DOMAINE DU FIEF GUERIN 1995 Loire	*Great fruit! Crisp and appley citrus flavours, ripe and well-balanced acid with some length.*	£5.00	JSS	(B)
MUSCADET DE SÈRVE ET MAINE SAUVION DU CLÉRAY 1995 Loire	*Evocative, honeyed, soft fruit nose and a ripe character on the palate; beautifully balanced and zesty.*	£5.40	LNR ROB CPW RBS	(B)
MUSCADET CARTE D'OR SAUVION 1995 Loire	*A hint of yeasty character, and some attractively ripe and fresh apple fruit.*	£5.50	LNR ROB CPW DBY BWC	(B)
CHÂTEAU BOULAY MONTLOUIS DE CRAY 1995, CHAPELLE DE CRAY Loire	*An approachable style; well-balanced with taut acidity and fruit. Will soften further.*	£5.70	WTK JCK TPW GWI CRM DBY MHW	(B)

FRANCE • LOIRE WHITE

VOUVRAY DOMAINE BOURILLON 1993 Loire	*Pleasantly sweet, with a fresh intensity of crisp acid underneath. A well-made wine.*	£6.00	BKW WCR	(B)
REUILLY BLANC DOMAINE HENRI BEURDIN 1995 Loire	*Cool, silver-green colour with gooseberry and grapefruit leaves; juicy, pronounced fruit on the palate.*	£6.10	BBR GI MWW ADN	(B)
ST MICHAEL CHÂTEAU GAUDRELLE 1993 Loire	*This is not a complex wine, but won praise from all for its softness and drinkability.*	£7.00	M&S	(B)
VOUVRAY CHAMPALOU RÉSERVE 1995 Loire	*A ripe pear flavour and excellent, soft, well-evolved fruit. Honeyed, ripe and clean.*	£7.30	BD SOM	(S)
CHÂTEAU MONCONTOUR 1993 Loire	*Clean and relatively simple apple acidity; quite tart and refreshing - a sound medium-dry Chenin.*	£7.40	U JN GI BEN RBS NIC	(B)
POUILLY FUMÉ CUVÉE JULES 1994, FOUASSIER Loire	*Clear gooseberry style with a ripe fruit background and succulent acidity; a thoroughly becoming wine.*	£7.50	TO	(B)
MENETOU SALON MOROGUES 1995, DOMAINE HENRY PELLE Loire	*A brilliant wine with deep colour and varietal fruit in a soft, creamy style.*	£7.90	Widely available	(B)
SANCERRE CAVES DU GUÉ D'ARGENT CUVÉE RESERVE 1995, SERGE LALOUE Loire	*A rich wine with real depth of fruit and fresh acid combining to give a stylish, warm finish.*	£8.00	ABY	(B)

FRANCE • LOIRE WHITE

SANCERRE HENRI BOURGOIS 'LES BONES BOUCHES' 1994 Loire	*Fine example with a discrete nose of vegetal, green fruit; a mouth-filling flavour.*	**£8.30**	SAF SOM	(B)
POUILLY FUMÉ SERGE DAGUENEAU ET FILLES 1994 Loire	*Creamy pineapple, toasty oak and vanilla nose; elegant, soft, rounded fruit palate – warming and clean.*	**£8.60**	ABY J&B	(B)
POUILLY FUMÉ JACQUES MARCHAND 1995 Loire	*Soft, aromatic style, some sweet almonds with a creamy, weighty palate and long, lemony finish.*	**£9.00**	MIS	(B)
SANCERRE DOMAINE DU CARROIR PERRIN 1995, PIERRE RIFFAULT Loire	*Young, pleasant, herbal nose with strong pungent citrus fruit in the mouth and refreshing acidity.*	**£9.00**	3D	(B)
VOUVRAY MARC BREDIF 1993 Loire	*A pleasant length of appley fruit and crisp acidity; well-concentrated and tasty.*	**£9.20**	Widely available	(B)
SANCERRE DOMAINE DE BELLECOURS 1995 Loire	*A lightly-coloured appearance hides an extreme gooseberry nose with an exotic fruit and lemon background.*	**£9.50**	WIN	(S)
SANCERRE VACHERON LES ROCHES 1995 Loire	*Charming number with a clean, grassy nose and sufficient acid to give a long finish.*	**£9.80**	U GI BEN RD MWW DBY ADN	(B)
SANCERRE LE CHANT DU MERLE, DOMAINE MICHEL THOMAS 1995 Loire	*Green malic acid, fat oily fruit and broad flavours; a lighter style with an elegant finish.*	**£10.00**	BD	(B)

FRANCE • LOIRE WHITE

MENETOU SALON DOMAINE DE CHATENOY 1995, PIERRE CLEMENT Loire	*Boiled sweets and a gooseberry, grassy nose; gentle fruit and smoky bacon on the finish.*	£10.00	ENO NIC	(S)
SANCERRE VACHERON LES ROCHES 1994 Loire	*Light fruit and oak notes on the nose with creamy acidity giving a light, subtle finish.*	£10.10	GI RD MWW RBS ADN	(B)
POUILLY FUMÉ CHÂTEAU DE TRACY 1995, COMTESSE D'ESTUTT D'ASSAY Loire	*Harmoniously ensembled; elegant, exotic, green fruit on the nose, well-balanced, lasting finish.*	£11.80	Widely available	(S)
SANCERRE LA CHÂTELAINE CUVÉE PRESTIGE 1993, JOSEPH MELLOT PÈRE ET FILS Loire	*Some floral notes and a green, appley character balance the acidity to produce an easy style.*	£12.00	WIN AMA	(B)
POUILLY FUMÉ DE LADOUCETTE 1993, BARON PATRICK DE LADOUCETTE Loire	*A friendly, tropical fruit wine with lychee and greengage; finishing with power and finesse.*	£13.20	Widely available	(B)
SANCERRE CUVÉE EDMOND 1993, LES VINS ALPHONSE MELLOT Loire	*A deeply-coloured well-made example with creamy oak, crisp appley acid and forward fruit.*	£17.20	AV	(B)
COMTE LAFOND GRAND CUVÉE BLANC 1993, BARON PATRICK DE LADOUCETTE Loire	*A strawberry on a well-crafted wine; smoky, flinty tones on the wonderfully drawn-out finish.*	£25.60	RD NIC	(S)
VOUVRAY LE PEU DE LA MORIETTE 1990, JEAN-CLAUDE PICHOT Loire	*An unctuous, 'moelleux' style with flavours of lovely barley sugar, honey and apple.*	£26.90	NIC	(S)

LOIRE • SPARKLING

SAUMUR RUBIS ROUGE BOUVET-LADUBAY NV Loire	*Wonderful and delicate with real style. A real must for a summer garden party.*	£9.10	SEL BNK JN MM	**B**
TRÉSOR BRUT BOUVET-LADUBAY NV Loire	*Green gooseberries on the nose and a sweet, ripe, creamy palate with very good length.*	£10.00	VWC VW MM	**B**

RHONE • RED

CO-OP CÔTES DE VENTOUX NV, LOUIS MOUSSET Rhône	*A rich, fresh pepper bouquet with vegetal undertones; a fresh, soft and balanced wine.*	£3.60	CWS	
VACQUEYRAS VIEUX CLOCHER 1993, ARNOUX ET FILS Rhône	*Spicy, herbal aromas; packed, toasted ripe fruit; this is clean and peppery with staying power.*	£4.00	SMF	
OAK AGED CÔTES DU RHÔNE GABRIEL MEFFRE 1995 Rhône	*Lovely, strawberry-plum fruit and velvety, soft new oak; this has excellent balance.*	£4.30	SAF VW CWS	
CÔTES DE RHÔNE-VILLAGES DOMAINE DE LA PRÉSIDENTE 1995, MAX AUBERT Rhône	*The warm, smoky nose leads into a concentration of rich jammy fruit and peppery spice.*	£4.90	GI SV	

GEORGES DUBOEUF DOMAINE DES MOULINS 1995 Rhône	*Bubblegum and juicy fruits on the nose combine with a fresh, clean, well-balanced palate.*	£5.00	LNR THR JN BWC BU WR TH	(B)
CÔTES DU RHÔNE MAITRE DE CHAIS 1995, MONBOUSQUET Rhône	*This ruby wine shows a perfumed, blackcurrant fruit intensity which combines well with sweet oak.*	£5.00	BUT RTW WER DBY COK NRW	(B)
LA CHASSE DU PAPE RÉSERVE 1994, GABRIEL MEFFRE Rhône	*Juicy, ripe plums on the nose precede an un-usually satisfying length and exciting finish.*	£5.00	SAF	(B)
CROZES-HERMITAGE CELLIERS DE NOBLENS 1993 Rhône	*A superb combination of complex fruit flavours flow from this concen-trated, well-balanced example.*	£5.00	SMF	(G)
VACQUEYRAS CUVÉE DU MARQUIS DE FONSEGUILLE 1994, LES CAVES DE VACQUEYRAS Rhône	*Plummy fruits abound and the nose is spicy, aro-matic and vegetal. Good length and aftertaste.*	£5.70	CWS	(B)
CROZES-HERMITAGE LOUIS MOSSET 1994 Rhône	*An elegant and subtle plum nose; rich and peppery raisin, red-currant and spice. Soft and youthful.*	£5.70	U CWS	(B)
DOMAINE DE LUNARD VINS DE PAYS DES BOUCHES DU RHÔNE 1989, FRANÇOIS MICHEL Rhône	*An attractive nose of sweet, ripe dark fruit becomes a harmonious palate of fruit and spice.*	£5.90	MK TW CAR	(B)
CÔTES DU RHÔNE-VILLAGES DOMAINE DE LA GRANDE BELLANE 1993, VALRÉAS Rhône	*Intense concentration of black pepper on the nose; nice fruit and stacks of tannins.*	£6.00	VWC CWS	(B)

FRANCE • RHONE RED

VALVIGNEYRE SYRAH CÔTES DU RHÔNE 1994, ALAIN PARET Rhône	*Good berry fruit and lavender nose. Clean and fresh and some creamy oak tannins.*	£6.00	Widely available	B
CÔTE DU RHÔNE BELLERUCHE, CHAPOUTIER 1994 Rhône	*Rich plums come through on the palate in a concentration of flavours with great length.*	£6.20	OD DBY MM GRT CNL	B
CROZES-HERMITAGE CAVES DES CLAIRMONTS 1992 Rhône	*Smooth fruits and spices on the nose. Classy palate with coffee. Quite dry but refreshing tannins.*	£6.50	W	B
CÔTES DU RHÔNE-VILLAGES CAVES DE RASTEAU CUVÉE PRESTIGE 1993, CAVES DES VIGNERONS DE RASTEAU	*Mouthwatering fruits with good concentration. A light, classy style with a soft, tannic finish.*	£6.60	Widely available	B
LES ABEILLES CUVÉE ANDRE ROUX 1994, LA CAVE DES VIGNERONS DE CHUSCLAN Rhône	*Good appearance with cooked fruits on nose. Fruity flavours and spicy tannins.*	£6.80	BD	B
CÔTES DU RHÔNE ROUGE 1993, GUIGAL Rhône	*Chocolate with berries and charred oak on a palate which is full and firm. Long finish.*	£7.00	Widely available	B
PERRIN RÉSERVE 1994, JEAN PIERRE & FRANCOIS PERRIN Rhône	*Good complex palate with outstanding balance of fruits, spices, acidity and tannins.*	£7.00	MIS	S
CAIRANNE DOMAINE RICHAUD 1993 Rhône	*Fresh, young purple colour. A warm plum nose and fruity palate. Chewy tannins.*	£7.50	ENO	

FRANCE • RHONE RED

MALT HOUSE VINTNERS ST JOSEPH 1993, CAVE DE TAIN L'HERMITAGE Rhône	*Cherry fruits with great vanilla oak flavours and hints of black pepper. Good, long finish.*	**£7.90**	MHV	(B)
GIGONDAS LAURUS 1993, GABRIEL MEFFRE Rhône	*Sweet, peppery nose with juicy fruits and rich berry flavours. Could be a future classic.*	**£8.00**	GA	(S)
MALT HOUSE VINTNERS CHÂTEAUNEUF-DU-PAPE 1995, LAURENT-CHARLES BROTTE Rhône	*Up-front berry fruits and peppery flavours dominate. Warming tannins and pleasing finish.*	**£8.70**	MHV	(B)
ST JOSEPH CUVÉE MÉDAILLE D'OR 1991, CAVE DE SAINT DÉSIRAT Rhône	*Big, rich fruits. Medium-bodied with good tannins. Great potential. A good wine.*	**£8.70**	CVR SMF W	(B)
ST JOSEPH LES NOBLES RIVES 1994, CAVE DE TAIN L'HERMITAGE Rhône	*Still young but showing good form. Fine mixture of ripe fruits and oak.*	**£9.30**	BOO DBY NIC	(B)
CHÂTEAUNEUF-DU-PAPE DOMAINE DE MATHIEU 1993 Rhône	*Mature colourings. Slightly cooked fruits on palate with sweet acidity. Traditional style; good finish.*	**£9.30**	SOM	(B)
LES GARRIGUES 1992, DOMAINE DE LA JANASSE Rhône	*Deep purple, garnet rim. Spicy nose with some fruit on middle-palate. Long finish.*	**£9.50**	ENO	(B)
CROZES-HERMITAGE CHÂTEAU CURSON 1994, DOMAINE POCHON Rhône	*Rich garnet colour. Big fruits and a good structure. Long, toasty, sweet finish.*	**£9.50**	J&B	(B)

DOMAINE DE LA MORDORÉE 1994, DELORME PROPRIÉTAIRE RÉCOLTANT Rhône	*Mulberries and a spicy nose follow on to the palate with an oaky, tannic finish.*	**£10.00**	NIC	**B**
CHÂTEAUNEUF- DU-PAPE LAURUS 1994, GABRIEL MEFFRE Rhône	*A big wine with lots of rich, stalky fruit; huge tannins and a well-structured finish.*	**£11.00**	GA	**B**
CORNAS LES SERRES 1990, DELAS FRÈRES Rhône	*Juicy, spicy, chocolatey aromas. Well-balanced with a pleasant finish and reasonable length.*	**£11.20**	FTH	**B**
CORNAS CHANTE-PEDRIX 1989, DELAS FRÈRES Rhône	*Sweet fruit on the nose; a a palate of concentrated oak, berry fruit and gripping tannins*	**£11.20**	CVR DBY WCR FTH	**S**
CHÂTEAUNEUF-DU-PAPE CHÂTEAU DE LA SOLITUDE 1994, DOMAINES PIERRE LANÇON Rhône	*Deep ruby, blackcurrant colour. Rich fruit nose and rich, cassis palate with soft tannins.*	**£11.50**	SMF DBY	**B**
CHÂTEAUNEUF-DU-PAPE DOMAINE CHANTE CIGALE 1993 Rhône	*Sweet and ripe with perfect acidity. Full, ripe, savoury fruits with large oaky spice.*	**£11.60**	Widely available	**B**
SEGURET CASA BASSA 1992, DOMAINE DE CABRASSE Rhône	*Strong nose of rich fruits and alcohol. Lots of fruit. Lovely, fresh wine.*	**£11.80**	SV HW	**B**
CUVÉE ELISE CHÂTEAUNEUF-DU-PAPE 1994, DOMAINE ST BENOIT Rhône	*This damson-coloured wine has great berry fruit combining with fresh, green spice.*	**£12.60**	WTR	**B**

FRANCE • RHONE RED

GRANDE GARDE CHÂTEAUNEUF-DU-PAPE 1995, DOMAINE ST BENOIT Rhône	*This well-structured wine explodes into a mass of liquorice and black berry fruit.*	**£12.60**	WTR	(S)
DOMAINE DU VIEUX TÉLÉGRAPHE CHÂTEAUNEUF-DU-PAPE 1993, HENRIE BRUNIER ET FILS Rhône	*Fine, structured wine with lovely fruit and hints of chocolate. Good length and depth.*	**£13.20**	Widely available	(S)
CHÂTEAUNEUF-DU-PAPE LA BERNADINE 1994, CHAPOUTIER Rhône	*Black, jammy fruits on the nose and a forest fruit palate with toasty oak. Good length.*	**£13.40**	Widely available	(B)
CORNAS CHAPOUTIER 1994 Rhône	*The green spices, sweet vanilla oak and firm tannins combine to give a mass of flavour*	**£13.80**	OD GI MM	(S)
CORNAS DOMAINE ROCHEPERTUIS 1991 Rhône	*A huge wine with great potential - smoky bacon, firm, full oak and fruit. Concentrated wine.*	**£14.50**	ENO J&B	(G)
CORNAS ALLEMAND 1991 Rhône	*A lovely, elegant nose with a touch of vanilla precedes a cream and chocolate palate. Very promising.*	**£15.10**	VWC J&B VW RW RAE	(B)
DOMAINE COMBIER CLOS DES GRIVES 1994 Rhône	*Aromatic, violet nose. A big, rich wine with bags of young fruit and oodles of style.*	**£15.50**	ENO	(B)
CHÂTEAUNEUF-DU-PAPE CUVÉE TRADITION 1989, DOMAINE DE MONPERTUIS Rhône	*A sound wine with complexity and a mature nose of white pepper and sweet spice.*	**£19.10**	EP	(B)

FRANCE • RHONE WHITE

CÔTE RÔTIE GUIGAL 1992 Rhône	*Rather subdued aroma is followed by a palate full of gentle, spicy fruit and chunky tannins.*	£20.10	Widely available	**B**
CÔTE RÔTIE CHAPOUTIER 1994 Rhône	*A fresh, light-bodied wine with pleasant style. Gentle spice and orange aromas. Sweet, ripe fruits.*	£23.30	OD MM GRT CNL	**B**
CHAPOUTIER MONIER DE LA SIZERANNE HERMITAGE 1994 Rhône	*Attractive, peppery nose complementing spicy and chocolatey fruit flavours. An earthy finish.*	£23.90	OD RD DBY MM GRT CNL	**S**

RHONE • WHITE

CHÂTEAUNEUF-DU-PAPE BLANC 1995, DOMAINE CHANTE CIGALE Rhône	*Fresh, fruity and elegant; full of lime, apple and vanilla with a crisply zingy palate*	£11.60	QUC COT COC DBY HOU NRW AMW MFS	**S**
CONDRIEU DOMAINE DE PIERRE BLANCHE 1994 Rhône	*A beautifully balanced concoction of rich peach fruit, almonds and vanilla, lifted by a complex, spicy character.*	£15.00	CHN	**G**
CONDRIEU LES CEPS DU NÉBADON 1993, PARET ET DEPARDIEU Rhône	*Grassy and oily on the nose with hints of botrytis, wet wool, pear, pepper and complex, honeyed peach fruit.*	£17.50	NI WCR ADN AMW	**G**
CONDRIEU GUIGAL 1994 Rhône	*Viscous and long with excellent balance; an immense weight of spicy vanilla and peach-kernel fruit.*	£21.50	IRV J&B HVW SHG SWS SOM	**S**

FRANCE • RHONE SPARKLING/FORTIFIED

CONDRIEU GUIGAL 1993 Rhône	*Lovely, creamy vanilla accompanies bright and well-defined soft fruit and complex, vegetal tones.*	**£22.80**	Widely available	(S)
CONDRIEU DOMAINE CUILLERON 1994 Rhône	*Lots of complex fruit including peaches, bananas, peach and vanilla. Rich and oily.*	**£25.00**	ENO	(B)

🍇

RHONE • SPARKLING

CLAIRETTE DE DIE NV, CAVE COOPERATIVE DE DIE Rhône	*Big and forward; fresh, fruity nose and massive mousse. Soft tropical palate with sweet length.*	**£6.70**	U W	(B)

🍇

RHONE • FORTIFIED

DOMAINE DE DURBAN MUSCAT DE BEAUMES DE VENISE 1994, LEYDIER ET FILS Rhône	*Light, elegant toffee apple flavour with toasty aspects. Refreshing underlying acidity provides good balance.*	**£11.10**	ABY	(B)
DOMAINE DE DURBAN MUSCAT DE BEAUMES DE VENISE 1995, LEYDIER ET FILS Rhône	*Fresh, grapey fruit. Ripe and luscious; gains balance from its fresh, lemony finish.*	**£11.10**	ABY	(B)

Pinpoint who sells the wine you wish to buy by turning to the stockist codes. If you know the name of the wine you want to buy, use the alphabetical index. If the price is your motivation, refer to the invaluable price guide index; red and white wines under £5, sparkling wines under £10 and champagne under £15. Happy hunting!

PROVENCE • RED

DOMAINE ST JEAN DE VILLECROZE 1990 Provence	*A mature, fresh-styled wine. Chocolatey, berry fruit flavours provide a tastey palate.*	**£7.00**	TW UNC MK CAR POR	**B**
CHÂTEAU ROUTAS CYRANO 1994, PHILIPPE BIELER Provence	*Elegant with good structure, providing a mouthful of soft fruits and lengthy tannins. Fine finish.*	**£10.50**	DBY	**B**

SOUTH WEST • RED/ROSE

CLOS LENVÈGE FUTS DE CHÊNE CUVÉE A L'ANCIENNE 1992, JACQUES BLAIS South West	*Deep colour and good use of oak. Excellent balance and good tannins. Good rounded wine.*	**£4.90**	MFS PHP OLW WBK DBY	**B**
CHÂTEAU TOUR DES GENDRES BERGERAC ROSÉ 1995 South West	*Wonderful balance of light raspberry fruit and zesty acidity with a gentle spritz.*	**£5.30**	GS RD	**S**
COMTE LA BARDE DES TENDOUX 1993, SOCAV & COMTE LA BARDE South West	*Strawberry sweetness on the nose with a touch of cedar and cigar box. Good finish.*	**£10.90**	ABY	**P**
COTEAUX L'ARDÈCHE RÉSERVE DES HAUTES TERRASSES 1995, UVICA South West	*Good, peppery, jammy blackcurrant fruit with hints of spice and pepper. Stylish.*	**£15.50**	YAP BD SMF PIM	**P**

SOUTH WEST • WHITE

Château de la Jaubertie 1995, Hugh Ryman South West	*Fresh, clean and extremely well-made, this is full of appealingly ripe, aromatic fruit.*	**£5.10**	VW DBY RYW CWS	**B**
Domaine des Cassagnoles Blanc de Blancs Sec 1995, J & G Baumann South West	*A delicious, clean and grassy nose with excellent intensity, clarity and impressive length.*	**£6.00**	BD	**S**
Jurançon Sec Grain Sauvage Blanc de Blancs 1995, Cave des Producteurs de Jurançon South West	*A spicy nose, promising oranges, cedar and roses gives way to a rich lemony palate.*	**£6.40**	NIC P	**B**
Savagnin Arbois 1989, Fruitière Vinicole d'Arbois South West	*Brilliant yellow gold in colour, Manzanilla sherry on the nose and perfect balance and length.*	**£15.00**	NIC	**B**

SOUTH WEST • SWEET WHITE

Château Theulet Monbazillac Cuvée Prestige 1994 South West	*Rich full honey and lime aromas. Smooth, ripe and rounded palate showing creamy, honeyed fruit.*	**£11.00**	GI BBR RBS	**B**
Château Grinou 1994, Guy Cuisset South West	*Soft marzipan and honey aromas. Concentrated, fat, peachy fruit balanced by some fresh citrus acidity.*	**£13.00**	ALZ	**S**

SOUTH WEST • SPARKLING

DOMAINE DE LAMOURE CRÉMANT DE LIMOUX 1992, DOMAINE MARTINOLLES South West	*Clean, ripe, full nose and delicious intense fruit palate giving good fizz.*	£8.50	CRM GI	B

LANGUEDOC ROUSSILLON • RED

"LES CAPITELLES" 1995, LES VIGNERONS DES TROIS TERROIRS Languedoc Roussillon	*A cherry and plum nose and a ripe fruit palate with a hot peppery finish.*	£3.90	GI	B
FITOU PRÉSTIGE DE PAZIOLS 1993, CAVE DE PAZIOLS Languedoc Roussillon	*Mint and blackcurrant nose, a light berry fruit palate with a comfortable balance of oak.*	£4.00	MWW	B
FITOU MILLÉSIME 1994, PRODUCTEURS DU MONT TAUCH Languedoc Roussillon	*A vegetal, peppery nose; a young, spiced palate of some complexity and an oaky finish.*	£4.00	TO SMF JS W MWW MRN U TH VLW	B
SAFEWAY FITOU 1994, LES CHAIS BEAUCAIROS Languedoc Roussillon	*A vibrant nose with just the merest hint of young fruit on the palate.*	£4.00	SAF	B
DOMAINE COMMANDERIE ST JEAN 1995, CHÂTEAU DE GREZAN Languedoc Roussillon	*Stewed blackberry and violet nose and a lively palate with sweet fruits, pepper and some length.*	£4.00	Widely available	S

Wine	Description	Price	Stockists	
SYRAH "LE MIDI" VIN DE PAYS D'OC 1995, LES VIGNERONS DES TROIS TERROIRS Languedoc Roussillon	*Intense fruitcake nose and a big, juicy blueberry body with pepper, tannin and good length.*	£4.20	CRM GI	(B)
LA SERRE MERLOT 1995 Languedoc Roussillon	*Youthful, cherry-cassis aromas. Plummy flavours with a hint of chocolate. Well-balanced, good claret.*	£4.40	HN SHG CHF BI	(B)
DOMAINE LA TOUR BOISÉE ROUGE 1994, MARIE-CLAUDE & JEAN-LOUIS POUDOU Languedoc Roussillon	*A fresh, young wine; good on the nose, high in tone and still improving.*	£4.50	PV WAW	(B)
DOMAINE DE PICHERAL 1995, GAEC DE PICHERAL Languedoc Roussillon	*An aroma of clouded raisins followed by soft, sweet fruit with a wisp of pepper.*	£4.50	A VER WES	(B)
'V' DE VIOLET 1995, EMILY FAUSSIE Languedoc Roussillon	*Warm nose of stalky plum leading into stewed fruit with high acid and some length.*	£4.50	BLS RAE	(B)
COSTIÈRES DE NÎMES CHÂTEAU ST LOUIS LA PERDRIX 1993 Languedoc Roussillon	*Cedar and raspberry nose and a spicy palate with baked plums, berry fruits and good length.*	£4.50	TO	(S)
COSTIÈRES DE NIMES CELLIER DU BONDAVIN 1994 Languedoc Roussillon	*Lightly peppery palate with a good fruit balance; rich and tight, but will open out.*	£4.60	B&B TRV LWE	(B)
LAPEROUSE VIN DE PAYS D'OC 1995, VAL D'ORBIEU & PENFOLDS Languedoc Roussillon	*A developed, spicy nose and a tannic palate with some weight and a little length.*	£4.70	TO TH VW SAF OD MWW WCR CWS	(B)

DOMAINE DE LA BAUME PHILIPPE DE BAUDIN MERLOT 1994, BRL HARDY Languedoc Roussillon	*Wonderful smoke and spice bouquet; broad Syrah palate balancing oak and plums.*	£4.80	Widely available	(B)
DOMAINE DE THÉLIN SYRAH 1992 Languedoc Roussillon	*Fine blueberry fruit nose with plums and violets combining with pepper on the palate.*	£4.90	WIM	(B)
CORBIÈRES LAGRASSE CHÂTEAU SAINT AURIOL 1993 Languedoc Roussillon	*A hearty middle-weight with a warm red-cherry nose; fair reach and a strong finish.*	£5.00	W	(B)
DOMAINE DE FONTBERTIÈRE CUVÉE FRANCK-EDWARD 1994, Languedoc Roussillon	*Mint and black fruits on the nose; a balanced, peppery palate with a weighty punch.*	£5.00	MWW	(B)
LA CLAPE CHÂTEAU MARMORIÈRES 1993 Languedoc Roussillon	*Smoky on the nose and a broad, ripe palate with excellent fruit complexity, balance and length.*	£5.00	MWW	(B)
MONTAGNE NOIRE 1995, LES PRODUCTEURS RÉUNIS FONCALIEU Languedoc Roussillon	*Apple nose followed by full ripe fruit, summer pudding, pepper and a long, spicy finish.*	£5.00	VLW	(B)
CHÂTEAU SAINT JAMES 1993, CHRISTOPHE GUELIO Languedoc Roussillon	*Chocolate and pepper on the nose; jammy yet slightly tannic fruit palate and sweet finish.*	£5.00	MWW	(B)
VIGNOBLES DES VALÉES PERDUES COTEAUX DE LANGUEDOC MONTPEYROUX Languedoc Roussillon	*Tobacco and leather on the nose, full-bodied, well-balanced, richly fruity and promising.*	£5.00	VW OD	(B)

DOMAINE ST EULALIE 1994, G BLANC Languedoc Roussillon	*An easy drinking wine with a concentrated nose, nice fruits and an oaky finish.*	**£5.10**	SHJ WON HHC BLS WIC CFT POR	**B**
FORTANT DE FRANCE CABERNET SAUVIGNON 1993 Languedoc Roussillon	*Showing plenty of fruit and leafy violets giving complexity. Some good oaked tannins to finish.*	**£5.20**	MWW SAF WCR	**B**
DOMAINE SAINT HILAIRE CABERNET SAUVIGNON 1992, A N HARDY Languedoc Roussillon	*Young wine with creamy berry fruits; well-balanced with robust oakiness. Good length and could improve.*	**£5.50**	GRT	**S**
LAITHWAITE OAK AGED SYRAH 1994, A & P DE BERTIER Languedoc Roussillon	*Interesting, vibrant violet and black cherry nose evolving to a full, fruity style on tasting.*	**£5.80**	BD	**B**
DOMAINE DES HORTENSIAS CUVÉE EXCEPTIONNELLE 1992, CAVE DES HAUTS COTEAUX DU MINERVOIS Languedoc Roussillon	*Wide-awake nose of melon and berries followed by developed and pleasantly tannic fruity palate.*	**£5.90**	BD	**B**
CORBIÈRES CHÂTEAU DU GRAND CAUMONT CUVÉE TRADITION 1994, FAMILLE RIGAL Languedoc Roussillon	*Pleasantly fruity with a hint of chocolate on the palate; balanced tannins and good prospects.*	**£6.00**	BD	**B**
ROUQUETTE 1994, CAVE LANGUEDOC ROUSILLON Languedoc Roussillon	*Rich nose with cedar and liquorice; well-structured plummy palate with a breath of sea-salt.*	**£6.00**	U POR	**B**
DOMAINE DE LA BAUME ESTATE MERLOT CUVÉE PROPRIÉTAIRE 1994, BRL HARDY Languedoc Roussillon	*A subdued lemon nose and a rich palate with blackcurrant, oak and a long finish.*	**£6.30**	A OD WR JS VWC MHW	**S**

FRANCE • LANGUEDOC ROUSSILLON ROSE

CHÂTEAU PECH LATT VIELLES VIGNES 1992 Languedoc Roussillon	*Light and balanced palate of fruit with just the right amount of oak. Young; could improve.*	£6.50	VR	**B**
CUVÉE HÉLÈNE DE TROIE CORBIÈRES 1993, CHÂTEAU HÉLÈNE Languedoc Roussillon	*A woody, fruity nose and good initial fruit on the palate; a steady finish.*	£6.90	PV TP WAW	**B**
MAS DE BRESSADES 1993 Languedoc Roussillon	*Sweet, mute nose and a palate of raspberries, chocolate and ginger precede a quick finish.*	£7.00	MWW	**B**
ALIQUIER & FILS FAUGÈRES 1993 Languedoc Roussillon	*Spicy, blackberry nose and a palate of peppery, mainly berry, fruits. Good balance and length.*	£7.30	VWC THP VW RW TAN RAE BI	**B**
MAS BRUGUIÈRE 1994, ISABELLE ET GUILHEM BRUGUIÈRE Languedoc Roussillon	*An austere, well-balanced wine with ripe cherries and chocolate to the fore, lasting through to the finish.*	£9.60	JN SEL RBS MFS	**B**

🍇
LANGUEDOC ROUSSILLON • ROSE

FORTANT SYRAH ROSÉ 1995, SKALLI FORTANT DE FRANCE Languedoc Roussillon	*Fresh, light, berry fruit with a slight spiciness. Soft cherry flavours and an attractive dry finish.*	£4.00	BTH VW TH WR	**B**
ST. MICHAEL ROSÉ DE SYRAH 1995, DOMAINES VIRGINIE Languedoc Roussillon	*Well-developed style combining robust straw-berry fruit with a sprinkling of pepper and fresh acidity.*	£4.00	M&S	**S**

LANGUEDOC ROUSSILLON • WHITE

WINTER HILL SEMILLON/CHARDONNAY 1995, FONCALIEU Languedoc Roussillon	*Bursting with buttery peach and ripe melon flavours; vanilla underlying rich, spicy fruit.*	**£3.70**	VLW W	**B**
CHEVALIER DE RODILAN SAUVIGNON BLANC 1995 Languedoc Roussillon	*Pale but fragrant with delicate gooseberry fruit on the nose; balanced with a fruity finish.*	**£3.80**	VER	**B**
DOMAINE DE LA TUILERIE CHARDONNAY 1995, HUGH RYMAN Languedoc Roussillon	*Dead simple and pleasantly light with a lemon and cheese nose and soft vanilla palate.*	**£4.00**	VW RYW SMF	**B**
TESCO DOMAINE SAUBAGNERE 1994, GRASSA Languedoc Roussillon	*Bright, with a fresh green tinge; the nose is full, buttery and honeyed. Soft and gentle.*	**£4.00**	TO	**B**
CHEVALIER DE RODILAN CHARDONNAY 1995 Languedoc Roussillon	*An elegant wine tasting of rich pineapple and toasty oak. A clean, medium-to-long finish.*	**£4.00**	VER	**S**
DOMAINE DE LA BAUME PHILIPPE DE BAUDIN SAUVIGNON BLANC 1995, BRL HARDY Languedoc Roussillon	*A refreshing, discrete, classic Sauvignon style, perfectly balanced, this wine reveals real gooseberry character .*	**£4.50**	Widely available	**S** WINE OF THE YEAR

Pinpoint who sells the wine you wish to buy by turning to the stockist codes. If you know the name of the wine you want to buy, use the alphabetical index. If the price is your motivation, refer to the invaluable price guide index; red and white wines under £5, sparkling wines under £10 and champagne under £15. Happy hunting!

Wine	Description	Price	Stockists	
PENFOLDS VAL D'ORBIEU LAPEROUSE 1995 Languedoc Roussillon	*This is a very attractive wine full of excellent, honeyed, apple flavours; a full, rounded finish.*	£4.50	TO TH VW SAF OD MWW WCR CWS	B
DOMAINE BASSAC SAUVIGNON 1995, LOUIS DECHON Languedoc Roussillon	*A ripe tropical fruit nose displaying high alcohol and acid with a full, fruity palate.*	£4.70	VR	B
DOMAINE LA BAUME PHILIPPE DE BAUDIN CHARDONNAY 1994, BRL HARDY Languedoc Roussillon	*Intense vanilla on the nose; excellent body with quite hot, brambly fruit and great length.*	£4.80	Widely available	B
LA BAUME CHAIS BAUMIÈRE CHARDONNAY 1994, BRL HARDY Languedoc Roussillon	*A full-bodied wine with rich, ripe, melon flavour and good acidity.*	£4.80	AWS BKT JS DBY	P
DOMAINE DE RIVOYRE BARREL FERMENTED CHARDONNAY 1994, HUGH RYMAN Languedoc Roussillon	*Tasters found this well-balanced, with a rich toasted flavour and creamy finish.*	£4.90	SAF DBY HOU RYW VLW SMF	P
GALET VINEYARDS SAUVIGNON BLANC 1995, GABRIEL MEFFRE Languedoc Roussillon	*A clean and gentle wine with well-defined varietal richness, juicy fruit and balanced acidity.*	£5.00	GA	
DOMAINE DE LA JALOUSIE CUVÉE BOIS 1993, YVES GRASSA Languedoc Roussillon	*Flowery, ripe tropical fruit nose and a juicy, buttery palate with a concentrated, oaky style.*	£5.00	TO	
MONTAGNE NOIRE CHARDONNAY 1995, LES PRODUCTEURS RÉUNIS FONCALIEU Languedoc Roussillon	*A good, oaky Chardonnay with a fruity nose and full-bodied, smoky, finish.*	£5.00	VLW	

LAROCHE GRANDE CUVÉE CHARDONNAY, 1995 Languedoc Roussillon	*Fudgey, cheesy nose and complex toasty palate with a peppery butterscotch finish.*	£5.00	WOC PF	**(S)** WINE OF THE YEAR
CUCKOO HILL VIOGNIER 1995, JEAN & LUC VIENNET Languedoc Roussillon	*Delightfully green and vegetal; lots of grass and gooseberries combined with ripe and attractive peachy fruit.*	£5.20	A MHW W	**(S)**
VIOGNIER DOMAINE DES SALICES 1995, J & F LURTON Languedoc Roussillon	*The nose combines rich apricot and melon fruit with a more earthy lemon/grapefruit flavour.*	£6.00	MWW	**(B)**
GALET VINEYARDS VIOGNIER 1995, GABRIEL MEFFRE Languedoc Roussillon	*Fruity and aromatic, displaying a floral, peachy nose typical of Viognier. A stylish and elegant wine.*	£6.50	GA MWW	**(B)**

🍇

LANGUEDOC ROUSSILLON • SWEET WHITE

DOMAINE DE LA JALOUSIE LATE HARVEST 1993, GRASSA Languedoc Roussillon	*Attractive, ripe, appley fruit balanced by clean fresh acidity. Ripe, rounded palate with a long, spicy finish.*	£5.00	TO	**(B)**

🍇

LANGUEDOC ROUSSILLON • FORTIFIED

SPAR MUSCAT ST. JEAN DE MINERVOIS NV, VAL D'ORBIEU Languedoc Roussillon	*Soft, ripe and sweet with intense spice. Lovely balance with its delightful boneyed richness and lemony acidity.*	£3.20	SPR	**(B)**

FRANCE • LANGUEDOC ROUSSILLON FORTIFIED

MUSCAT ST JEAN DE MINERVOIS PETIT GRAINS, LES VIGNERONS DE SEPTIMANIE Languedoc Roussillon	*Soft, sultana fruit nose. Sweet, honeyed palate with peachy fruit. Perfumed, grapey finish.*	£4.20	JS PLA MGN WTR TAN	**B**
NOILLY PRAT NV Languedoc Roussillon	*Hints of orange peel and bone-dry quinine. Just the way Bond likes it!*	£6.30	JO JS TH W TEL GDS	**B**
RIVESALTES HORS D'AGE FORCAREAL NV, J P HENRIQUES Languedoc Roussillon	*Enticing nose of gentle, raisiny fruit and caramel. Rich toffee and muscova- do sugar on the palate.*	£6.30	SWS DBY COK POR NRW WCR	**S**
MUSCAT DE FRONTIGNAN VIN DE LIQUEUR NV, FRONTIGNAN CO-OP Languedoc Roussillon	*Intense, raisiny style with fat, rounded, concentra- tion. Luscious and sweet; good balance.*	£6.70	NIC SMF GRT	**F**
DOMAINE CAZES MUSCAT DE RIVESALTES 1994 Languedoc Roussillon	*Fresh, perfumed nose with aromas of pink grapefruit, orange peel and sweet grapes.*	£10.60	ENO RBS NIC CNL	**C**
MAS AMIEL 1993, CHARLES DUPUY MAURY Languedoc Roussillon	*Full of rich berry fruits, this wine shows good maturity with hints of golden marmalade .*	£11.50	NIC	**)**

GERMANY

Despite the fact that it is the source of some of the world's finest white wines, Germany is still a country overlooked by many searching for a quality wine. Help appears to be at hand, however, in the form of a recent wealth of information on the Riesling grape within the wine press describing its versatility and resilience. These wines deserve a wider market.

WHITE

ERBEN KABINETT 1994, FRANZ WILHELM LANGGUTH ERBEN Rheinhessen	*Full-flavoured, this is a good, grapey wine with the steeliness characteristic of the Mosel.*	**£4.00**	JS	(B)
LANGENBACH SOLO 1995, HERMANN KENDERMANN WEINKELLEREI Rheinhessen	*Zingy and grapey, fresh fruit and a touch of spice. This is very well-made and highly refreshing.*	**£4.00**	BU WR TH	(B)
SOMERFIELD GEWÜRZ-TRAMINER HALBTROCKEN 1993, WINZERGENOSSEN-SCHAFT RIETBURG Pfalz	*The bouquet is promisingly floral and delicate, giving way to a palate full of smooth, creamy fruit.*	**£4.30**	SMF	(B)
SCHLOSSBERG RIESLING SPÄTLESE 1989, WEINGUT SCHLOSS LIESER Mosel-Saar-Ruwer	*Petrolly and limey aromas precede a refreshing, crisp palate. Very stylish – a great summer drink.*	**£4.50**	NRW	(B)
ERDENER TREPPCHEN RIESLING 1991, WEINGUT MÖNCHHOF Mosel-Saar-Ruwer	*Lots of soft, lush fruit makes this sweet and lemony with a hint of diesel. Very pleasant.*	**£5.00**	RW W	(B)

GERMANY • WHITE				
HOCHHEIMER HÖLLE RIESLING KABINETT 1995, GEHEIMRAT ASCHROTT'SCHE ERBEN Rheingau	*Excellent, ripe, and with tones of boneyed apples – a lovely open nose full of powerfully tropical fruit.*	£5.00	A	(S)
OCHFENER BOCHSTEIN RIESLING KABINETT 1994, WEINGUT REICHSGRAF VON KESSELSTATT Mosel-Saar-Ruwer	*A classy, youthful and rather tight Riesling nose precedes a zingy palate containing good, ripe, appley fruit.*	£6.00	O AMA	(S)
RIESLING 1993, WEINGUT GRANS-FASSIAN Mosel-Saar-Ruwer	*Harmonious, gentle and rich. The nose hints at class and the palate follows through.*	£6.50	MWW HAY WMK	(B)
TRITTENHEIMER-ALTÄRCHEN RIESLING KABINETT 1992, WEINGUT GRANS-FASSIAN Mosel-Saar-Ruwer	*Classy, though still rather youthful; traces of waxy botrytis on the nose. Very elegant.*	£7.00	MWW HAY	(B)
BERNKASTELER BADSTUBE RIESLING KABINETT 1994, WEINGUT REICHSGRAF VON KESSELSTATT Mosel-Saar-Ruwer	*A delicious bouquet of blackcurrants, with lemon, mango, some mellow honey and some crackling acidity.*	£7.00	CWS	(S)
DEIDESHEIM RIESLING 1989, DEINHARD Pfalz	*A heavily spiced, peachy nose and lots of full-bodied, ripe fruit. Very classy.*	£7.10	JEH HCK CNL MFS AMA	(B)
OPPENHEIMER SACKTRÄGER RIESLING 1993, WEINGUT KÜHLING-GILLOT Rheinhessen	*Exotically spicy aromas of pears, grapes and citrus fruits with a high level of residual sugar.*	£7.50	WSC	(B)
KASELER NIES'CHEN RIESLING KABINETT 1994, WEINGUT REICHSGRAF VON KESSELSTATT Mosel-Saar-Ruwer	*Classically varietal, racy Riesling character, full of beautifully balanced fruit and hints of sweetness.*	£8.20	TP ADN AMA	(B)

GERMANY • WHITE				
KOBERNER WEISENBERG RIESLING SPÄTLESE 1994, WEINGUT FREIHERR VON SCHLEINITZ Mosel-Saar-Ruwer	*A sweetly floral, aromatic nose with some lovely lemony herbaceous hints with a touch of watermelon.*	£8.20	WSC	(S)
RIESLING 1994, WEINGUT FRITZ HAAG Mosel-Saar-Ruwer	*A fresh and elegant floral nose with a lemony palate that is refreshing and slightly sharp.*	£8.40	J&B L&W	(B)
KOBERNER WEISENBERG RIESLING 1994, WEINGUT FREIHERR VON SCHLEINITZ Mosel-Saar-Ruwer	*A delicate and elegantly flowery nose, gently lemony and slightly spicy.*	£8.40	WSC	(S)
SCHLOSS JOHANNISBERGER RIESLING 1994 Rheingau	*A tight and smoky nose with some tart, appley fruit which will soften in time.*	£8.60	S&D GI MHW PTR BUT DBY AMA	(B)
ÜRZIGER WÜRZGARTEN RIESLING SPÄTLESE 1994, WEINGUT MÖNCHHOF Mosel-Saar-Ruwer	*Fresh, spicy, lemon zest; lots of fleshy fruit and ripely acidic citrus fruit. Lovely.*	£9.00	J&B	(B)
RIESLING KABINETT 1994, WEINGUT J J PRÜM Mosel-Saar Ruwer	*A fine and delicate, flowery nose which is faintly spritzy and very elegant with harmonious, peach-like acidity.*	£9.00	J&B	(S)
LANGENLONSHEIMER SONNENBORN RIESLING SPÄTLESE 1994, WEINGUT WILLI SCHWEINHARDT Nahe	*Lean and lithe - aromas of apple pie and lots of grippy apple fruit on the palate.*	£9.80	WSC	(B)
WEHLENER SONNENUHR RIESLING KABINETT 1994, WEINGUT DR LOOSEN Mosel-Saar-Ruwer	*Richly coloured, this is warm and ripe, full of rich lemon and honey aromas.*	£10.00	Widely available	(B)

GERMANY • WHITE

SCHLOSS JOHANNISBERGER RIESLING KABINETT 1994 Rheingau	*An earthy nose marks this austere and very dry wine which contains peppery apple fruit that lingers well.*	£10.20	GNW PTR WER BUT DBY	**B**
SINGLE ESTATE SOMMERHÄUSENER STEINBACH SILVANER SPÄTLESE 1994, WEINGUT ERNST GEBHARDT Franken	*Honeyed fruit and spicy petrolly aromas – a rich wine which is peppery on the tongue.*	£11.00	WSC	**B**
WEHLENER SONNENUHR RIESLING KABINETT 1993, WEGELER-DEINHARD Mosel-Saar-Ruwer	*Well-rounded spiciness and some botrytis, a green but very drinkable wine with some breeding.*	£11.00	PF	**B**
BRAUNEBERGER JUFFER SONNENUHR RIESLING SPÄTLESE 1990, WEINGUT FRITZ HAAG Mosel-Saar-Ruwer	*Signs of some development, a high degree of concentrated, rich citrus fruit and excellent balance.*	£11.50	J&B	**S**
ÜRZIGER WÜRZGARTEN RIESLING SPÄTLESE 1989, WEINGUT DR LOOSEN Mosel-Saar-Ruwer	*A clean, zingy sherbet nose, lively, fresh and ripe. Typically Riesling in an easy style.*	£13.60	NI BOO JN SHG HW	**B**
ERDENER TREPPCHEN RIESLING SPÄTLESE 1994, WEINGUT DR LOOSEN Mosel-Saar-Ruwer	*An intriguingly perfumed aroma of boiled sweets and violets. Some cassis on the palate.*	£13.90	BBR NI BOO SHG LWE NY HW ADN	**B**
WEHLENER SONNENUHR RIESLING SPÄTLESE 1990, WEGELER-DEINHARD Mosel-Saar-Ruwer	*A classic Riesling nose; flinty, grapefruity and a touch austere with a wonderfully fresh finish.*	£14.70	WIM BEN	**B**

Pinpoint who sells the wine you wish to buy by turning to the stockist codes. If you know the name of the wine you want to buy, use the alphabetical index. If the price is your motivation, refer to the invaluable price guide index; red and white wines under £5, sparkling wines under £10 and champagne under £15. Happy hunting!

GERMANY • SWEET WHITE

NACHFOLGER WEISSER BURGUNDER AUSLESE TROCKEN 1994, WEINGUT WILLI SCHWEINHARDT Nahe	*Excellent, full-fruit aroma with some spice and almond and the crisp pithiness of grapefruit.*	£15.00	WSC	(B)
GEHEIMRAT 'J' RHEINGAU RIESLING SPÄTLESE DRY 1989, WEGELER-DEINHARD Rheingau	*Botrytis and lemon zest with some petrolly, floral aromas. A well-developed palate that would be good with food.*	£16.00	HAR	(B)

SWEET WHITE

KIRCHHEIMER SCHWARZER BEERENAUSLESE NV, ZIMMERMANN-GRAEF Pfalz	*Elegant style, quite floral with hints of lemon zest. Quite raisiny with exotic, peachy fruit.*	£4.30	W CWS	(S)
TESCO STEINWEILER KLOSTER LIEBFRAUENBERG AUSLESE NV Pfalz	*Big, rich fruit – rather raisiny, and more than a hint of botrytis.*	£5.30	TO	(B)
KOBERNER WEISENBERG RIESLING AUSLESE 1993, KONRAD HÄHN Mosel-Saar-Ruwer	*Greeny gold, this has a lovely, ripe, spicy nose with super balance and concentration.*	£10.50	WSC	(B)
OPPENHEIMER SACKTRÄGER RIESLING AUSLESE 1992, WEINGUT KÜHLING-GILLOT Rheinhessen	*Delightful crisp, green-apple nose. Lightly honeyed with great zesty acidity. Will last for ages.*	£13.40	WSC	(B)
OPPENHEIMER SACKTRÄGER RIESLING TROCKENBEEREN-AUSLESE 1992, WEINGUT KÜHLING-GILLOT Rheinhessen	*Full, rich, botrytised sweetie with excellent complexity. Combines fresh, ripe, tropical fruit and fine acidity.*	£37.00	WSC	(G)

SPARKLING

DEINHARD YELLO CHARDONNAY/RIESLING NV	*Savoury nose; dry, lemony palate with biscuit tones, good length and a sweetish finish.*	**£5.90**	MRN WFL U CHF MTL FEN AMA CWS

ITALY

Diversity of wines matches the diversity of climate and terrain. Huge, mouth-filling reds such as the Barolos of Piedmont can be contrasted with the delicate whites of Fruili. This variation is derived from the very different characteristics of the wine-growing regions. The trend is to produce wines which are more palatable to the general consumer; thus, fruit content and quality are high on the agenda.

PIEDMONT • RED

BARBERA D'ASTI BRICCO ZANONE 1994, TERRE DA VINO Piedmont	*A mature colour; a slightly rubbery nose, but vigorously fruity on the palate. Good.*	£4.70	OD WST	(B)
DOLCETTO D'ALBA SETTIMO 1993, AURELIO SETTIMO Piedmont	*Deep colouring and vibrant fine tannins. A big wine with a fruity style. Very enjoyable.*	£5.30	PV WAW	(B)
BARBERA D'ALBA FIULOT PRUNOTTO 1995, CASA VINICOLA ALFREDO PRUNOTTO Piedmont	*Deep colour. A pleasing, bitter cherry character; good balance with quite young tannins.*	£6.80	L&W V&C LUC SV BLN MM W	(B)
BRACHETTO DEL PIEMONTE 1994, BATASIOLO Piedmont	*Full of cherries on the nose and ripe apples on the palate; good length and acidity.*	£9.60	MON	(G)
NEBBIOLO D'ALBA OCCHETTI 1994, CASA VINICOLA ALFREDO PRUNOTTO Piedmont	*A balsamic, fruity and complex nose, with a tannic, acidic palate. Still a little young.*	£10.40	HN SV BLN V&C MM	(S)

BARBARESCO MONTESTEFANO 1993, CASA VINICOLA ALFREDO PRUNOTTO Piedmont	*Closed and peppery on the nose. Very tannic with enjoyable rich fruit coming through.*	£20.20	L&W HAR SV DIR V&C BLN	(B)
BAROLO MONVIGLIERO RISERVA 1990, TERRE DEL BAROLO Piedmont	*Perfumed, delicate nose. Rich, round and full of fruit with good concentration and length.*	£25.00	IT	(S)

TUSCANY • RED

SALVANZA SANGIOVESE DI TOSCANA 1993, GESTIONI PICCINI Tuscany	*Deepish ruby colour. A warm, slightly porty nose and palate. Eucalyptus and new oak present.*	£6.00	SAF	(B)
POLIZZANO CHIANTI 1995 Tuscany	*Young purple colour; damsons on the nose. Slightly malolactic taste with tannins; chalky finishing touch.*	£6.00	SCA POR DBY NOX NRW	(B)
I SASSI CHIANTI CLASSICO 1994, MELINI Tuscany	*Young garnet colouring. A complex nose of caramel, leather and cherry. Soft and mouth-filling. Very good.*	£7.20	MON	(B)
CASTELLO DI BROLIO CHIANTI CLASSICO 1994 Tuscany	*Ruby hue. Blueberry, spicy nose. On the palate, sweet fruit and some drying tannins.*	£7.50	ENO VIL V&C	(B)
PODERE CAPACCIA CHANTI CLASSICO 1992, GIANPAOLO PACINI Tuscany	*A good ruby colour; cherries on the nose and a good balance. Nice finish.*	£8.50	SEL V&C	(S)

MARCHESI ANTINORI CHIANTI CLASSICO RISERVA 1993 Tuscany	*Attractive raspberry/plum fruit and soft, sweet cherries with delightful fruit-stone bitterness on the finish.*	£8.80	Widely available	(B)
LE VOLTE 1994, TENUTA DELL'ORNELLAIA Tuscany	*Deep ruby colour. Creamy, slightly rusty nose. Rich with good tannins and fruits.*	£8.80	ENO SEL CPW CWI V&C WCR CWS	(S)
VILLA CERNA RISERVA 1993, CECCHI Tuscany	*Youthful ruby colour. Soft, warm fruit flavours which are predominantly cherry on the palate.*	£9.00	IT	(B)
BERARDENGA CHIANTI CLASSICO 1993, FATTORIA DI FELSINA Tuscany	*Dark purple colour. Rich fruit aromas and well-balanced on the palate. A great wine.*	£9.30	ENO V&C AMW	(S)
LAMAIONE MERLOT DELLA TENUTA DI CASTELGIOCONDO MONTALCINO 1993, MARCHESI DE' FRESCOBALDI Tuscany	*Deep ruby to garnet. Soft and rich on the nose, rich and smooth on the palate.*	£12.00	OD	(S)
FRESCOBALDI CHIANTI RUFINA MONTESODI 1991, MARCHESI DE' FRESCOBALDI Tuscany	*A lovely, burnt cherry nose precedes a medium-bodied, rich fruit palate. Refreshing use of acid.*	£13.20	PIM CF WIN V&C MM	(B)
ST. MICHAEL BRUNELLO DI MONTALCINO ANNATA 1990, RAINER ZUROCK Tuscany	*A powerful and rich wine. Structured flavours of earthily rural fruit on the palate. Nicely developed tannins.*	£14.00	M&S	(S)
CASALFERRO CASTELLO DI BROLIO 1993, BARONE RICASOLI Tuscany	*Rich ruby garnet. Delicate, opening sour fruit; masses of oak. High acid, young tannins – good wine.*	£14.20	ENO VIL V&C	(B)

BRUNELLO DI MONTALCINO FRESCOBALDI 1991, Tuscany	*Ripe, tannic and fruity on the nose. Rather acidic taste with subtle tannins. Crisp, short finish.*	**£14.30**	OD U V&C MM	**B**
IL LATINI 1988, SONIA CHECCUCCI LATINI Tuscany	*Rich garnet colouring. A complex, mature bouquet with rich fruit on the palate. Lovely.*	**£15.10**	TRV L&W	**S**
BRUNELLO DI MONTALCINO COL D'ORCIA 1991 Tuscany	*Good fruit on the nose with chocolate hints. Ripe fruit on the palate. Good length.*	**£15.60**	LU V&C RAV	**S**
BRUNELLO DI MONTALCINO CASTELLO BANFI 1991 Tuscany	*Slightly dusty and chalky on the nose. Ripe fruit with firm, closed stucturing; nice balance.*	**£16.40**	BUT DBY V&C	**S**
BRUNELLO DI MONTALCINO 1991, TENUTA DI ARGIANO Tuscany	*A hot, spicy nose followed by ripe, fruity, chocolatey flavours. Good structure and nice length.*	**£16.70**	Widely available	**G**
BRUNELLO DI MONTALCINO 1991, FATTORIA DEI BARBI Tuscany	*A slightly acidic and tannic nose. Full of ripe fruit and tannins on the palate. Wonderful.*	**£17.40**	ENO VIL JN CFT WMK V&C AMA	**S**
RUFFINO NERO DEL TONDO VINO DA TAVOLA 1993 Tuscany	*Very good colour, concentrated berries and cherry fruit; aggressive tannins. An enjoyable, complex mouthful.*	**£19.50**	ALI	**B**
BRUNELLO DI MONTALCINO COL D'ORCIA RISERVA 1990 Tuscany	*A stalky and liquorice nose that follows to the palate. Bitter fruit, firm tannins. Balanced and delicious.*	**£19.50**	LU V&C RAV AMA	**G**

ITALY • OTHER REGIONS RED

BRUNELLO DI MONTALCINO FRESCOBALDI RISERVA 1990 Tuscany	*Old-fashioned style; bitter, hot, alcoholic palate. Full tannins and fruit on the nose with a delicious vanilla palate.*	£20.50	WIN V&C AMA	(G)
BRUNELLO DI MONTALCINO 1991, POGGIO ANTICO Tuscany	*A ripe and spicy nose; firm, hot and spicy palate. Good length, nicely balanced.*	£22.10	HAR BLN RBS NIC V&C	(S)
ANTINORI TIGNANELLO 1993 Tuscany	*Deep red colouring. Very fruity and perfumed nose. Mellow, pleasant, good length and nice tannins.*	£23.00	Widely available	(B)
ORNELLAIA 1992, TENUTA DELL'ORNELLAIA Tuscany	*Black cherry and elderflower on the nose. Deep, sherbety and sweet on the palate.*	£28.10	Widely available	(S)
ANTINORI SOLAIA 1993 Tuscany	*Vanilla pod concentration with hints of cherry and hedgerow fruit. Showing good breeding.*	£41.30	Widely available	(S)

OTHER REGIONS • RED

KWIK SAVE MONTEPULCIANO D'ABRUZZO 1995, GRUPPO ITALIANO VINI Abruzzo	*Deep red, some purple. Lots of fruit with high acids and some tannins. Grapey with good length.*	£3.00	KWI	(B)
SAFEWAY SICILIAN RED 1995, CALATRASI Sicily	*Ripe loganberries with fresh black pepper on the nose. Soft redcurrant flavours. Medium finish.*	£3.00	SAF	(B)

LAZIO ROSSO CASALE DEL GIGLIO 1995 Latium	*This wine has an interesting, sharp nose; slightly farmyardy. Bitter palate.*	**£3.40**	TO SMF	(B)
VILLA MANTINERA MONTEPULCIANO DI MOLISE 1994, VINI CLITERINA Molise	*Mature, spicy, plummy bouquet. A full, rich, plummy flavour. Super fruit/tannin balance. Good length.*	**£3.60**	CWS	(B)
PUGLIAN RED 'THE COUNTRY COLLECTION' 1995, CANTELE Puglia	*Good colour with bright cherries on the nose. Well-structured, fresh and vibrant.*	**£3.60**	CRS MRW VW SAF OD CWS	(B)
SOMERFIELD GRILLI DI VILLA THALIA 1993, CALATRASI Sicily	*This has berries and orange peel on the nose. Loganberry flavours with a long finish.*	**£3.70**	SMF	(S)
TORREVENTO CASTEL DEL MONTE ROSSO 1993 Puglia	*A deep colour. Subtle nose although there are strong tannins and fruit on the palate.*	**£4.00**	OD	(B)
PRINCIPATO MERLOT/CABERNET 1994, CA'VIT Trentino Alto Adige	*Mid-deep colour. Sweet summer fruit on the nose. A bitter aftertaste but initially fine.*	**£4.00**	Widely available	(B)
TABURNO ROSSO 1994 Campania	*A bouquet of perfumed roses on the nose and rather good, ripe cherries on the palate.*	**£4.00**	TO	(B)
MERLOT PIAVE 1995, RICORDI CA' VENDRAMIN Veneto	*Bright purple with lots of juicy fruit on the nose. Round soft taste. A tasty, simple wine.*	**£4.00**	BWC TWB	(B)

SAFEWAY CASA DI GIOVANNI RED 1994, CALATRASI Sicily	High plummy fruit nose. Well-balanced fruit with damsons and plums persisting to the finish.	£4.00	SAF	(B)
MERLOT TRENTINO BRIONE 1995, CONCILIO Trentino Alto Adige	Good deep colour; complex, attractive nose with a substantial, youthful, chocolatey taste. Commercial style.	£4.30	TO FUL	(B)
SANGIOVESE SAN CRISPINO RIVA 1993, CANTINE RONCO Romagna	A good complex nose. On the palate there is some oak and a little fruit.	£4.40	FDL SSM OD BLN V&C WST	(B)
VALPOLICELLA CLASSICO IL MASO 1994, CASA VINICOLA ZONIN Veneto	A lovely, mature nose with secondary aromas. Taste; soft, attractive chocolates, oaks and creaminess. Balanced.	£4.60	EP HOT CVR	(B)
PRIMITIVO DEL SALENTO VINO DA TAVOLA 1994, AZIENDA VINICOLA CANTELE Puglia	Rich and chocolatey on the nose. A good powerful balance and great depth of fruit.	£4.60	IT OD BU WR TH CWS	(S)
MONTEPULCIANO D'ABRUZZO BARONE CORNACCHIA 1993 Abruzzo	Sweet, freshly-trodden fruit; rustic with tannins. Good length, could develop well.	£4.60	MWW V&C	(S)
VALPOLICELLA VIGNETI CASTERNA PASQUA 1993 Veneto	A good colour with a slightly closed nose; black fruits on the palate. Good dry intensity.	£4.80	TP SMF	(B)

Pinpoint who sells the wine you wish to buy by turning to the stockist codes. If you know the name of the wine you want to buy, use the alphabetical index. If the price is your motivation, refer to the invaluable price guide index; red and white wines under £5, sparkling wines under £10 and champagne under £15. Happy hunting!

MONTEPULCIANO D'ABRUZZO JORIO 1993, UMANI RONCHI The Marches	*This has a deep ruby colour with a mature spicy blackberry bouquet. Lasting tannic finish; a vibrant wine.*	£5.00	ENO VIL RBS V&C SMF WCR	**B**
SANTA BARBARA SQUINZANO 1993 Puglia	*Deep red colour. A tarry, rich nose. Depth, structure and ripe fruit. Good all-round wine.*	£5.30	A CTL MHW V&C	**B**
VILLA PIGNA ROZZANO 1994 The Marches	*Deep colour; sweet, ripe juice fragrances with good fruit and some tannins on the palate.*	£5.50	A WST	**B**
TAURINO NOTARPANARO ROSSO DEL SALENTO 1988, AZIENDA AGRICOLA COSIMO TAURINO Puglia	*Rich, fruity nose – a nice bouquet. Complex balanced taste; warm and pleasant palate. A short finish.*	£5.60	MWW V&C SOM W	**S**
SALICE SALENTINO VENDEMMIA SAN MARTINO 1991, FRANCESCO COLUCCI Puglia	*Ruby garnet colour; rich blackcurrant nose. Slight tabacco, oaky, soft, warm and rich fruits. Balanced acidity.*	£5.80	BD	**B**
COPERTINO RISERVA 1993 Puglia	*A rich chocolate nose with a slight, stalky blackcurrant aroma. There is a soft fruity flavour on the palate.*	£5.80	ENO VIL MRF DBY HVW V&C WCR SOM	**S**
SALICE SALENTINO RISERVA 1992, FRANCESCO CANDIDO Puglia	*Rich garnet colour. Good fruit aromas. A soft balanced flavour with fine acidity and tannins.*	£5.90	Widely available	**B**
TRENTINO MERLOT 1995, CONCILIO Trentino Alto Adige	*Attractive depth of colour. Masses of sweet fruit and oak on nose with good balance; a long, lingering finish.*	£6.00	BD	**S**

CASALE DEL GIGLIO PETIT VERDOT 1994 Latium	*A good colour; smoky on the nose. Lots of pruney fruit on the palate.*	£6.00	HOU TO	(S)
VILLA PIGNA CABERNASCO VINO DA TAVOLA ROSSO 1992 The Marches	*Leafy on the nose with capsicum, oak and dusty fruit. Good structure.*	£6.00	WST TO	(S)
BARBAGLIO ROSSO DEL SALENTO 1993, CO-OPERATIVA SANTA BARBARA SAN PIETRO Puglia	*A deep opaque black-currant colour. Excellent structure with powerful fruit. Good depth.*	£6.10	CTL V&C VW	(G) WINE OF THE YEAR
TAURINO NOTARPANARO ROSSO DEL SALENTO 1986 Puglia	*Ruby to garnet colour. Warm, rich fruity nose. Rich flavours, good balance; soft tannins.*	£6.40	MWW V&C SOM	(B)
VIGNETO SAN LORENZO ROSSO CONERO 1993, UMANI RONCHI The Marches	*Deep ruby colouring. A slightly closed nose and tough palate but good fruit; some oak.*	£6.50	Widely available	(S)
SALICE SALENTINO ROSSO 1990, CANTELE Puglia	*Good curranty aroma. Stunning, rich fresh fruit flavours with nice rounded tannins.*	£6.60	RD	(B)
CIAFRE VINO DA TAVOLA DI CONTROGUERRA 1994, AZIENDA AGRICOLA DINO ILLUMINATI Abruzzo	*An attractive aroma of grass and wet stones - pungent and herbal with a hint of greengages.*	£6.90	BLN V&C	(B)
AGONTANO ROSSO CONERO 1993, GAROFOLI The Marches	*Dark ruby colouring. Massive fruit and good structure on the nose. Fruity, tannic, hot palate.*	£7.50	IT	(G)

FRACIA VALTELLINA SUPERIORE 1990, NINO NEGRI Lombardy	*Bright colour. Light earthy fruity nose. Easy fruit with light tannins to finish.*	£7.70	ENO VIL V&C	B
AMARONE DELLA VALPOLICELLA TENUTA IL MASO 1992, CASA VINICOLA ZONIN Veneto	*Ruby to blackcurrant colour. A sweet chocolatey nose with good fruit, rich and firm acidity.*	£7.70	EOR HOT CVR	B
DUCA SANFELICE ROSSO RISERVA 1990, LIBRANDI Calabria	*Browny-red colouring. Mature savoury aromas with red fruits on the palate. A good balance.*	£8.80	ENO CWI V&C	S
ROCCA RUBIA CARIGNANO DEL SULCIS RISERVA 1992, C S SANTADI Sardinia	*Medium ruby colour. Faint pine needles on the nose and a good balance of fruits.*	£8.80	Widely available	G
ZANNA MONTEPULCIANO D'ABRUZZO VECCHIO 1991, ILLUMINATI Abruzzo	*Deep colour. Deep nose of rich tarry fruit. Good concentration of fruit. Good long finish.*	£9.00	BLN V&C	B
TOMMASI AMARONE RECIOTO DELLA VALPOLICELLA CLASSICO 1991, TOMMASI Veneto	*Getting tired and drying but the fruit is still apparent. Almost port in style.*	£9.70	U	B
GRUMELLO VALTELLINA SUPERIORE RISERVA 1990, NERA Lombardy	*A sweet summer fruit nose. Balanced, soft tannins, red berry fruit flavours. Thin on finish.*	£10.50	CD	B
AZIENDA AGRICOLA LA PRENDINA VIGNETO DEL FALCONE CABERNET SAUVIGNON 1993, GOILIETTO PIONA	*Oaky and extremely agreeable. Touches of walnut with cedar tones. Consistent and extremely smooth. Nice wine.*	£11.00	V&C	B

DUCA D'ARAGONA CANDIDO ROSSO DEL SALENTO 1990, FRANCESCO CANDIDO Puglia	*Blackcurrant colouring. Soft, honeyed nose with fruit aromas. Well-balanced with rich, drying tannins.*	£11.10	ENO VIL RD DBY CWI V&C SOM AMA **(B)**
CUMARO ROSSO CONERO 1993, UMANI RONCHI The Marches	*Huge leathery, meaty nose, complemented by a long, hot palate. Bags of tannins and fruit.*	£11.10	Widely available **(G)**
GUERRIEDI RIZZARDI FONTIS VINEALE MINUS 1994 Veneto	*Fine nose and well-integrated. A touch of bitter fruits with a good finish.*	£11.50	HBJ F&M HAR SEL **(B)**
SFURSAT VALTELLINA SUPERIORE 1994, NINO NEGRI Lombardy	*A delicious robust red which is rich and mellow. A very classic, pure example of its type.*	£12.30	ENO VIL BUT CWI V&C **(S)**
VALPOLICELLA RECIOTO CLASSICO CAPITEL MONTE FONTANA 1991, AZIENDA AGRICOLA TEDESCHI Veneto	*Ripe and slightly sweet style of wine with good fruit flavours and balanced finish.*	£13.30	WIN V&C SOM **(B)**
AMARONE CLASSICO DELLA VALPOLICELLA BOLLA 1989 Veneto	*Deep rich colour, a nose with hints of cherries, smoky oak, and a touch of chocolate. Chewy and chunky. Very good.*	£13.90	WIM WNS GER CD LU V&C **(S)**
TERRE BRUNE 1992, C S SANTADI Sardinia	*Ruby to garnet colours with vibrant fruits and oak. Full aroma and a rich, fruity palate.*	£15.20	ENO VIL RD HVW CWI V&C SOM AMA **(G)**
LUMEN MONTEPULICIANO D'ABRUZZO ILLUMINATI 1993, AZIENDA AGRICOLA DINO ILLUMINATI Abruzzo	*Good, deep ruby colour, high tannin and lots of ripe fruit on the palate, still young.*	£18.00	BLN V&C **(S)**

WHITE

BIANCO DEL LAZIO GABBIA D'ORO VINO DA TAVOLA 1995, CANTINA GADORO Latium	*A very fragrant, aromatic nose bursting with fascinating, truffley, minerally fruit. A full, well-balanced palate.*	£2.70	A	**B**
FILIPETTI EXTRA DRY NV Piedmont	*Wonderful delicate and refreshing with good fruit content – super length.*	£3.30	SAF WST	**B**
SEGESTA SICILIAN WHITE 1995, FIRRIATO Sicily	*Lovely, fresh yet gentle fruit hinting at pear drops and bubble gum. Soft, light and clean.*	£3.70	FUL OD	**B**
SOAVE CLASSICO CORTE OLIVI 1995, CANTINE LENOTTI Veneto	*Pale, almost water-white with tinges of green, the flavour is delicate and soft; agreeably quaffable.*	£3.80	A WST	**B**
TESCO ORVIETO CLASSICO ABBOCCATO NV, BARBI Umbria	*Enticing aromas of ripe melon and honey. Mix of green apple fruit, honey and limes.*	£3.90	TO	**S**
BIDOLI SAUVIGNON BLANC 1995 Friuli Venezia Giulia	*Clean, refreshing Sauvignon character with loads of sharp fruit and an agreeable finish.*	£4.00	WST	**B**
CANTINA TOLLO BIANCO NV Abruzzo	*Very dry, clean and crisp; a wine with excellent positive bubblegum fruit, fine balance and length.*	£4.00	A V&C	**B**

ITALY • WHITE				
LE TRULLE CHARDONNAY DEL SALENTO 1994, AZIENDA VINICOLA CANTELE KYM MILNE Puglia	Perfectly clean and simple nose with a subtle lemon and vanilla custard palate.	£4.40	Widely available	(B)
MALT HOUSE VINTNERS PINOT GRIGIO 1995, BIDOLI Friuli Venezia Giulia	A fresh and easy-drinking style, full of apples and apricots. Well-balanced, simple and lively.	£4.60	MHV WST	(B)
BIDOLI PINOT GRIGIO CA PRADAI 1995 Friuli Venezia Giulia	Sophisticated, elegant and stylish, this shows intense apple and citrus fruit with peachy hints.	£4.80	A OD GRT WST	(B)
VIGNETO CARAMIA CHARDONNAY DEL SALENTO 1995 Puglia	Oak nose, ripe melon and mango palate with creamy oak; balanced acid and fresh length.	£4.80	Widely available	(S)
GRECO DI PUGLIA 1995, KYM MILNE Puglia	Very well-balanced, fresh and zesty with a touch of delightful aromatic fruit. Good stuff.	£5.00	TO OD	(B)
LA VIS CHARDONNAY 1995 Trentino Alto Adige	Light-weight and simple with faint fruit and clean finish. A great summer drink.	£5.00	A V&C	(B)
ALASIA CHARDONNAY DEL PIEMONTE 1995 Piedmont	Attractive peach and lychee nose, full palate of chunky flavours with good length and finish.	£5.20	Widely available	(B)
RUFFINO LIBAIO 1995, TENIMENTI RUFFINO Tuscany	An unusually creamy, herbal nose. The palate is dry, crisp and full of rich flavours.	£6.00	RBS NY CD V&C	(B)

ITALY • WHITE				
Soave Vigneto Monte Grande 1995, Azienda Agricola Pra Veneto	*Gently aromatic with tones of apples, lemons and pears, this is fresh yet softly creamy.*	£7.00	SAN MHW JUS	B
Castello della Sala Chardonnay 1995, Marchesi Antinori Umbria	*Faint nose and fine palate with twist of lime, tropical fruit and a long finish.*	£7.40	V&C DIR GSH HOL SV BLN	B
Soave Classico Superiore Vigneto La Rocca 1994, Leonildo Pieropan Veneto	*Soft, floral fruit offset by a hint of bitter almonds and clean citrus flavours.*	£8.10	ENO WSO BEN HW V&C	B
Terre di Franciacorta Bianco Bellavista 1995, Bellavista Lombardy	*A balanced wine with pear and apple flavours well woven. Tremendous richness and length.*	£9.00	CD LU V & C V&C	B
Puiatti Pinot Grigio 1995 Friuli Venezia Giulia	*Spritzy wine with a light, lemon and pear drop character and a suggestion of nuttiness.*	£9.90	ENO J&B CWI V&C SOM	B
Jermann Chardonnay 1994, Vinnaioli Jermann Friuli Venezia Giulia	*Lovely and refreshing Chardonnay showing a complex, fruity palate balanced by crisp acidity.*	£11.00	ENO	B
Alteserre 1994, Bava Piedmont	*Excellent ripe aromatic fruit - dry and fresh with hints of citrus fruits and herbs.*	£12.80	NI MHW	B
Castello della Sala Cervaro 1994, Marchesi Antinori Umbria	*Delightful smoky nose; a palate filled with elegant nectarine, lemon and sweet vanilla. Wonderful!*	£19.40	HAR V&C L&W WIM SV BLN AMA	G

FORTIFIED

PELLEGRINO MARSALA VERGINE VINTAGE 1962, CARLO PELLEGRINO Sicily	*Salted nut aromas. Richer palate of dried fruits and bitter almonds.*	**£13.90**	WIN DBY	(B)

NEW ZEALAND

DESPITE BEING BADLY AFFECTED by heavy rains last year, New Zealand is still host to some of the most delicious and invigorating Sauvignon Blancs sold on the international market. In addition, there is an increasing production of Chardonnay, Gewürztraminer and reds – in particular Pinot Noir – which offer interesting and exciting alternatives to the rest of the world.

CABERNET SAUVIGNON

TIMARA CABERNET SAUVIGNON/MERLOT 1994, MONTANA WINES Marlborough/ Hawkes Bay	*Excellent, soft, sweet red-currant fruit with well-integrated oak. Attractive cedary finish; very well-made.*	£4.70	Widely available	B
MONTANA CABERNET SAUVIGNON 1994, MONTANA WINES North Island	*Herbaceous and cedary fruit aromas. A wine with some complexity. Drink now.*	£5.70	Widely available	B
ST. MICHAEL SAINTS HAWKE'S BAY CABERNET/MERLOT 1994, MONTANA WINES North Island	*Good, oaky, berry fruit nose. Showing well balanced fruits, herbs and hints of mint.*	£7.00	M&S	B
JEWELSTONE MISSION CABERNET/MERLOT 1994 North Island	*Good fruit flavours on the palate, with plums and raspberries dominating. Good acidity and tannins.*	£7.20	AMW HAW PIM	B
VILLA MARIA CABERNET/ MERLOT RESERVE 1991 North Island	*Medium-bodied colourings with smooth, smoky undertones on the nose. Superb juicy, berry fruit.*	£7.40	WR BU DBY FEN WCR	B

NEW ZEALAND • RED

VINTAGE SELECTION CABERNET/MERLOT 1993, LINCOLN VINEYARDS North Island	*Blackcurrant purple with leafy, green Cabernet aromas. Structured tannins with a good fruit back-up.*	£7.90	WIL BEC ALM PTR DBY	Ⓑ
ENIGMA 1995, CHIFNEY WINES North Island	*Burnt aromas reminiscent of a Côtes de Rhône. Ripe, dark fruit with a hint of cassis.*	£9.00	GGW	Ⓑ
MARA ESTATE CABERNET SAUVIGNON 1994, BABICH North Island	*Earthy, musky nose with touches of hedgerow jamminess. Excellent balance with firm but discreet tannins.*	£10.00	PF WIM	Ⓢ
AWATEA CABERNET/MERLOT 1993, TE MATA North Island	*Spice and cream on the palate with fresh fruit, cloves and cinnamon. Finely balanced.*	£13.10	SHG AMW AMA BU WR	Ⓢ
TE MOTU CABERNET /MERLOT 1994, WAIHEKE VINEYARDS North Island	*Rich ruby colourings with strawberries and cream on the nose. Liquorice, cinnamon and spice on the palate.*	£19.50	FSW GNW WWT FNZ	Ⓢ

PINOT NOIR

CORBANS PRIVATE BIN PINOT NOIR 1994 South Island	*A wonderful juicy Pinot Noir that has a strawberry vanilla nose with dry cherry character.*	£9.90	JCK WTR CEN CDE CAX MHW	Ⓑ
PALLISER ESTATE OF MARTINBOROUGH PINOT NOIR 1994 North Island	*Deep red fruit, cranberry juice; crisp and tart. Good colour; oak and tomato aromas. A balanced wine.*	£10.40	ABY TH BWI J&B DBY MHW BU WR	Ⓑ

NEW ZEALAND • RED

MARTINBOROUGH VINEYARD PINOT NOIR 1994 North Island	*Fresh cherry-red, good fruit concentration; light lively style. A real pleasure to drink.*	£10.90	Widely available	B
GIESEN PINOT NOIR 1995 South Island	*Highly peppery, sneezing dust nose; fruit dominated by pepper and mustard flavours, with matured Pinot .*	£11.00	MOR	B
VAVASOUR PINOT NOIR RESERVE 1994 South Island	*Lovely and rich fruit comes out on the nose and palate. This is an outstanding Pinot Noir.*	£11.20	DBY NY HOU	B
NEUDORF MOUTERE PINOT NOIR 1994 South Island	*Fine nose, juicy fruit and clean, smooth, integrated flavours. Good balance and complexity; subtle but elegant.*	£13.90	SEL P ADN AMA	B
BAZZARD ESTATE HUAPAI PINOT NOIR 1994, CHARLES & KAY Auckland	*Mid-garnet colour, complex nose; rich, juicy bramble fruit; marked acids and tannins. Will develop nicely.*	£14.10	GGW	B

OTHER • RED

SACRED HILL CABERNET/ MERLOT 1994 North Island	*Aromas and flavours of cassis and rhubarb with hints of tobacco. Rich cherry tannins on finish.*	£9.20	SCA WIL SEL LWE FEN WOC	B
CORBANS PRIVATE BIN MERLOT/CABERNET SAUVIGNON 1994 South Island	*Slightly vegetal nose. Rich fruit with fairly excited tannins. Good for a couple more years.*	£10.00	JCK WTR CEN MHW CDE CAX BU WR	B

CHARDONNAY

MONTANA MARLBOROUGH CHARDONNAY 1995 South Island	*Intense nose and complex palate full of characterful flavours; good acid balance, length and finish.*	**£5.30**	Widely available	(B)
VILLA MARIA PRIVATE BIN CHARDONNAY 1995, MALBOROUGH South Island	*Smooth, rounded, spicy peach palate with flinty hints of oak.*	**£5.70**	BU WR TH	(B)
VILLA MARIA PRIVATE BIN CHARDONNAY 1995 North Island	*Fresh and clean with tropical fruit nose; full well-balanced palate and a lively finish.*	**£6.00**	U VDV VW MWW DBY FEN WCR	(S)
ST. MICHAEL SAINTS CHARDONNAY 1995, MONTANA WINES North Island	*Slightly lean, enjoyable light lemons and gooseberries which are heavily oaked. A good summer number.*	**£7.00**	M&S	(B)
MATUA VALLEY EASTERN BAYS CHARDONNAY 1995, North Island	*Unpronounced tropical fruit nose with a faintly-oaked middle palate, acid balance and a nice fresh aftertaste.*	**£7.70**	TP JS GRT	(S)
CHURCH ROAD RESERVE CHARDONNAY 1994, MONTANA WINES North Island	*On the palate there is soft oak, tropical fruit and almonds balanced with good acidity.*	**£7.70**	Widely available	(S)
MISSION JEWELSTONE CHARDONNAY 1994 North Island	*Clean, neutral, lightly nutty ripe-style with medium length. Opens up once exposed.*	**£7.90**	HAW PIM AMW	(B)

NEW ZEALAND • WHITE

LINCOLN VINEYARDS PARKLANDS 1994 North Island	*Golden green colour; complex, nutty lanolin nose with a delicious citrusy lemon zing on the palate.*	**£8.00**	AMW ALM CRM DBY POR NRW	(S)
CHURCH ROAD CHARDONNAY 1994, McDONALD WINERY North Island	*Lovely buttermilk and zesty citrus aromas complemented by tastes of sprightly pineapple and grapefruit.*	**£8.00**	Widely available	(S)
HAWKES BAY CHARDONNAY WHITE LABEL 1994, MORTON ESTATE North Island	*A delicious, oily vanilla Chardonnay which resembles ripe apples on the palate; needs time.*	**£8.50**	LNR CPW ROB DBY POR BWC	(S)
MERLEN CHARDONNAY 1994 South Island	*Almondy nose and nutty character. A well balanced, complex, smooth mouth-filling flavour.*	**£8.60**	ISW HVW GRT	(B)
WAIRAU RIVER CHARDONNAY 1994 South Island	*Attractive, ripe, honeyed melon nose, a complex oily fruit palate, with impressive length and a creamy finish.*	**£8.80**	LEA RD NY SOM	(S)
SACRED HILL WHITECLIFF CHARDONNAY 1995 North Island	*Ripe toasted tropical fruit nose; fresh, lively creamy, well-integrated palate with lingering toffee finish.*	**£8.80**	SCA WIL SEL LWE FEN	(S)
CHARDONNAY KEMBLEFIELD 1994 North Island	*Appealing, richly tropical nose. The palate, though lacking complexity, has a lemon lightness.*	**£9.00**	FUL D THP	(B)
OMAKA SPRINGS ESTATE CHARDONNAY 1995 South Island	*Fresh and light on the nose, a big middle palate with a nutty taste. Still slightly green.*	**£9.10**	A&N AMW ETV	(B)

LAWSON'S DRY HILLS CHARDONNAY 1994 South Island	Delicate nettle nose, fresh, full, lemony flavours which are nicely honeyed. A spicy, zingy young finish.	£9.40	SHG BI	(S)
JACKSON ESTATE RESERVE CHARDONNAY 1994 South Island	Solid yet soft nose; good, fleshy, nutty and full style, long acidity and hint of sweetness.	£9.50	VIL BNK SV HW TAN AMW	(B)
PASK GIMBLETT ROAD CHARDONNAY 1994 North Island	Attractive pineapple and beeswax nose; excellent ripe tropical fruits. A full-bodied palate with good length.	£9.50	HOT SHJ WIC BLS L&W	(G)
CORBANS PRIVATE BIN CHARDONNAY 1994 North Island	Good summer wine of deep yellow colour. A cocktail of very ripe fruits. Firm, short finish.	£9.80	Widely available	(B)
VILLA MARIA MARLBOROUGH CHARDONNAY RESERVE 1994, South Island	Pungent almost garlicky nose with acidity a bit sharp at first. Good lemony fruit and depth.	£10.00	AR	(B)
ROCKWOOD RESERVE CHARDONNAY 1995 North Island	Rich, ripe, rounded character with attractive, smoky lemon fruit and a long buttery finish.	£10.00	LWE	(S)
ORMOND ESTATE CHARDONNAY 1993, MONTANA WINES North Island	Toasty vanilla pod aromas exude and give way to a rich, tropical fruit mouthful.	£10.30	Widely available	(B)
CORBANS PRIVATE BIN MARLBOROUGH CHARDONNAY 1994 South Island	A sherbet nose showing touches of vanilla extract and grapefruit. A complex palate of fruit salad.	£10.40	JCK WTR CEN MHW CDE CRM CAX	(S)

NEW ZEALAND • WHITE

RENWICK ESTATE CHARDONNAY 1993, MONTANA WINES South Island	*Deep yellow colour, rich butter nose produced by well-integrated oak given zip by a twist of lemon.*	£10.50	Widely available	**B**
ORMOND ESTATE CHARDONNAY 1994, MONTANA WINES North Island	*Good balance between oak and acidity creating an enjoyable buttery, nutty and tropical fruit mouthful.*	£10.50	TBC CLA BNK CPW SEA FEN VLW WCR	**S**
PALLISER ESTATE OF MARTINBOROUGH CHARDONNAY 1994 North Island	*Good golden colour, ripe rich fruit. Though lacking complexity a nicely made wine with length.*	£10.60	TH BWI ABY HVW DBY MHW BU WR	**B**
HAWKES BAY CHARDONNAY BLACK LABEL 1994, MORTON ESTATE North Island	*Exciting palate of creamy coconut and melon, good acidity and balance. Lovely complexity and cracking finish.*	£10.70	LNR DBY BWC	**B**
MARTINBOROUGH VINEYARD CHARDONNAY PALLISER ESTATE 1994 North Island	*An open, floral nose complemented by zesty lemon and nutty palate; medium length.*	£10.70	Widely available	**B**
CLIFTON CHARDONNAY 1994, OKAHU ESTATE North Island	*A yeasty, burnt nose which tends to suffocate the subtle fruits found on the palate.*	£11.00	GGW	**B**
GIESEN CHARDONNAY 1995 South Island	*A rich tropical fruit nose and sweet honeydew melon palate with good balance and a nice, appley finish.*	£11.00	MOR	**B**
CLIFTON CHARDONNAY 1994, OKAHU ESTATE North Island	*Refreshingly traditional style; soft elegant palate combining tropical fruits and almond oaking; great complexity.*	£12.00	GGW	**S**

NEW ZEALAND •WHITE

NEUDORF MOUTERE CHARDONNAY 1994 South Island	*Abundant honey and melon leading to a palate with plenty of creamy coconuts and tropical fruit.*	**£16.80**	MAR BH SEL NY P ADN MFS AMA	(G)

SAUVIGNON BLANC

WAIRAU RIVER SAUVIGNON BLANC 1995 South Island	*A herbaceous nose with good neutral character, carried through on palate and finish.*	**£8.00**	Widely available	(B)
JACKSON ESTATE SAUVIGNON BLANC 1995 South Island	*Intense tropical fruit notes and grass in a sound wine with outstanding balance and weight.*	**£8.10**	Widely available	(B)
GROVE MILL SAUVIGNON BLANC 1995 South Island	*A typical New Zealand Sauvignon, with outstanding herbaceous aromas and a lovely white berry palate.*	**£8.20**	Widely available	(S)
LAWSON'S DRY HILLS MARLBOROUGH SAUVIGNON BLANC 1995 South Island	*A youthful number with plenty of varietal character, forward fruit and smoky flavour on the finish.*	**£8.40**	SHG BI W	(S)
MARA ESTATE SAUVIGNON 1994, BABICH WINES North Island	*Integrated oak, vanilla and tropical fruit style; full in the mouth, harmonious and balanced.*	**£9.00**	PIF WIM	(B)
PALLISER ESTATE OF MARTINBOROUGH SAUVIGNON BLANC 1995 North Island	*An intense gooseberry and boiled sweet nose with an abundant, zingy acid character and a juicy palate.*	**£9.20**	Widely available	(S)

NEW ZEALAND • WHITE

NAUTILIS MARLBOROUGH SAUVIGNON BLANC 1995 South Island	*Herbaceous, with pine on the nose and a pleasant green tinge. A soft, acid style.*	£9.20	D JN HVW MWW DBY MM AMA	**B**

OTHER • WHITE

TESCO NEW ZEALAND DRY WHITE NV North Island	*Fresh fruit, melons and fruit salad; this is lovely fresh, clean and nicely balanced wine.*	£4.00	TO	**B**
TIMARA DRY WHITE 1995, MONTANA WINES South Island	*Full-bodied, tropical pineapple fruit and nettle aromas. Plenty of fruit and lots of length.*	£4.30	Widely available	**B**
NOBILO WHITE CLOUD 1995, HOUSE OF NOBILO North Island	*Honey and lime aromas with a delicate, grapey flavour. Attractive balance of fruit and fresh acidity.*	£4.80	Widely available	**B**
VILLA MARIA PRIVATE BIN CHENIN/ CHARDONNAY 1995 North Island	*An enticingly fresh and rather light aroma hinting of gooseberries and honey with crisp apple fruit.*	£5.20	TO BKW VDV DBY WCR	**B**
STONELEIGH RIESLING 1994, CORBANS WINES South Island	*Delightful, peachy fruit, spicy lime and an 'almost perfect balance of acid and residual sugar'.*	£5.50	Widely available	**S**
VILLA MARIA PRIVATE BIN RIESLING 1995, South Island	*A light, floral nose with lifted, fruit salad tones and a clean, very well balanced palate.*	£6.20	VDV DBY BU WR TH	**B**

NEW ZEALAND • SPARKLING

MILLTON VINEYARD SEMILLON/CHARDONNAY 1995 North Island	Fresh capsicum with a hint of botrytis and packed with deliciously soft, herby fruit.	£6.20	SAF VER CWI CWS	(B)
PALLISER ESTATE OF MARTINBOROUGH RIESLING 1994 North Island	A muscatty wine showing plenty of good pineapple and peardrop character with a suggestion of blackcurrants.	£6.80	ABY HVW P	(B)
PATUTAHI ESTATE GEWÜRZTRAMINER 1994, MONTANA WINES North Island	Fleshy and waxy with lots of excellent, toasty, floral spice and subtle hints of honey.	£10.70	WTS P&R EP JBR G&M COK SEA FEN	(B)

SWEET WHITE

VILLA MARIA NOBLE RIESLING RESERVE 1991 North Island	Ripe peach and apple fruit; honeyed, with a rich, creamy palate. Fresh, lemony acidity.	£9.90	OD DBY	(S)
GIESEN BOTRYTISED RIESLING 1995 South Island	Full, spicy marmalade aromas. Rich and honeyed complemented by some tangy grapefruit. Soft, gentle finish.	£20.00	MOR	(B)

SPARKLING

ST. MICHAEL BLUFF HILL NEW ZEALAND BRUT SPARKLING NV, MONTANA WINES South Island	Crisp, lean style with a lively, yeasty lemon nose, raspberry fruit and a dry, lemon finish.	£7.00	M&S	(B)

NEW ZEALAND • SPARKLING				
NAUTILUS CUVÉE MARLBOROUGH BRUT NV South Island	*Bright, clean, apple blossom nose and ripe, appley palate. Pleasant now and set to improve.*	**£10.50**	JN MWW DBY WCR SOM AMA	**S**
JACKSON ESTATE SPARKLING 1992 South Island	*Good, creamy style with a full, lemon nose; balanced, toasty flavour and a crisp finish.*	**£19.50**	GDS HW AMW	**B**

NORTH AMERICA

THE UNITED STATES, AND CALIFORNIA in particular, is leading the
New World from the front in the production of quality reds,
not to mention producing a few excellent whites. Many a judge
was pleasantly surprised to discover the identity of these wines
after the Challenge, especially when they had described one as
'the perfect Burgundy'. Canada is also producing some novel
wines worthy of exploration.

CALIFORNIA • CABERNET SAUVIGNON

REDWOOD TRAIL CABERNET SAUVIGNON 1993, STERLING VINEYARDS California	*Blackberry fruits, hints of pepper, rich tannins and sweet oak give this wine a long finish.*	**£4.90**	CLA OD CVR COK SEA	(S)
MOUNT KONOCTI CABERNET SAUVIGNON 1993, KONOCTI CELLARS California	*Tasters found a tempting smoky, blackcurrant nose. Oak and fruit marry well on the palate.*	**£6.20**	VWC SHG BEN VW	(B)
QUIVIRA DRY CREEK CABERNET CUVÉE 1992 California	*High complexity with lots of sweet-and-sour fruits. Mint and dusty spice add to a big, tannic finish.*	**£7.00**	A	(B)
CYPRESS CABERNET SAUVIGNON 1993, J LOHR WINERY California	*Minty nose and a nice, soft, plummy palate with new oak. Good balance, cedary finish.*	**£7.00**	ENO	(S)
CONCANNON CABERNET SAUVIGNON 1993 California	*Peppery/minty nose and a strawberry character with hints of spice. A palate with depth.*	**£7.50**	GNW AWS PWW TAN NI	(B)

NORTH AMERICA • CALIFORNIA RED

VILLA MOUNT EDEN CABERNET SAUVIGNON 1992, MOUNT EDEN VINEYARDS California	*Rich, plummy, earthy nose. Velvety, soft plums and nice spice. Good complexity, lengthy tannins. Fabulous wine.*	£7.50	BB AWS WCR	(S)
PARK WEST CABERNET SAUVIGNON 1993 California	*Lots of ripe fruits and great vanilla oak. Tannins are rich and full. Long, hot finish.*	£7.50	CFH WWI PAT	(S)
FIRESTONE CABERNET SAUVIGNON 1993 California	*Medium-bodied with soft, ripe fruits. Appealing oak. A smooth, rich wine with a fine and refreshing finish.*	£9.50	WSO MWW	(B)
RAYMOND NAPA VALLEY CABERNET SAUVIGNON 1991 California	*Fruitful and cedary nose leads to mature, ripe cassis fruit. Classy tannins, long finish.*	£9.50	FS	(S)
AUDUBON COLLECTION CABERNET SAUVIGNON UNFILTERED 1993, AUDUBON CELLARS California	*Complex with fine, fruity aromas, showing rich fruits and hot spices with smooth firm tannins.*	£9.50	SEL	(G)
LYETH RED 1990 California	*Berry-fruit nose. Ripe blackcurrants with lots of acidity. Has good tannins and length. A refreshing wine.*	£9.70	BH T&W CEB NY HW P	(S)
LOHR ESTATES SEVENOAKS CABERNET SAUVIGNON 1993, J LOHR WINERY California	*Good intensity, soft plum character. Rich fruits and nice balance of wood on palate.*	£10.00	ENO	(B)
JEKEL SANCTUARY CABERNET SAUVIGNON 1993 California	*Strongly oaked with spicy fleshy fruit. Good, lengthy finish with fine structure and balance.*	£10.00	MWW	(B)

GALLO SONOMA CABERNET SAUVIGNON 1992, ERNEST & JULIO GALLO California	*Oaky nose. Pleasing proportion of fruit and oak on the palate; good tannins and rich finish.*	£10.60	Widely available	**B**
BERINGER VINEYARDS NAPA VALLEY CABERNET SAUVIGNON 1993 California	*Cedar and ripe berry-fruits nose. Soft and balanced with a lovely, spicy-oak finish.*	£10.60	LNR CPW HD MWW MTL SMF IVY	**S**
SIMI CABERNET SAUVIGNON 1990 California	*Notes of raspberry and redcurrant on the nose. Tannins and fruit are well-married. Long finish.*	£12.50	COR HOL TP SEL RBS NY SOB PIM	**B**
DYNAMITE CABERNET SAUVIGNON 1993, CARMENET VINEYARD California	*Clear red with clean, herbaceous aromas. Soft, ripe, fruity palate. Has firm but discreet tannins.*	£12.80	HN WSO SHG BI	**B**
FREEMARK ABBEY CABERNET SAUVIGNON 1992 California	*Evidence of cinnamon, mint, raspberry and blackcurrant on the nose. Has a fruity, creamy palate.*	£13.50	HWL PAT	**S**
FREI RANCH CABERNET SAUVIGNON 1992, ERNEST & JULIO GALLO California	*Deep and velvety in the glass. Rich berry fruit with suggestions of strawberry, cassis and fig. Memorable finish.*	£14.20	EP SEL A&N SOB THP E&J	**G**
STAG'S LEAP DISTRICT CABERNET SAUVIGNON 1991, CLOS DU VAL WINERY California	*Ruby-red colour with a farmyardy nose. Savoury vegetal notes and delicious, ripe fruit.*	£14.50	WSO NAD WMK	**B**
LAUREL GLEN TERRA ROSA CABERNET SAUVIGNON 1993 California	*Has a plummy, black-curranty nose and intense fruit on palate. Ripe tannins, a good structure, fruity finish.*	£14.50	BKW OD WCR	**S**

RIDGE SANTA CRUZ MOUNTAINS CABERNET SAUVIGNON 1992 California	*Delicious, summer-pudding flavour in the mouth with touches of mint, cassis and vanilla on the finish.*	£15.90	Widely available	B
SHAFER STAG'S LEAP DISTRICT CABERNET SAUVIGNON 1992 California	*Soft cedar on the nose. A vegetal edge on the palate with slightly tight young tannins.*	£16.70	RBS WTR VLW WCR	B
ARROWOOD SONOMA COUNTY CABERNET SAUVIGNON 1991 California	*Burnt-rubber nose. Ripe, modern style with buttery, smoky, vanilla oak and splendid, full-bodied oak.*	£18.00	SEL	B
RUBICON 1981, NIEBAUM-COPPOLA ESTATE California	*Complex cassis, strawberry and earthy complexity mingle on the palate. Developing well.*	£19.00	RD	S
FREEMARK ABBEY CABERNET SAUVIGNON 1990 California	*Tarry wood on the nose. Strawberries on the palate with a slightly dry finish.*	£19.90	SEL VH PAT	B
CECCHETTI SEBASTIANI CELLARS CABERNET SAUVIGNON 1993 California	*Purple ripeness in the glass. Hedgerow fruit precedes ripe vanilla and spice on the palate.*	£20.00	TWB	S
BERINGER NAPA VALLEY PRIVATE RESERVE CABERNET SAUVIGNON 1991 California	*Beautifully extracted fruit on the palate with touches of new oak and a green freshness.*	£21.60	LNR MWW CPW	B
MONDAVI UNFILTERED NAPA RESERVE CABERNET SAUVIGNON 1990 California	*Sweet, ripe fruit with a rather earthy, slightly rustic palate. Will mature well, but is drinking nicely now.*	£27.90	MWW CLA SOB MM	B

NORTH AMERICA • CALIFORNIA RED

RIDGE MONTE BELLO CABERNET SAUVIGNON 1991 California	*An abundance of juicy, summer-fruit flavours complemented by vanilla extract and cedary oak.*	£39.90	MWW ADN AMA M&V	(G)
OPUS ONE 1992, BARON PHILIPPE DE ROTHSCHILD & ROBERT MONDAVI California	*Aromas of delicious chocolate, vanilla pod and blackcurrants. The palate is creamy and full.*	£46.50	Widely available	(G)

CALIFORNIA • PINOT NOIR

PARDUCCI PINOT NOIR 1994 California	*Trace of oak and slight greenness; lengthy finish. A substantial wine which will develop.*	£6.50	GS	(S)
FLEUR DE CARNEROS PINOT NOIR 1994 California	*Excellent Pinot; sweet fragrance with good depth. Soft, rich fruit balanced with silky tannins.*	£9.20	MWW NAD MFS AMA	(G)
CARNEROS CREEK PINOT NOIR 1994 California	*Good, clean, ripe rhubarb nose, firmly structured fruit, good tannins, warm ripe finish.*	£9.50	MD RTW AMA	(S)
CARNEROS CREEK SIGNATURE RESERVE PINOT NOIR 1993 California	*Depth of colour, complex vegetal and concentrated fruit nose, with fruit and mocha tones on the palate. An elegant wine.*	£11.00	NAD AMA	(S)
ROCHIOLI PINOT NOIR 1993 California	*Bright colour. Full, ripe Pinot character on the nose. Full, quite sweet, ripe fruit and very good length.*	£11.50	JN DBY RW RAE	(G)

CALERA PINOT NOIR 1993 California	*Attractive, redcurrant nose, good soft fruit and high acidity. An austere finish with hints of pepper and leather.*	**£12.20**	BEN CPW DBY MWW MHW SOM	**B**
SAINTSBURY CARNEROS PINOT NOIR 1994 California	*Ripe, forest fruits, cherries and good oak give a complex nose and palate with great length.*	**£12.70**	Widely available	**S**
AU BON CLIMAT PINOT NOIR 1994 California	*Full, ripe, sweet berries; earthy nose; full, rich, ripe fruit and earthiness on palate. This wine has great elegance.*	**£14.90**	Widely available	**G**
MONDAVI CARNEROS PINOT NOIR 1993 California	*Good, clean Pinot nose, good Pinot character: fresh brambles; some tannins; balanced, with a long finish.*	**£16.60**	CLA TP OD BEN	**B**
MONDAVI NAPA RESERVE PINOT NOIR 1992 California	*Excellent in class, jammy fruit, nicely integrated tannins. Dry but soft, this has a very good, long finish.*	**£18.60**	CLA BEN HOT MWW SOB MM	**G**
SAINTSBURY CARNEROS RESERVE PINOT NOIR 1994 California	*Pale crimson. Attractive fruity nose of raspberry and cherry. A fine, fruity cherry palate, good structure and vanilla.*	**£20.80**	HAR CHF SEL NY SOM P ADN	**B**
THE FAMOUS GATE CARNEROS PINOT NOIR 1993, DOMAINE CARNEROS California	*Good fruit and tannins, well-balanced, integrated oak, good length. Though still young, this will be good.*	**£22.50**	PF TP	**B**
BEARBOAT PINOT NOIR 1994 California	*Mid-garnet, gamey nose with crushed cherries and oak tones, full, rounded palate, great potential.*	**£23.00**	ENO	**S**

CALIFORNIA • ZINFANDEL

SOUTH BAY VINEYARDS ZINFANDEL, CALIFORNIA DIRECT California	*Tasters found elegant, sweet fruit (notably strawberries), with a creaminess and a slight touch of stalkiness.*	£5.00	JS	(S)
SUTTER HOME AMADOR COUNTY RESERVE ZINFANDEL 1990 California	*A stylish wine now displaying some maturity, flavour expands beautifully in the mouth with an ample finish.*	£7.40	VHW VIL SHG WAC MTL MFS AMA	(G)
VILLA MOUNT EDEN ZINFANDEL 1994, MOUNT EDEN VINEYARDS California	*A plummy nose marks this rich, spicy wine showing jammy fruit and excellent structure.*	£8.80	BB AWS SHG NY WCR	(G)
KENWOOD ZINFANDEL 1992 California	*An opulent, earthy and ripe, spirity nose with an inviting balance of fruit, oak and spice.*	£9.00	VWC VNO VW	(G)
CLINE CELLARS ZINFANDEL 1994 California	*Palate of ripe fruit and mint; cherry wood and leafy notes. A super-rich wine.*	£9.40	WTR RBS NY VLW TRO	(S)
GALLO SONOMA ZINFANDEL 1992, ERNEST & JULIO GALLO California	*An intense, distinctive nose of baked fruit surrounds fresh acidity and creamy tannins.*	£9.70	SEL EP A&N SOB MTL E&J FTH	(B)
VOSS ZINFANDEL 1993 California	*Beautifully structured, ripe and juicy fruit with distinctive oak. A smooth and fine wine.*	£10.00	TH BU WR	(S)

KENWOOD NUNS CANYON ZINFANDEL 1993 California	*Complexity of the palate is indicated by the layers of forest fruits, spice, chocolate and oak.*	£10.00	VNO VWC VW	(G)
FREI RANCH VINEYARDS ZINFANDEL 1993, ERNEST & JULIO GALLO California	*A rich, deep wine with dark, ripe fruit and herbal and cedar notes elegantly played.*	£11.50	EP A&N SOB SEL E&J	(B)
RIDGE GEYSERVILLE ZINFANDEL 1992 California	*Silky, animal notes, cedar and chocolate; sublime, ripe fruit and blackcurrants. Harmonious wine.*	£15.90	Widely available	(G)

CALIFORNIA • OTHER RED

ASDA CALIFORNIA RED NV, ARIUS CELLARS California	*A superb nose of raspberries, loganberries and herbs precede a light, subtle, yet rich, strawberry palate.*	£3.00	A	(S)
SOMERFIELD CALIFORNIA DRY RED NV, SEBASTIANI VINEYARDS California	*An immensely forward and fresh wine with a lovely black-cherry and forest-fruits style.*	£3.50	SMF	(B)
PARDUCCI PETITE SIRAH 1993 California	*A fragrant, spicy wine with a rich, berry-fruit flavour and a touch of tobacco and spice .*	£5.60	VWC	(S)
PARDUCCI PETITE SIRAH 1994 California	*Tasters found rich, herbal, oak and chocolate aromas leading to ripe fruit flavours and a strong finish.*	£6.20	ROD J&H VW MFS	(G)

CONCANNON PETITE SIRAH 1994 California	An immensely rich and concentrated brambley wine with lashings of spice and fruit. Rounded and lasting.	**£7.20**	GNW AWS PWW TAN NI SEL DBY	(G)
FETZER BARREL SELECT MERLOT 1993 California	Creamy, plummy nose. Rich and plentiful tannins with a long, fine finish. A really great wine.	**£7.40**	WIN MHW	(S)
CLOS DE GILROY AMERCIAN GRENACHE, BONNY DOON VINEYARD California	Young, jammy style with a good proportion of fruits and light tannins. Easy drinking.	**£7.80**	Widely available	(S)
CA' DEL SOLO BIG HOUSE RED 1994, BONNY DOON VINEYARD California	Cooked plums, spice and chocolate on nose. Ripe fruits and rich tannins give great length.	**£7.90**	Widely available	(G)
CONCANNON PETITE SIRAH RESERVA 1992 California	A very dark and full-bodied but smooth wine unfolding lots of oak, cinnamon and cedar.	**£9.00**	GNW DBU PWW TAN NI	(S)
PELLEGRINI 1994 California	Light, fruity aroma with light structure. Enjoyable juicy fruits and good, smooth, tannic finish.	**£9.10**	WTR RBS NY VLW	(B)
WHEELER WINERY MERLOT 1992 California	Mature, spiced-cedar nose. Well-balanced acidity with tannins giving good length.	**£9.20**	HW SV NY P	(B)
NOCETO SANGIOVESE 1994 California	A soft, earthy wine with a deep-red colour. Well-balanced oak, fruit and acid.	**£10.20**	ENO NY HW V&C ADN	(B)

QUPÉ SYRAH 1993 California	*A big, purple-black wine, very soft and full of sweet, ripe fruit – fragrant and juicy stuff.*	**£10.70**	JUS WAC SEL NY HOU GRT AMA	**S**
JADE MOUNTAIN PROVENCALE 1994 California	*Dark purple in colour, lots of full, juicy fruit, young tannins and green spice.*	**£10.90**	CT BOO DBY NY	**S**
QUPÉ SYRAH 1994 California	*Soft, sweet character and rich, ripe fruits with spices. Pleasing finish.*	**£11.00**	HN SEL WAC TP NY GRT	**B**
SWANSON MERLOT 1993 California	*An earthy, berry-fruit nose with a touch of mint and a full, rich, jammy fruit palate.*	**£14.50**	HN LEA AV DBY SOB	**B**
JADE MOUNTAIN SYRAH 1993 California	*Ripe and robust, an instantly impressive wine – vibrantly chewy and juicy, crammed with youthful tannin.*	**£15.80**	SAN CEB DBY NY HOU MFS	**G**
BERINGER HOWELL MOUNTAIN MERLOT 1992 California	*Vanilla oak, berry fruit and cinnamon on the nose. Raspberry and liquorice on the palate.*	**£20.00**	LNR HD CPW MWW BWC	**S**

CALIFORNIA • CHARDONNAY

KINGS CANYON CHARDONNAY 1995, HUGH RYMAN/ ARCIERO WINERY California	*Musky, lemon-peel nose; intense, ripe lemon and apricot palate with good balance and length.*	**£4.00**	RYW BU WR TH	**B**

AUGUST SEBASTIANI CHARDONNAY 1994, SEBASTIANI VINEYARDS California	*Complex and evolved, minerally nose with a nutty edge. A long and balanced, honeyed palate.*	**£4.90**	MTL SMF PIM	**B**
COPPERIDGE CHARDONNAY NV, ERNEST & JULIO GALLO California	*Clean, lean start with a good closed nose. Big and generous with a fruity middle and finish.*	**£5.00**	FTH WMK THP	**B**
KINGS CANYON BLACK LABEL CHARDONNAY 1995, HUGH RYMAN/ ARCIERO WINERY California	*Rich crème caramel on the nose and a vibrant palate of rich, slightly oily fruit.*	**£5.00**	TDS RYW BU WR TH	**B**
CHARDONNAY RANCH SERIES 1995, H SUTER California	*A lovely, long wine with a creamy, grapefruit flavour and a nose showing caramel hints.*	**£5.00**	VWC VW	**S**
CARTLIDGE & BROWNE CHARDONNAY 1995 California	*Vanilla-custard nose with bready oak. An excellent, soft-fruit palate and a mellow, burnt-wood aftertaste.*	**£5.00**	W	**S**
STERLING VINEYARDS CHARDONNAY 1994 California	*Wonderful and fruity with an elegant palate and powerful nose. Definitely to be tried.*	**£6.30**	CLA OD SEA RAV	**B**
FETZER SUNDIAL CHARDONNAY 1995 California	*Clean and vibrant, fresh, juicy, young style; ripe and interesting. Very good, modern style.*	**£6.40**	Widely available	**B**
CONCANNON CHARDONNAY 1994 California	*A lovely almond nose. On the palate creamy peaches and vanilla vie with crisp, lemon acidity.*	**£7.50**	GNW AWS PWW TAN NI	**S**

CK Cellars Saint Helena Chardonnay 1995 California	*Restrained but integrated nose, good fruit/orangey acid balance with mild oak. Long finish.*	£7.90	BD	S
Fetzer Bonterra Chardonnay 1993 California	*Full, young colour. On the palate a luscious, round cocktail of butterscotch, nuts and citrus zip.*	£8.70	OD VR SEL DBY SOM	S
Villa Mount Eden Chardonnay 1994, Mount Eden Vineyards California	*An enchanting, herbaceous nose is nicely complemented by a delicious, fat, smoky, tropical-fruit palate.*	£8.80	BB AWS SHG NY POR WCR	G
Gravelstone Chardonnay 1994, Jekel Vineyards California	*Exudes interesting crème caramel and asparagus aromas. Creamy, soft fruit on the middle palate and lovely acidity.*	£9.00	MWW	B
Beringer Napa Valley Chardonnay 1994 California	*Aromas of cinnamon and baked apples precede flavours of tastes of rich butterscotch and zesty acid.*	£9.50	LNR CPW HD ROB MWW BWC	S
Benziger Chardonnay Vintner's Selection 1993 California	*Gentle, appealing, nutmeg aromas. Extremely refined oak supporting a lucious, peachy palate. Complex wine.*	£9.50	WCR WAV	S
Olivet Lane Chardonnay 1994, Pellegrini Vineyards California	*Smooth, velvety, lychee-and-kiwi-fruit cocktail with a medium-bodied, creamy vanilla backbone on the palate.*	£10.00	PON WTR VLW	S
Rutherford Hill Jaeger Vineyard Chardonnay 1993 California	*Tasters enjoyed this delicious citrussy Chardonnay with its hints of lemon sorbet and rich vanilla.*	£10.30	AV	

EDNA VALLEY CHARDONNAY 1993, EDNA VALLEY VINEYARDS California	*Lovely, deep-straw colour. Chunky, honeyed almonds on the nose and tropical-fruit flavours on the palate.*	£11.00	LEA BEN BI	(S)
GALLO SONOMA STEFANI VINEYARD CHARDONNAY 1994, ERNEST & JULIO GALLO California	*Good, earthy, organic nose, interesting palate with gentle, floral fruit, lots of oak. Long finish.*	£11.20	A&N SOB SEL THP MTL E&J	(B)
ACACIA CHARDONNAY 1994 California	*Sweet, mango nose; buttery, lactic style with interesting spice, medium body, good complexity and balance.*	£11.30	HN HAR SHG GGW BI	(B)
GALLO SONOMA CHARDONNAY LAGUNA RANCH VINEYARD 1994, ERNEST AND JULOI GALLO California	*A firm, nutty nose is followed by what tasters called an evocative mouthful of fresh and juicy wine.*	£11.50	EP SEL A&N SOB THP MTL E&J	(S)
SIMI CHARDONNAY 1993 California	*Sherry-style nose with a good balance of fruit and oak, but this is slightly lacking in complexity.*	£11.70	COR HOL TP SEL RBS NY SOB PIM	(B)
CALERA CHARDONNAY 1994 California	*Very good, lemony fruit and a restrained use of oak mark this as a wine which is complex and enriching.*	£11.80	BEN MWW SOM	(B)
SAINTSBURY CARNEROS UNFILTERED CHARDONNAY 1994 California	*Neutral, soft nose, ripe and juicy palate with a good, nutty, toasty edge and walnutty finish.*	£12.10	HAR MES CHF BEN SEL WCR SOM	(B)
CRICHTON HALL CHARDONNAY 1993 California	*Pale-yellow colour and enchanting, honeyed nose. A well-made, easy-drinking, melony wine.*	£12.50	SEL ALD SOB PAT GRT	(B)

MARIMAR TORRES CHARDONNAY 1993 California	*Grapefruit aromas give way to a well-rounded, full-bodied, apricotty mouthful. Nice wine.*	£13.00	PAL SEL MRF HVW ALD COK MFS	**B**
CHALK HILL CHARDONNAY 1993 California	*Wonderful coffee and toast hints on the nose. Elegantly used oak and good balance.*	£13.00	J&B	**S**
SAINTSBURY CARNEROS RESERVE CHARDONNAY 1994 California	*A ripe, fruity nose leads on to a complex, full, rich, fruit-salad mouthful. Charming*	£15.30	GRT NI CHF BEN CNL SOM ADN MFS	**S**
SWANSON CHARDONNAY 1993 California	*Honey, mango and peach aromas precede a palate with a lovely balance between fruit and oak.*	£15.50	HN LEA PAV AV DBY SOB AMA	**G**
BIEN NACIOLO GOLD COAST VINEYARDS CHARDONNAY 1994, AU BON CLIMAT California	*On the palate there are lovely and very ripe tropical fruits, pre- dominately lychees.*	£15.60	Widely available	**G**
MONDAVI CARNEROS CHARDONNAY 1994, ROBERT MONDAVI WINERY California	*A complex, root ginger and citrus nose is fol- lowed up by a weighty, fruit-packed palate.*	£16.00	OD	**S**
ESTATE CHARDONNAY 1993, ERNEST & JULIO GALLO California	*Pale lemon colour, burnt toast and lime citrus on the palate with a good long finish.*	£19.80	Widely available	**B**

Pinpoint who sells the wine you wish to buy by turning to the stockist codes. If you know the name of the wine you want to buy, use the alphabetical index. If the price is your motivation, refer to the invaluable price guide index; red and white wines under £5, sparkling wines under £10 and champagne under £15. Happy hunting!

CALIFORNIA • OTHER WHITE

GEYSER PEAK SAUVIGNON BLANC 1995 California	*Elegant style with green pea and gooseberry aromas and flavours and a tart finish.*	**£6.00**	VWC VW	**B**
FIRESTONE JOHANNESBERG RIESLING 1995 California	*A delightful nose of fragrant tea, apricots and delicate peaches marks this full, open and fruity wine.*	**£6.50**	TH BU	**S**
MERITAGE WHITE 1993, BERINGER VINEYARDS California	*Fine and well-balanced with delicious, tropical fruits and vanilla tones. Pleasing depth and good length.*	**£8.00**	LNR	**B**

CALIFORNIA • SWEET WHITE

AUDUBON LATE HARVEST SAUVIGNON BLANC 1992 California	*Very sweet and honeyed palate. Lots of ripe, pineapple fruit with some fine citrus acidity.*	**£8.50**	SEL	**B**

CALIFORNIA • SPARKLING

SCHARFFENBERGER BRUT NV California	*Toasty, coconut and mushroom nose with a creamy, fruity and biscuity palate. Balanced acid and finish.*	**£13.00**	A SEL SOB VW HAR	**S**

WINE OF THE YEAR

SONOMA PACIFIC TETE DE CUVÉE 1985 California	*Crisp, very clean with yeasty nose and mild green apple acidity. This has a reasonable length and finish.*	**£21.00**	ENO	**B**

CALIFORNIA • FORTIFIED

QUADY'S STARBOARD BATCH 88 NV California	*Inky, deep colour. Jammy plum and toasty oak. Sweet, concentrated, long but one-dimentional.*	**£7.40**	Widely available	**B**

CANADA • RED

CAVE SPRING CELLARS CABERNET/MERLOT 1994 Niagara Peninsula	*Herbaceous, crunchy, green-pepper nose with leafy overtones. Soft cassis, attractive berry fruit with a sweet cherry finish.*	**£7.40**	DBY	**S**

CANADA • WHITE

ST DAVID'S BENCH CHARDONNAY 1994, CHATEAU DES CHARMES Ontario	*Buttery malolactic influences on the palate. Harmonic structure, gentle, persistent finish – a fine wine.*	**£10.00**	GI	**S**

Pinpoint who sells the wine you wish to buy by turning to the stockist codes. If you know the name of the wine you want to buy, use the alphabetical index. If the price is your motivation, refer to the invaluable price guide index; red and white wines under £5, sparkling wines under £10 and champagne under £15. Happy hunting!

CANADA • SWEET WHITE

REIF ESTATE ICEWINE RIESLING 1994 Ontario	*Sweet, pink-grapefruit aromas. Has a ripe-peach and honeyed-apple palate cut by some fresh, citrussy acidity.*	**£25.50**	AMA	(B)
PAUL BOSC ESTATE ICEWINE 1994, CHATEAU DES CHARMES Ontario	*Fresh grapefruit with gentle spiciness. Intense honeyed palate; creamy with lots of concentrated tropical fruit.*	**£30.00**	GI	(S)

CANADA • FORTIFIED

SOUTHBROOK FARM LAILEY VINEYARD FRAMBOISE NV Ontario	*Delighted our tasters with pure, raspberry fruit. Essence of crushed raspberries with fresh brambley flavours.*	**£6.50**	AMA	(B)

OREGON • RED

OREGON PINOT NOIR RESERVE 1993, WILLAMETTE VALLEY VINEYARDS Oregon	*A soft, easy-drinking style. Full of rich damson fruit with a long, velvety finish.*	**£9.40**	Widely available	(B)
FIRESTEED PINOT NOIR 1993 Oregon	*Fresh, clean Pinot on the nose. Rich, ripe flavours; high extract; full-bodied and very complex.*	**£9.40**	BKW JN DBY CWI NY HOU VLW WCR	(S)

OREGON • WHITE

ARGYLE RIESLING 1992, DUNDEE WINE COMPANY Oregon	*Aromas of marzipan, ripe fruit and botrytis, layered with a generous bouquet of honey.*	£8.30	BKW NEI WCR ADN
OREGON DRY RIESLING 1992, WILLAMETTE VALLEY VINEYARDS Oregon	*An oily Riesling style; lightly honeyed with a citrussy finish.*	£8.40	AV SEL CWL CC SCA THP
WILLAMETTE VALLEY VINEYARDS CHARDONNAY 1993 Oregon	*Wonderful and elegant with delicate aromas and a lovely palate of fine fruits.*	£8.60	AV CC SCA CWL SEL THP CWI FEN

WASHINGTON • RED

SADDLE MOUNTAIN GRENACHE 1994, STIMSON LANE Washington State	*This deep-red wine starts with aromas of ripe, dark fruit with a strawberry and liquorice flavour*	£4.50	BB AWS WCR AMW
PINOT NOIR COLUMBIA WOODBURNE CUVÉE 1993 Washington State	*Good, young red, authentic nose with sweet, fruit rich and complex with very good balance.*	£6.60	COK FTH
CONEY & RUN MERLOT 1993 Washington State	*Berry fruits and rich tannins with staying power add depth. Plums and spiced oak for the finish.*	£7.50	ROB EP TP

COLUMBIA CREST MERLOT 1993 Washington State	*Beautiful Merlot fruit that still remains structured and disciplined despite a fresh approach.*	£8.30	VIL U SHG NY WCR	B
PAUL THOMAS COLUMBIA VALLEY CABERNET/ MERLOT 1994 Washington State	*Good forest fruits on the nose and palate, with a nice addition of spices to the tannins.*	£8.30	BBR CWL SCA THP WIL SEL LWE WOC	B
COLUMBIA CREST CABERNET SAUVIGNON 1993 Washington State	*A big, fruit-packed nose is nicely followed by blackcurrants and vanilla on the palate.*	£8.60	BB AWS VIL SHG MRF MTL WCR ETV	B
HEDGES RED MOUNTAIN ESTATE 1991 Washington State	*Rich, baked, vegetal hints to the nose precede some delicious, chewy, cedary fruit. Well-balanced.*	£15.00	WCR	B
HEDGES RED MOUNTAIN RESERVE 1992 Washington State	*Delicate on the nose with touches of eucalyptus and cedar. Liquorice fruit on the finish.*	£15.00	WCR	S
CHATEAU STE MICHELLE COLD CREEK MERLOT 1993 Washington State	*Lots of spirited new oak with soft, fleshy Merlot fruit. Good, firm tannins; long finish.*	£20.50	BB AWS	B

WASHINGTON • WHITE

CHATEAU STE MICHELLE CHARDONNAY 1994 Washington State	*An interesting vanilla peach nose. Delicious, complex palate of baked bananas, caramelly toffee and spicy oranges.*	£8.80	BB AWS SHG WCR	S

PORTUGAL

Too OFTEN THOUGHT OF as a nation producing dry, astringent reds and watery whites, this year's Challenge showed the true potential of this country and its diverse grape varieties. New investment from the EC and technical expertise from flying winemakers have helped raise the standard of the wines generally. Bright Brothers Douro 1995 is a prime example of this, being a great Red Wine of the Year. Needless to say, some ports were outstanding.

RED

ALTA MESA 1994, SÃO MAMEDE COOP Estremadura	*Vibrant magenta. Fresh, juicy fruit. Slightly dusty on palate: Good length. Pleasant, firm tannins.*	£3.20	U THP VW WCR	**B**
SAFEWAY FALUA VINHO REGIONAL RIBATEJO 1995, FALUA SOCIDADE DE VINHOS Ribatejo	*Cherry red. Simple, raspberry-red fruit nose. Smoky flavour with a pleasant, peppery finish.*	£3.20	SAF	**S**
MEIA ENCOSTA DÃO RED 1994, SOCIDADE DOS VINHOS BORGES Dão	*Dense morello cherry. Earthy, red fruit aroma. Some complexity of flavour. Short, green tannin finish.*	£3.80	BES	**B**
VILA-REGIAN 1993, SOGRAPE Douro	*Light, brick-red in colour. Tarry nose. Clean, light fruit. Fruit and tannin in balance .*	£4.00	OD GI	**B**
JOSÉ DE SOUSA REGUENGOS DE MONSARAZ 1992, JOSÉ MARIA DA FONSECA SUCCS Alentejo	*Traditional style. Sweet, porty aroma with pruney flavour. Soft, balanced tannins.*	£4.50	MWW MHW	**S**

PORTUGAL • RED

FIUZA CABERNET SAUVIGNON 1994, FIUZA & BRIGHT Ribatejo	*Sweet fruits and earthy aromas. Jammy flavours and rich tannins create a full-bodied wine.*	£5.00	BU WR TH	(S)
QUINTA DA LAMELAS 1995, QUINTA DA ROSA VINHOS Douro	*Deep fuchsia pink. Plummy with hint of carrot, cherry and oak. Structured tannins. Nicely balanced.*	£5.00	BU WR TH	(S)
BRIGHT BROTHERS DOURO 1995 Douro	*Fuchsia colour. Intense concentration. Young cherry, floral nose. Spicy tannin and ripe fruit. Long satisfying finish.*	£5.00	VW TH BU WR	(G) WINE OF THE YEAR
FIUZA CABERNET SAUVIGNON 1994, FIUZA & BRIGHT Ribatejo	*Deep extracted red. Complex nose, raspberry, pepper, smokey oak. Elegant sweet fruit flavours. Well balanced.*	£5.00	HOC BU WR TH	(G)
DUQUE DE VISEU 1991, SOGRAPE Dão	*Woody, pruney nose. Sweet, alcoholic fruit. Smooth and fleshy. Ready to drink now.*	£5.50	GI CWS	(B)
DUQUE DE VISEU 1992, SOGRAPE Dão	*Dark red. Herbaceous nose. Good depth of flavour. Soft fruit with spice and cedar. Green, hard finish.*	£5.50	GI CWS	(B)
QUINTA DO CRASTO DOURO RED 1994 Douro	*Deep red. Young looking. Vanilla, cedary oak. A soft, fleshy, grapey fruit which has a clean, fresh finish. Balanced.*	£5.50	ENO SEL ADN	(B)
QUINTA DE PANCAS 1995, SOCIADE AGRICOLA PORTO DA LUZ Estremadura	*Deep, dense, purple colour. High alcohol. Ripe, minty fruit. Well structured, spicy and tannic. Long finish.*	£5.50	Widely available	(B)

VINHA DO MONTE 1993, SOGRAPE Alentejo	Bright red. Leathery, green olive nose. Soft, ripe, redcurrant fruit and spicy oak.	£5.90	SAF GI VW SPR	(S)
TINTO DA ANFORA 1991, J.P. VINHOS Alentejo	Brick red. Raspberry, caramelised rice pudding aroma. Soft, sweet berry flavour. Toasty oak finish. Great length.	£6.10	Widely available	(G)
DUAS QUINTAS RESERVA 1992, ADRIANO RAMOS PINTO Douro	Deep, dark red. New World style. Chocolate, ripe redcurrant and blackcurrant. Soft tannins. Well-made.	£6.70	Widely available	(G)
GARRAFEIRA 1987, JOSÉ MARIA DA FONSECA SUCCS Bairrada	Brick red. Ripe, plummy fruit with some sweetness. Good, rounded concentration. Firm tannin on the finish.	£7.00	MHW	(B)
HERDADE ESPORÃO CABERNET SAUVIGNON 1993, FINAGRA Alentejo	Spicy nose – cinnamon, mint and cedar with good balance of acidity and fruit on the finish.	£7.00	BU WR	(B)
DUAS QUINTAS RESERVE 1991, ADRIANO RAMOS-PINTO VILA NOVA DE GAIA Douro	Dark purple. Intense cranberry, violet and pepper. Soft fruit and tannin. Well structured. Long and delicious.	£8.60	HWL NI JN SHG J&B VLW	(B)
QUINTA DA URTIGA RAMOS-PINTO NV Douro	Dense clear red. Fresh, grapey nose. Raisiny palate. Well balanced, lacks concentration. Long finish.	£9.00	Widely available	(B)
QUINTA DOS ROQUES RESERVA 1992, QUINTA DOS ROQUES VITIVINICULTURA & AGROPECUARIA Douro	Purplish red. Concentrated, plummy nose, blackcurrant, cedar and oak. Well balanced wine, will keep.	£9.10	MFS LV SAS LEA WNS HVW	(S)

RESERVA ESPECIAL CASA FERREIRINHA 1986, CASA FERREIRINIIA Douro	*Deep, complex wine showing signs of age. Jammy, turpentine, liquorice nose. Hard, tannic finish.*	£12.40	OD GI SEL	**B**

WHITE

SAINSBURY'S DO CAMPO WHITE 1995, J P VINHOS Terras do Sado	*Slightly nutty, developed aroma indicative of a warm climate and a surprisingly zesty, lime fruit flavour.*	£3.00	JS	**B**
QUINTA DE PEDRALVITES 1995, SOGRAPE Bairrada	*A very aromatic, Muscatty nose, grapey and nettley with a clean crisp taste that lingers well.*	£6.00	WSO GI	**B**

PORT

SOMERFIELD THE NAVIGATORS LATE BOTTLED VINTAGE PORT 1989, REAL VINICOLA Douro	*Lightish colour. Soft, raisiny nose echoed on palate. Hot finish.*	£6.50	SMF	**B**
SOMERFIELD THE NAVIGATORS VINTAGE CHARACTER PORT NV, REAL COMPANHIA VELHA Douro	*Deep, mid-red. Young, ripe fruit. Very sweet and alcoholic. This needs time to mature.*	£6.50	SMF	**B**
TESCO FINE VINTAGE CHARACTER PORT, ROYAL OPORTO WINE COMPANY Douro	*Deep, clear red. Sweet nose. Concentrated chocolate and sweet fruit acid with the alcohol nicely balanced.*	£6.50	TO	**G**

COCKBURN'S 10 YEAR OLD TAWNY NV, COCKBURN SMITHES & CIA Douro	*Dark, caramel colour. Slightly medicinal nose. Chocolate and raisins on the palate. Lacks intensity. Hot finish.*	£6.70	ADD	B
WAITROSE VINTAGE CHARACTER PORT NV, SMITH WOODHOUSE Douro	*Medium red. Stewed fruit and peppery nose. Wet wood, sweet and fiery.*	£6.80	W	B
THRESHER CHARTER LATE BOTTLED VINTAGE PORT 1987, SILVER & COTENS	*Young, purple colour. Tight nose. Lovely, black-currant flavour. Medium body. Firm tannin. Needs time.*	£8.00	TH BU WR	S
WARRE'S WARRIOR FINEST RESERVE NV. Douro	*Pale red. Boiled sweet and stalky nose, chocolate mint flavours, cloying sweetness, slightly bitter finish.*	£8.50	Widely available	B
QUINTA DO NOVAL LATE BOTTLED VINTAGE 1990 Douro	*Light brown-red. Heavy, heady, spicy nose. Juicy, simple fruit. Hot, slightly flat finish.*	£8.70	Widely available	B
COCKBURN'S SPECIAL RESERVE PORT NV Douro	*Mid red. Closed nose. Sweet peppery attack. Well balanced mid palate with a big spiritous finish.*	£9.00	Widely available	B
QUINTA DA URTIGA RAMOS-PINTO NV Douro	*Dense, clear red. Fresh, grapey nose. Raisiny palate. Well balanced, lacks concentration. Long finish.*	£9.00	Widely available	B
QUINTO DO CRASTO LATE BOTTLED VINTAGE 1988 Douro	*Maturing colour. Minty chocolate nose. Soft fruit palate. Firm structure. Showing bottle age. Fiery spiritous finish.*	£9.00	ENO MWW WCR ADN	S

QUINTA DE LA ROSA FINEST RESERVE Douro	*Mid deep red. Baked nose. Concentrated plum, pepper and caramel flavours. Nice balancing spirit and acid.*	£9.10	Widely available	**B**
SANDEMAN SIGNATURE VINTAGE CHARACTER NV Douro	*Deep red, slightly oxidised nose. Spicy, young fruit. Complex and balanced mid palate; young, chaffy finish.*	£9.70	OD LWL HAR EP CRM MTL CWS	**B**
FORTNUM & MASON LATE BOTTLED VINTAGE PORT 1990, BURMEST Douro	*Clear, mid-red. Green, stalky nose. Vegetal, chocolate and mint flavours. This is balanced but closed.*	£10.00	F&M	**B**
QUINTA DO NOVAL LATE BOTTLED VINTAGE 1989 Douro	*Deep, brick red. Prune and tea nose. Cherry and spicy flavours. Firm acid. Hot finish.*	£10.00	MAR WWC MFW BAB SHG HHC MTL	**S**
CÁLEM QUINTA DA FOZ PORT 1992, A CÀLEM & FILHO Douro	*Intense, dark colour; soft nose. Powerful prune, raisin and liquorice flavour. Sweet and hot. Bitter finish.*	£10.00	WIM U	**S**
RAMOS PINTO LATE BOTTLED VINTAGE PORT 1989, Douro	*Deep red. Burnt, jammy hot nose. Concentrated, chocolate mint and spice flavours. Balanced wine. Worth cellaring.*	£10.00	HHC WRW CLA TP SHG BEN GHL	**S**
TAYLOR'S LATE BOTTLED VINTAGE PORT 1990, TAYLOR'S FLADGATE & YEATMAN VINHOS Douro	*Deep, dark, inky wine. Very concentrated fruit; alcohol and tannin. Slightly medicinal. Tough, needs time.*	£10.70	Widely available	**B**
BURMESTER VINTAGE CHARACTER SWEET RUBY NV Douro	*Dense, dark red. Treacley, oaky nose. Fresh, clean damson/ plum palate. High acid. Not cloying.*	£11.20	HBJ ROS	**B**

WARRE'S SIR WILLIAM 10 YEAR OLD NV Douro	*Intense, mid red with deep, pruney nose; plum, mint and liquorice flavours. Fat and alcoholic.*	£11.20	IRV C&B AV DBY MTL	**S**
QUINTA DO NOVAL 10 YEAR OLD TAWNY PORT Douro	*Strawberry colour. Concentrated nose of caramelised dates. Quite simple, sweet wine with long finish.*	£12.00	JCB U WTR VIL HVW FEN WOC W	**B**
BARROS LATE BOTTLED VINTAGE 1985, BARROS ALMEIDA & CA. Douro	*Young red colour. Some maturity in the nose. Fleshy fruit. Harmonious on the mid palate, with a long finish.*	£12.50	AWS	**B**
QUINTA DO NOVAL COLHEITA TAWNY 1976 Douro	*Light tawny colour. Caramelised, fresh fruit nose. Nutty, creamy palate. Sweet and simple. Hot finish.*	£13.40	VWC BEN VW NIC	**B**
SMITH WOODHOUSE TRADITIONAL LATE BOTTLED VINTAGE 1984 Douro	*Light colour. Sappy nose. Pleasant mouth-feel, some fruit and tannin. Austere and young.*	£14.00	C&B J&B VIL	**B**
MARTINEZ 10 YEAR OLD TAWNY NV, MARTINEZ GASSIOT Douro	*Caramel tawny colour. Raisiny, toffee nose. Oak unbalanced. Simple, nutty palate. Finished with some length.*	£14.30	WIC RTW SHG CPW LWE RBS CNL AMW	**B**
WARRE'S TRADITIONAL BOTTLE MATURED 1982 Douro	*Dark colour. Jammy, luscious nose - complex plum, coffee and liquorice flavours. Not too sweet. Long finish.*	£14.50	Widely available	**G**
FONSECA QUINTA DO PANASCAL 1984 Douro	*Brick red colour. Closed fruit cake nose and intense fruity palate harmonising with spirit. Good ageing potential.*	£14.80	Widely available	**S**

DELAFORCE VINTAGE 1985 Douro	*Brown, old nose. Nutty, spicy fruit. Some concentration and elegance. Drying out in the finish.*	**£15.00**	OD POR	**B**
QUINTA DO TUA 1987 Douro	*Young, deep garnet colour. Sweet, minty, fruity nose. Ripe fruit palate, but lacks length and complexity.*	**£15.00**	SEL CAT ADD	**B**
TAYLOR'S 10 YEAR OLD PORT NV, TAYLOR'S FLADGATE & YEATMAN VINHOS Douro	*Dark orange tinged. Chocolate, raisins and musty oak. Deep nutty flavour. Concentrated with good length.*	**£15.10**	Widely available	**S**
QUINTO DO CRASTO VINTAGE PORT 1985 Douro	*Dark red colour. Floral yeasty nose. Warm raisiny fruit. Lacking concentration. Short finish, needs time.*	**£15.70**	ENO SEL WCR	**B**
QUINTA DO CRASTO SINGLE QUINTA VINTAGE 1985, SOCIEDAD AGRICOLA DA QUINTA DO CRASTO Douro	*Medium deep red jammy. Stalky rose petal nose. Rich, young, juicy, spicy fruit. Attractive style.*	**£15.70**	SEL WCR	**B**
QUARLES HARRIS 1983 VINTAGE PORT 1983 Douro	*Dark red wine. Concentrated Christmas cake nose. Supple fruit. Full bodied and alcoholic. Long rounded finish.*	**£16.10**	NAD BUT NEI MHW TAN	**B**
QUINTA DO VAU VINTAGE PORT SINGLE QUINTA 1988, HOUSE OF SANDEMAN Douro	*Nice mouthful – strong and alcoholic with great complex fruits and powerful aromas.*	**£16.30**	CRM OD SEL	**B**
GOULD CAMPBELL VINTAGE PORT 1983 Douro	*Lovely deep red colour. Plummy cocoa nose. Firm tannin. Full balanced wine. Dry finish.*	**£16.50**	BBR BUT NEI THP J&B WOI	**B**

TAYLOR'S QUINTA DE VARGELLAS 1984, TAYLOR'S FLADGATE & YEATMAN VINHOS Douro	*Deep red wine. Lovely, chocolate and pepper nose. Ripe, raisin flavours. Intense, balanced and with a long finish.*	£17.60	Widely available	**G**
QUINTA DO SAGRADO VINTAGE 1988 Douro	*Bright young colour. Young plummy and green tea nose. Delicious concentrated damson flavour. Complex and balanced.*	£17.70	LAU	**S**
BURMESTER 10 YEAR OLD TAWNY NV Douro	*Dark red colour. Raisined, earthy nose. Spicy Christmas cake flavours. Sticky finish with good length.*	£18.00	HBJ RID SEL	**B**
FONSECA GUIMARAENS 1978 Douro	*Light red wine with unfocused nose. Rather soft fruit and not too sweet.*	£18.10	Widely available	**B**
SMITH WOODHOUSE VINTAGE PORT 1980 Douro	*Opaque red with traditional nose. Full Christmas pudding flavours. Lovely long and chocolatey finish.*	£18.20	TH VIL OD	**S**
BURMESTER COLHEITA RESERVA 1985 Douro	*Light to mid brick colour. Quiet nose. Nutty spiritous flavour. Crisp finish.*	£18.50	HBJ SEL	**B**
QUINTA DO BOMFIM 1984, DOW Douro	*Dark, rich, red berry fruit and a hint of rubber. Firm, tannic and alcoholic. Classy wine.*	£18.60	Widely available	**S**
CROFT VINTAGE 1991 Douro	*Opaque red. Stalky, light nose. Peppery, simple fruit. Alcohol unbalanced. Sharp finish. Needs time.*	£19.20	PF U OD SEL J&B FEN	**P**

WARRE'S CAVADINHA 1984, Douro	*Dark red colour, quite intense, baked fruit nose; fruit cake palate. Full, long finish.*	£19.40	Widely available	(B)
CHURCHILL'S QUINTA DA AGUA ALTA VINTAGE 1987, CHURCHILL GRAHAM Douro	*Lovely, dark red youthful colour. Great concentration – chocolate, mint, spice, fruit and walnuts.*	£20.30	SAN BTH GDS SV WSC HW TAN MFS	(G)
WARRE'S 1980 VINTAGE PORT 1980 Douro	*Browning with a jammy nose and damson jam flavours. Has a fleshy mouth feel with a spiritous finish.*	£20.70	Widely available	(S)
DOW 20 YEAR OLD TAWNY NV Douro	*Dark colour. Smoky bacon aroma. Sweet raisiny fruit fading. Clean acidity. Great balance. Long and complex.*	£22.30	Widely available	(S)
CHURCHILL'S VINTAGE 1991, CHURCHILL GRAHAM Douro	*Opaque colour. Light, stalky nose. Complex fruit. Chewy, structured tannin. Well balanced, very traditional port.*	£23.10	Widely available	(S)
GRAHAM'S PORT 1985 Douro	*Young bright red. Violet and liquorice nose. Juicy fruit with some spicyness. Can stand some ageing.*	£24.40	VWC JN SHG CPW J&B VW DBY G&M	(B)
DUQUE DE BRAGANCA 20 YEAR OLD TAWNY NV, AA FERREIRA Douro	*Pale orange-brown colour. Coarse, alcoholic nose, and Christmas pudding aromas with great, rich character.*	£24.50	WTK HOU WNC BEC NI DBY COK	(B)
QUINTA DO NOVAL 20 YEAR OLD TAWNY PORT Douro	*Fading red. Boiled sweets and earthy oak nose. Elegant soft palate. Good balance and length.*	£25.40	JCB JAK BUY CFT VIL MHW WOC	(B)

QUINTA DO NOVAL 1971 TAWNY COLHEITA Douro	*Light tawny colour. Perfumed earthy nose. Concentrated dry fruit and toast flavour. Firm acid and alcohol.*	£25.50	VLW NIC	S
VINTAGE PORT RAMOS PINTO 1983 Douro	*Ruby coloured ripe fruit nose. Full but simple palate. Finish is quite dry but fiery.*	£26.00	RWI SHG	B
GRAHAM'S 1980 VINTAGE PORT Douro	*Deep red colour with a very fruity nose. Minty flavours, quite sweet. Fairly long finish.*	£28.60	OD TH RTW SHG J&B G&M SOB	B
TAYLOR'S 20 YEAR OLD TAWNY PORT, TAYLOR'S FLADGATE & YEATMAN VINHOS Douro	*Dark brown. Smoky, perfumed and woody with intense toffee and green walnut flavour. Great length and balance.*	£30.60	Widely available	S
RAMOS PINTO 30 YEAR OLD TAWNY, ADRIANO RAMOS PINTO Douro	*Pale red-brown. Baked smoked Muscat nose with toffee. Long delicious sweet finish.*	£40.00	EP	S

MADEIRA

BARBEITO ISLAND RICH 5 YEAR OLD MALMSEY NV, VINHOS BARBEITO Madeira	*Elegant style showing delightful flavours of caramel, toasted nuts and apricots. Great balance and wonderful complexity.*	£11.00	PF	
BLANDY'S 5 YEAR OLD PALE DRY SERCIAL NV, MADEIRA WINE COMPANY Madeira	*Mixed pecan nut and butterscotch aromas. Smoky toffee and spicy caramel flavours balanced by citrus fruit.*	£11.10	Widely available	

BLANDY'S 5 YEAR OLD RICH MALMSEY NV, MADEIRA WINE COMPANY Madeira	*Caramelised nut aromas. Rich, sweet palate with ripe prune and raisin flavours. Fine balance.*	£11.20	Widely available	(B)
BLANDY'S 5 YEAR OLD BUAL NV, MADEIRA WINE COMPANY Madeira	*Wonderfully complex, mixing raisins, coffee, caramel and light butterscotch flavours with spicy and savoury overtones.*	£11.20	Widely available	(G)
COSSART GORDON 5 YEAR OLD SERCIAL NV Madeira	*Baked oranges, raisin and chocolate flavours mixed with a generous, pleasant sprinkling of warm vanilla.*	£12.50	Widely available	(G)
BARBEITO CHRISTAVÃO COLOMBO NV, VINHOS BARBEITO Madeira	*Very balanced and harmonious style showing spicy, dried fruit and caramel flavours.*	£14.00	PF	(B)
BLANDY'S 10 YEAR OLD RICH MALMSEY NV, MADEIRA WINE COMPANY Madeira	*Rich savoury aromas mingled with burnt caramel and coffee. Lively citrus acidity provides balance.*	£15.80	Widely available	(B)
COSSART GORDON 10 YEAR OLD VERDELHO MADEIRA Madeira	*Multi-flavoured with its coffee and toffee, caramel and vanilla flavours. Soft, woody finish.*	£16.10	WOI ADN BU WR	(B)
HENRIQUES & HENRIQUES 10 YEAR OLD MALMSEY MADEIRA NV Madeira	*Mouth-filling showing a full raisiny palate mixed with delicious flavours of coffee, caramel, nuts and sweet butterscotch.*	£16.10	CWL P&R EVI LEA DBY TAN VEX TRO	(G)

Pinpoint who sells the wine you wish to buy by turning to the stockist codes. If you know the name of the wine you want to buy, use the alphabetical index. If the price is your motivation, refer to the invaluable price guide index; red and white wines under £5, sparkling wines under £10 and champagne under £15. Happy hunting!

COSSART GORDON 10 YEAR OLD MALMSEY NV Madeira	*Hints of coffee, chocolate and burnt raisins. Fresh acidity provides excellent balance on finish.*	**£17.50**	BBR C&B TH J&B JAV MM CNL **B**
COSSART GORDON 15 YEAR OLD RICH MALMSEY NV Madeira	*Complex, aged Malmsey showing rich palate of ground coffee beans, dark chocolate, nuts and raisins.*	**£21.10**	TH C&B MM AMA BU WR **S**

FORTIFIED

SETÚBAL MOSCATEL SUPERIOR 1965, JOSÉ MARIA DA FONSECA SUCCS Setúbal	*Rich, treacle nose. Lots of Christmas pudding-type fruit with hints of burnt muscovado sugar.*	**£16.90**	MHW MOR AMA **B**

SOUTH AFRICA

A S THE BOUNDARIES surrounding South Africa disappear, so the international market begins to enjoy and acknowledge the quality of its wines. The Pinotage grape is a particular asset to this rising nation. Investment, technical assistance and market understanding, all of which are well under way, will ensure that the potential of this country is realised over the next five years.

RED

OAK VILLAGE VINTAGE CABERNET SAUVIGNON 1994, VINFRUCO Coastal Region	*Cedar and blackcurrant leaf aromas. Sweet blackcurrant/damson fruit with interesting complexity. Good balance.*	**£4.00**	TO SPR	(B)
SIMONSVLEI WYNKELDER RESERVE PINOTAGE 1995 Coastal Region	*A deep, red, soft and spicy wine combined with a hint of chocolate and a warm finish.*	**£4.50**	OD SAF	(B)
CAPE AFRIKA PINOTAGE 1993 Coastal Region	*A ripe and tasty wine with stewed plums, cedar scents and a good clean finish.*	**£4.50**	CWS	(B)
CAPE VIEW MERLOT 1995, KYM MILNE AT BOTELLARY CO-OP Coastal Region	*Cassis nose, palate and finish with a good balance of mints, pepper and soft tannins.*	**£4.50**	VW	(B)
LA COTTE GRAND ROUGE 1995, FRANSCHHOEK VINEYARDS Cape	*This shows firm, ripe, characterful fruit with intense, rich oak and soft tannins. Good finish.*	**£5.00**	ABB SKW IVY	(B)

SOUTH AFRICA • RED

RUITERVLEI ESTATE WINE CINSAULT 1995 Coastal Region	*Shows an attractive peppery, earthy nose; rich and spicy with soft and mellow fruit.*	**£5.00**	BKW WCR	**S**
WINELANDS SHIRAZ/CABERNET SAUVIGNON 1995, KYM MILNE	*Ripe power; an almost opaque glassful, bursting with eucalyptus, chocolate and creamy new oak.*	**£5.00**	BU TH WR	**G**
OAK VILLAGE CABERNET SAUVIGNON 1992, VINFRUCO LIMITED Coastal Region	*Good cassis/cedar wood nose, good fruit palate, and an array of tannins for length.*	**£5.20**	THP CWS	**B**
KWV PINOTAGE/SHIRAZ 1993 Western Cape	*This is an easy drinking style of wine which has a smoky oak and ripe fruit character.*	**£5.20**	BCL LOH CHH ECA G&M	**B**
KWV MERLOT 1993 Coastal Region	*Spicey and fruity nose. Plummy fruits and fine tannins with a long and spicy finish.*	**£5.30**	BCL GDS ECA SEL G&M HOU	**S**
WELMOED WINERY CABERNET SAUVIGNON 1993 Coastal Region	*Sweet berry fruit with hints of liquorice and vanilla. Rich style showing supple silky summer fruits.*	**£5.50**	BKW MFS WCR	**B**
CLOS MALVERNE RESERVE 1994 Coastal Region	*This full-bodied rich wine redolent of pepper and leather has potential to develop further.*	**£5.70**	VWC SV DBY HW	**B**
BACKSBERG CABERNET SAUVIGNON 1993 Coastal Region	*Wonderful melange of summer fruits - strawberries, redcurrants and blackberries. Slight smokiness on the finish.*	**£5.70**	Widely available	**S**

SOUTH AFRICA • RED

BAY VIEW CABERNET SAUVIGNON/PINOTAGE 1994, LONGRIDGE Coastal Region	*Powerful wine showing lovely blackcurrant and oak, balancing well with good structure and intensity.*	£5.90	TPA VIL MTL MHW FEN	(S)
VILLIERA ESTATE CRU MONRO LIMITED RELEASE 1993 Coastal Region	*Young, blackberry ice-cream nose with soft fruity flavours and oak. Easy drinking.*	£6.00	FDL WST BU WR	(B)
SAVANHA CABERNET SAUVIGNON 1995 Western Cape	*Wonderful and fruity, showing typical Cabernet aromas with a full and dense flavour. A real winter warmer.*	£6.00		(B)
FAIRVIEW ESTATE SHIRAZ 1993, CHARLES BACK Coastal Region	*Medium weight with some fine fruits. Pleasing acidity and sweet oak give good depth.*	£6.00	Widely available	(B)
FAIRVIEW ESTATE SHIRAZ/MERLOT 1993 Coastal Region	*Deep garnet coloured, a wine displaying a minerally texture but a full soft and fruity flavour.*	£6.00	FUL	(B)
BOSCHENDAL ESTATE LANOY 1992 Coastal Region	*Some complexity with the flavours ranging from peppered cinnamon to fruit tannins and a leafy texture.*	£6.20	NRM NAD ROD VIL JAV POR	(B)
BEYERSKLOOF PINOTAGE 1995, BEYERS TRUTER Coastal Region	*Attractive, vibrant fruit and a firm structure proceed a perfumed nose. Good length.*	£6.30	Widely available	(B)
JACANA PINOTAGE 1995, HUGH RYMAN Coastal Region	*A pleasant, smooth and rich wine which has a minty aroma with spicy fruit and finish.*	£6.50	OD RYW VLW	(B)

SOUTH AFRICA • RED

SAXENBURG MERLOT 1994 Coastal Region	*Merlot fruits with good tannins and appealing spiciness. Longish finish with juicy aftertastes.*	£6.50	WR FUL ECA	**B**
FAIRVIEW ESTATE CARBENET SAUVIGNON 1994, CHARLES BACK Coastal Region	*Has a clean nose with hints of leather. Red fruit flavours are improved by plummy tastes and lasting tannins.*	£6.60	J&B JS VW LWE VLW GRT ADN	**S**
NEETHLINGSHOF CABERNET SAUVIGNON 1992 Coastal Region	*Attractive, mature style with mellow berry fruits and hints of tomato leaves. A gentle, soft, vanilla finish.*	£6.80	LOH CAP NG ECA CPW G&M HOU	**B**
SAXENBURG SHIRAZ 1994 Coastal Region	*Spicy, rich and very peppery, this has a full, intense palate with chewy berry flavours.*	£7.00	ECA DBY IVY	**S**
CLOS MALVERNE AURET CABERNET/MERLOT RESERVE 1994 Coastal Region	*Elegant style, rich ripe fruits give depth and balance with firm tannins. Well made wine.*	£7.10	BTH WIL SEL SV DBY	**S**
WARWICK ESTATE CABERNET SAUVIGNON 1992 Coastal Region	*Lots of ripe fruits and smoky oak give this wine a fresh style. Well balanced tannins.*	£7.40	VWC VW DBY RW RAE WR	**B**
CATHEDRAL CELLARS TRIPTYCH 1993, KWV Coastal Region	*Heavy weight wine with hot fruits and big tannins. Spiced oak showing on middle palate.*	£7.60	WIL SEC JEH CAP ECA DBY G&M	**B**
FAIRVIEW ESTATE SHIRAZ RESERVE 1993, CHARLES BACK Coastal Region	*Big, rich, sweet fruits and lots of liquorice with smooth, oaky tannins. Great potential.*	£7.90	W BBR J&B COK GRT	**G**

NEIL ELLIS CABERNET SAUVIGNON 1992 Coastal Region	*Interesting palate with ripe fruits and cedar wood. Gripping hot tannins.*	**£8.40**	Widely available	B
WARWICK FARM TRILOGY 1992, NORMA RATCLIFFE Coastal Region	*Shows good fruit and sweet spice. Soft but full with a good backbone of tannins.*	**£8.70**	DBY RW RAE BU WR	B
TALANA HILL 1992, JAN BOLAND COETZEE Coastal Region	*Very pungent blackcurrant spicy nose and palate. Juicy tannins and dryish finish.*	**£8.80**	SEL FTH	B
JORDAN CABERNET SAUVIGNON 1993, JORDAN ESTATE Coastal Region	*Aromas of smoked blackcurrants. Flavours of hot fruit and dry tannins that last.*	**£9.00**	L&W FSW GAR TP CFT GHL NY	B
STELLENRYCK CABERNET SAUVIGNON 1989, THE BERKELDER Coastal Region	*Sweet soft cassis nose with plenty of spice and wood. The palate has depth and complexity.*	**£9.30**	Widely available	B
THELEMA MOUNTAIN CABERNET SAUVIGNON 1992 Coastal Region	*Wood and berry fruits with hints of spice. Warm tannins with a fine structure.*	**£9.30**	Widely available	S
UITERWYK PINOTAGE 1994, UITERWYK Coastal Region	*This full and rich wine has lots of fruit and spice with weight and grip.*	**£9.40**	SAF BEN DBY RBS NY L&W	B
PLAISIR DE MERLE CABERNET SAUVIGNON 1994, STELLENBOSCH FARMERS WINERY Coastal Region	*Attractive wine with a little bit of Ribena fruit coupled with a good, robust structure.*	**£9.70**	Widely available	B

SOUTH AFRICA • WHITE

MEERLUST RUBICON 1991 Coastal Region	*Attractive Cabernet berry fruit with a touch of smokiness and a suggestion of spiciness. Has good balance.*	**£10.40**	Widely available	**B**
RUSTENBERG SUPERIOR CABERNET SAUVIGNON 1982 Coastal Region	*Ripe, warm and delicious. Packed with delicate aromas, juicy flavours and a long complex finish.*	**£12.20**	AV MFS	**B**

WHITE

PAARL HEIGHTS COLOMBARD 1995, BOLAND WYNKELDER Coastal Region	*An excellent varietal aroma - this is crisp and fresh and full of herbaceous, nettley fruit.*	**£3.60**	Widely available	**B**
SAUVIGNON BLANC WELMOED WINERY 1995 Coastal Region	*Green and herbaceous, this wine holds plenty of gooseberry; fruit-piercing acidity with lasting finish.*	**£4.00**	CCL GNW QR MFS CWS	**B**
LONG MOUNTAIN CHARDONNAY 1995 Western Cape	*A stylish South African Chardonnay with a light fruity flavour which is medium in length.*	**£4.20**	DIO PEA CEN CRM SAF WWI CAX VW	**B**
KWV CHENIN BLANC 1995 Western Cape	*Has a fresh, steely nose with a hint of sweetness and lots of good, zippy, bubblegum fruit.*	**£4.40**	Widely available	**B**
KWV SAUVIGNON BLANC 1995 Western Cape	*Clear, varietal character shouts from this easy-drinking, refreshing wine. Clean aromas and delicate finish.*	**£4.60**	Widely available	**B**

SOUTH AFRICA • WHITE			
LONGRIDGE BAY VIEW CHENIN BLANC 1995 Coastal Region	*Scrumptious, sweet, fruity bouquet and a big, broad, balanced palate of peach and oak.*	£4.70	TPA VIL WWI FEN RAV (B)
FAIRVIEW CHENIN BLANC 1995 Coastal Region	*Lovely and ripe with sweet, honeyed, vegetal fruit. Has excellent mineral and zesty lemon flavours.*	£4.70	VLW GRT W (B)
WATERSIDE WHITE 1995, GRAHAM BECK WINES Robertson	*Superb and rich aroma of banana and toast. Fat, full style.*	£4.70	EP (B)
WEST PEAK SAUVIGNON BLANC 1995, NOOITGEDACHT CELLARS Coastal Region	*Aromas of blackcurrant leaf and nettles laid with alcohol and fruit give an interesting wine.*	£4.90	Widely available (B)
LA COTTE CHENIN BLANC 1995, FRANSCHHOEK VINEYARDS Cape	*Touches of pear, apple and asparagus with mineral and herbaceous flavours. Crisp and fresh.*	£5.00	ABB SKW IVY (B)
NEDERBURG CHARDONNAY 1995 Coastal Region	*Wonderful and rich Chardonnay showing South Africa at its best. A real must to try.*	£5.50	Widely available (B)
GOEDVERWACHT ESTATE COLOMBARD 1995, BONNIEVALE Robertson	*This was mistaken for Sauvignon by several tasters. This is crisp, fresh and fruity in a melony, gooseberry way.*	£5.50	EP NG PM A WM MRF (B)
VILLIERA ESTATE SAUVIGNON BLANC 1995 Coastal Region	*An earthy Sauvignon style with asparagus and sharp gooseberries. Slightly green character but excellent length.*	£5.70	TH SSM WST BU WR (B)

SOUTH AFRICA • WHITE

FAIRVIEW ESTATE SEMILLION 1995, CHARLES BACK Coastal Region	*Floral nose and clean palate with slight oak, citrus peel, pear-drops and a hot finish.*	£6.00	OD	(B)
LONGRIDGE CHARDONNAY 1995 Coastal Region	*Clean, complex, fresh, elegant nose. On the palate there are light fruit/floral flavours.*	£6.40	TPA HWM VIL SOB RAV	(B)
KLEIN CONSTANTIA SAUVIGNON BLANC 1995 Constantia	*Nice yellow wine with a pea pod nose, followed by some yeasty and burnt characteristics.*	£6.70	Widely available	(B)
STELLENRYCK CHARDONNAY 1995, THE BERGKELDER Coastal Region	*Pale lemon in the glass with a vanilla nose. Rich mouthful with gentle pineapple mid-palate.*	£6.90	Widely available	(B)
HILL TOP CHARDONNAY 1995, CHARLES BACK Coastal Region	*A pale/green edge, predominant bouquet with plenty of balanced fruit. This is friendly but it lacks character.*	£7.00	THP	(B)
RIETVALLEI CHARDONNAY 1995, THE BERGKELDER Coastal Region	*Mid intensity, light floral bouquet, mildly oaked and crisp, fruity palate earthy finish.*	£7.00	NG CAP CLA	(B)
SAXENBURG CHARDONNAY 1995 Coastal Region	*Good, creamy oak slightly smothers peachy palate. Lingering acid producing a medium-intensity wine.*	£7.00	IVR ECA	(B)
BOSCHENDAL ESTATE LIGHTLY WOODED CHARDONNAY 1995 Coastal Region	*A light, smoky and fruity nose. A lively wine with a grapefruit taste and some complexity.*	£7.20	TO VIL	(B)

SOUTH AFRICA • SPARKLING

NEIL ELLIS CHARDONNAY 1995 Coastal Region	*A lovely, honeyed mandarin nose; very correct with a fruity palate and a long finish.*	£7.60	BOO MWW DBY LWE RBS COK MTL FTH	(B)
CHAMONIX CHARDONNAY 1994, CAPE CHAMONIX Franschhoek	*A full-bodied, rich, toasty aroma is followed by impressive lemon acidity and tropical taste.*	£7.70	LWE FEN	(S)
HAMILTON RUSSELL VINEYARDS CHARDONNAY 1995 Western Cape	*Fresh, young and delicate with a wealth of tropical flavours. This wine has elegance and harmony.*	£8.80	Widely available	(S)

ROSE

CAPE COUNTRY CAPE BLUSH 1995, KWV Western Cape	*Attractive rose petal and strawberry jam aromas. Sweet, ripe fruit flavours in the mouth.*	£4.00	BCL ECA	(B)

SPARKLING

CUVÉE KRONE BOREALIS BRUT 1992, TWEE JONGE GEZELLEN Western Cape	*Fresh and attractive nose and a sweetish featherweight palate wafting away to a downy finish.*	£7.00	NG GNW MFS W	(B)
GRAHAM BECK MADEBA BRUT NV Robertson	*Toasty nose, boney fruit palate; good structure, balance and length. An excellent introduction to sparkling.*	£7.30	L&W JS VW	(G)

CHARLES DURET BLANC DE BLANCS CHARDONNAY NV Robertson	*Clean, ripe, toasty flavours on the nose, citrus fruit on the palate. Good, balanced structure.*	**£8.00**	WEP	(B)
PIERRE JOURDAN BLANC DE BLANCS NV, CABRIESE ESTATE Franschhoek	*Rich, malt aroma and seemingly mature, concentrated lemon palate with a good balance of acidity.*	**£12.00**	NG	(B)

FORTIFIED

KWV RED MUSCADEL 1975 Robertson	*Rich toffee and raisin nose. Nutty with hints of spice. Tangy with a clean fruit finish.*	**£6.10**	ABY GDS ECA W	(B)
KWV WHITE JERIPIGO 1979 Boberg	*Ripe, seductive nose of smooth caramel and molasses. Silky caramel palate with hints of orange peel.*	**£6.60**	ABY ECA CFT W AMA	(B)
LATE BOTTLED CAVENDISH VINTAGE 1979, KWV Coastal Region	*Light tawny colour. Creamy orange and nutmeg nose. Smoky, caramel flavour. Balanced, stylish, aged wine.*	**£7.30**	Widely available	(S)

SOUTH AMERICA

A CONTINENT ON THE FAST TRACK of wine production. Value-for-money, clean, sunshine wines are beginning to emerge, and the quality is far more consistent than ever before. Generic and foreign expertise, backed up by heavy investment in machinery, has helped to create some delicious world-beating wines, such as the two Chilean Gold medal winners — the first ever.

ARGENTINA • RED

BODEGA ESCORITIVELA MENDOZA RED 1995 Mendoza	*A flowery, fragrant bouquet and a clean structure combine with strawberry flavours. Good length too.*	£3.00	SAF	B
LA AGRICOLA CABERNET SAUVIGNON 1995 Mendoza	*Soft, fragrant, bramble fruit aromas. Impressive fruit flavours on the palate which precede a good finish.*	£3.80	BKW WCR	B
ETCHART TINTO 1994, ARNALDO ETCHART Mendoza	*Straightforward, rich and packed with hot, heavy fruit yet not overpowering. Satisfying, fresh and clean.*	£3.80	CWS PEA SLM CDE DIO CLA CAX	B
BALBI VINEYARD MALBEC 1995, ALLIED DOMECQ ARGENTINA Mendoza	*Summer fruits on nose and berry fruit on palate makes for an simple easy drinking wine.*	£4.00	OD VW	B
BODEGAS LURTON MALBEC 1995, JACQUES LURTON Mendoza	*The youthful berry fruit content, soft tannin and creamy, oaked finish give a fine glassful.*	£4.00	FUL	B

Wine	Description	Price	Stockists	
VISTALBA ESTATE SYRAH 1995, CASA NIETO SENETINER Mendoza	*Pepper and ink - a soft, ripe style, full of smoky black fruit and brambly cooked apples.*	£4.60	BOO VW HVW NY HOU NRW TRO	B
ST. MICHAEL MALBEC OAK CASK RESERVE 1992, BODEGAS TRAPICHE Mendoza	*Black cherries, herbs and bubblegum on the nose. Fruity palate finishing with a mature oakiness.*	£5.00	M&S	B
ALAMOS RIDGE MALBEC 1994, NICOLAS CATENA Mendoza	*The rich colour and classy bouquet are brought together by sweet cassis fruits and smooth tannins.*	£5.50	HN SHG CHF GGW BI	B
BODEGA NORTON PRIVADA 1993 Mendoza	*Good blackcurrant and black cherries hinting spices and mint. Smooth long tannic finish.*	£6.90	LNR BOO JN	P
ARNALDO ETCHART 1990 Salta	*The wine shows leafy blackcurrants on the palate with acidic spices. The tannins are light but good.*	£7.30	PEA B&B WTR CDE CEN CAX	
ARNALDO ETCHART 1993 Salta	*Sweet, plummy fruits and tarry oak contents. Good blackcurrant, balanced well with the tannins.*	£7.30	PEA B&B WTR CDE CEN CAX	
WEINERT MERLOT 1990, BODEGAS Y CAVAS DE WEINERT Mendoza	*Well developed Cabernet fruits. Rich vanilla wood and ripe blackcurrants with good complexity, balance and length.*	£8.60	LEA OSW WDI BOL NI HVW CNL	
WEINERT MALBEC 1991, BODEGA Y CAVAS DE WEINERT Mendoza	*Deep, damson red with a powerful smoky nose, well knit tannins and concentrated fruit.*	£8.90	Widely available	

CATENA AGNELO VINEYARD CABERNET SAUVIGNON 1993 Mendoza	*Intense liquorice and hot plum nose. Touch of mint on the palate, soft cherry tannins.*	**£9.60**	FUL WSO HN BEN GGW BI (B)
TRAPICHE MEDALLA TINTO 1993 Mendoza	*Very deep colour with a big concentrated nose. Ripe sweet fruit with balance and endurance.*	**£11.00**	GI (B)

ARGENTINA • WHITE

ETCHART CHARDONNAY 1995, ARNALDO ETCHART Salta	*A lightly oaked Argentinian Chardonnay with full, complex grapefruit, and marmalade flavourings.*	**£4.90**	TH PEA SLM CLA CAX BU WR (B)

CHILE • RED

ENTRE RIOS CHILEAN RED NV, VINOS DE CHILE Lontué	*This classy wine is well-made with its faultless balance of fruits, tannins, acidity and oak.*	**£3.00**	MRS (B)
VINO DE CHILE NV, XPOVIN Central Valley	*A black cherry and liquorice aroma is followed by a light tangy flavour. Pleasant finish.*	**£3.30**	U WCR (B)
CONO SUR CABERNET SAUVIGNON 1994 Chimbarongo	*Herbaceous leafy nose complements developed berry fruits, powerful oak and warming tannins.*	**£3.80**	A OD FUL KWI THP WST W (B)

LAS COLINAS CABERNET SAUVIGNON 1994, VIÑA TOCORNAL Maipo Valley	*Jammy fruit; plenty of rich wood and tannins. Will benefit from a little more time.*	£3.90	SA WST BU WR TH	B
ANDES PEAKS CABERNET SAUVIGNON 1994, SANTA EMILIANA Rapel	*Offers blackberry and hints of redcurrants; woody spice and smooth, blended tannins.*	£4.00	Widely available	B
SANTA CAROLINA MERLOT/CABERNET SAUVIGNON 1995 Central Valley	*The berry fruits and touches of minty oak give it rich depth. Good, oaky finish.*	£4.40	EP ECA G&M HOU MTL	S
CANEPA MERLOT 1994, JOSÉ CANEPA Maipo Valley	*Medium bodied with fine balancing acidity. Soft plum jam fruits add to long juicy finish.*	£4.50	BKW WCR SPR	
SANTA CAROLINA CABERNET/MERLOT 1995 Central Valley	*Pungent berry fruits; good balance of tannins and acidity with a sweet oaky finish.*	£4.50	EP ECA G&M HOU MTL PIM WCR	
PALMERAS ESTATE OAK AGED CABERNET SAUVIGNON 1994, VIÑA SANTA EMILIANA Rapel	*Hot, spicy nose. Soft fruit in competition with old oak. Well developed tannins; mature length.*	£4.70	Widely available	
CANEPA CABERNET SAUVIGNON 1995, JOSÉ CANEPA Maipo Valley	*Lots of herby spices; full fruit flavours with lasting oak and a good strong tannic finish.*	£4.80	BKW NUR TO U WCR SPR	
LA PALMA CABERNET /MERLOT RESERVA 1995, VIÑA LA ROSA Rapel	*Liquorice and herbaceous nose; lovely, ripe berry fruits. Good concentration of flavours. Will improve.*	£5.00	WCR	

CARMEN MERLOT 1995 Maule Valley	*Peppery with green tannins and good fruits. Will mellow but is a great winter warmer now.*	**£5.10**	CRM TP GI DBY VW	(B)
MONTES NOGALES ESTATE CABERNET/MERLOT OAK AGED RESERVA 1994, DISCOVER WINES Curico	*Light aromas with good fruit on palate. A delightful, light young wine.*	**£5.40**	Widely available	(B)
CALITERRA MAIPO ESTATE CABERNET SAUVIGNON 1994 Maipo Valley	*Wonderful! Delicious blackcurrant essence. Simple example of Cabernet Sauvignon. A very nice wine.*	**£5.40**	OD FUL NIC MHW WCR BU WR TH	(B)
CARMEN CABERNET SAUVIGNON RESERVA 1994 Maipo Valley	*Fruity; very much New World. Summer fruits and subtle oakiness. Blended tannins give excellent smoothness.*	**£5.60**	OD BBR WSO GI DBY CWS	(B)
ERRAZURIZ ESTATES MERLOT RESERVA 1995 Aconcagua	*Full bodied wine with rich, dark colouring. Ripe fruit, wood and big tannins – great potential.*	**£5.70**	OD DBY WMK	(B)
VIÑA GRACIA CABERNET SAUVIGNON RESERVA 1993 Cachapoal Valley	*Closed but complex aromas with hints of almonds. A well made light young wine.*	**£5.90**	PAT	(B)
VIÑA GRACIA CABERNET SAUVIGNON RESERVA 1994 Maipo Valley	*Rich and fruity with almonds and cherries. Excellent balance, good length. Totally satisfying. Will keep.*	**£5.90**	PAT	(S)
ST. MICHAEL CABERNET SAUVIGNON RESERVA 1994, CARMEN VINEYARDS Maipo Valley	*Wonderful deep red colour. Gorgeous blackcurrant content with sweet oak and well balanced tannins.*	**£6.00**	M&S	(S)

VIÑA TARAPACA GRAN RESERVA 1990, VIÑA TARAPACA EX ZAVALA Maipo Valley	*Complex wine. Flavours range from rusty wood to lovely open fruit. Balanced tannins, long finish.*	£6.00	SHG WAV	**B**
CALITERRA CABERNET SAUVIGNON RESERVA 1994 Maipo Valley	*Fruit and oak give good balance with soft, smooth tannins. A great drink with great potential.*	£6.10	Widely available	**S**
CARMEN MERLOT RESERVA 1994 Maule Valley	*Youthful forest-fruit style. Good acidity and clean tannins – a great future.*	£6.20	OD BKW GI DBY SOB WCR CWS	**B**
ERRAZURIZ ESTATES CABERNET SAUVIGNON RESERVA 1993 Aconcagua	*Rich red with leafy peppery nose and minty flavours mixed with new oak. An elegant wine – has potential.*	£6.50	TO DBY	**S**
LA PLAYA CABERNET SAUVIGNON ESTATE RESERVA 1990 Maipo Valley	*Fairly rich nose with good, ripe fruits. Sweet vanilla oak and long fruity tannins.*	£6.80	WSG	**F**
ERRAZURIZ ESTATES DON MAXIMIANO RESERVA 1993 Aconcagua	*Ripe Chilean fruitiness with bubbling, curranty grape juice. Touches of pomegranate and damson flavours.*	£6.90	FUL WR BU VW DBY HOU WMK WCR	**I**
CANEPA PRIVATE RESERVE CABERNET SAUVIGNON 1994, JOSÉ CANEPA Maipo Valley	*Good Cabernet fruit is well structured,with a touch of wood and long tannins.*	£7.00	TO MWW A SEL SWS	**I**
CASABLANCA SANTA ISABEL CABERNET SAUVIGNON 1995, VIÑA CASABLANCA Casablanca	*Fragrant plums and berries. Smooth tannins, cherry jam finish. Great to drink; better to save.*	£7.00	MOR OD HAY NY WCR AMA	**S**

MONTES ALPHA CABERNET SAUVIGNON 1992, DISCOVER WINES Curico	*Mulberry plum on nose. Some complexity with good fruits on mid-palate.*	**£8.60**	Widely available	(B)
VALDIVIESO LONTUE NV Lontue	*A lovely deep, rich colour and big, approachable, spicy cough-linctus nose. Packed with fruit.*	**£10.00**	TLC BI	(S)
SANTA RITA CASA REAL 1993 Maipo Valley	*Chocolate nose with touches of Marmite and minty leafiness on the palate. A well balanced, fine wine.*	**£10.50**	OD CFT MWW DBY	(B)
CARMEN GOLD RESERVE CABERNET SAUVIGNON 1993 Maipo Valley	*Sweet, vegetal, earthy nose. Medium weight blackcurrant fruit with soft, smooth tannins. Developing well.*	**£11.00**	OD GI DBY	(B)
SANTA INÉS CABERNET/MERLOT 1995 Maipo Valley	*A minty, black fruit flavour with depth and strong tannins for a warming finish.*	**£14.60**	TO FUL RAV	(B)

CHILE • WHITE

SANTA CAROLINA WHITE 1995 Maule Valley	*An excellent clean nose with hints of greengage, gently aromatic and crisp on the palate.*	**£3.40**	TE BTH OD WWI ECA G&M HOU WCR	(B)
LA PALMA SAUVIGNON BLANC 1996, VIÑA LA ROSA Rapel Valley	*A serious and fresh wine with vibrant gooseberry fruit and a long and insistent finish.*	**£3.99**	W	(B)

Wine	Tasting Note	Price	Availability	
ANDES PEAK SAUVIGNON BLANC DES PEAK 1995, VIÑA SANTA EMILIANA Bio-Bio	*A very drinkable wine. Ripe Sauvignon nose with hot alcohol and fresh acid.*	£4.00	Widely available	Ⓟ
VIÑA CARTA VIEJA SAUVIGNON BLANC 1996 Maule Valley	*An attractive wine with peardrops and concentrated fruit. Well balanced and good length.*	£4.00	MWN MWW PIM	Ⓟ
ST. MICHAEL CASA LEONA CHARDONNAY 1995, VIÑA PEUMO Rapel	*Herbaceous lemon nose and a clean, zesty passion fruit palate. Good weight and nice length.*	£4.00	M&S	Ⓟ
SANTA INES SAUVIGNON BLANC 1996 Maipo Valley	*Fresh grapefruit aromas with ripe, concentrated fruit in a modern Sauvignon style.*	£4.00	TO	Ⓢ
ANDES PEAKS CASABLANCA CHARDONNAY 1995, VIÑA ST EMILIANA Casablanca	*Quiet lemon nose with fresh, fruity palate. Little depth but has length and lovely finishing acidity.*	£4.10	Widely available	Ⓢ
SANTA CAROLINA CHARDONNAY 1995 Lontue Valley	*Cardamon nose, enough tropical fruit to show through prickly acid. Short finish.*	£4.40	Widely available	Ⓘ
CALITERRA CHARDONNAY 1995 Curico	*Full, tropical nose and fresh and creamy peach palate. Well-integrated and showing fine length.*	£4.50	Widely available	Ⓘ
ROWAN BROOK OAK AGED CHILEAN CHARDONNAY RESERVE 1995, JOSÉ CANEPA Mataquito Valley	*Bright golden in colour, tasting of passion fruit and liquorice with medium long finish.*	£4.50	A	Ⓘ

SOUTH AMERICA • CHILE WHITE				
CHILEAN CHARDONNAY 1995, V M LIMITED Rancagua	*Good honey nose and warm-hearted tropical fruit palate with nice legs and length. Going places.*	£4.70	NUR	**B**
CASTILLO DE MOLINA SAUVIGNON BLANC 1995, VIÑA SAN PEDRO Lontué	*This is a simple medium weight wine showing Sauvignon fruit style and a sweet finish.*	£5.00	MRS RBS	**B**
CASABLANCA WHITE LABEL CHARDONNAY 1995, VIÑA CASABLANCA Casablanca	*Clear simple nose; balanced, ripe, tropical fruits on the palate and a complex finish.*	£5.40	Widely available	**B**
LA FORTUNA CHARDONNAY RESERVE 1995 Lontue Valley	*Biscuity, melon nose and palate with good acidity and reasonable length. A smooth, melting finish.*	£5.40	PF VIL IVY TRO AMA CWS	**S**
CALITERRA CASABLANCA ESTATE CHARDONNAY 1995, VIÑA CALITERRA Casablanca	*A good balance of vibrantly fresh flavours with orange on the nose and lychee fruit.*	£5.50	Widely available	**B**
ECHEVERRIA CHARDONNAY RESERVA 1995 Central Valley	*Clean and light bouquet with good acidity, creamy citrus flavour and fresh finish*	£5.60	SKW BLV VIL MTL PIM WOI	**B**
CONCHA Y TORO TRIO CHARDONNAY 1995 Rapel Valley	*A glorious kiwi nose with toasty oak and a lively tropical fruit flavour.*	£5.60	WSC AMA BU WR TH	**G**
SANTA CAROLINA RESERVA CHARDONNAY 1995 Maipo Valley	*A wine with subtle oakiness, light citrus aroma and tasting of pear drops.*	£5.80	OD SAF ECA CFT G&M HOU PIM	**B**

CASABLANCA SANTA ISABEL ESTATE SAUVIGNON BLANC 1995 Casablanca	*Honeyed and ripe fruit nose with a touch of leaf. Pleasant rounded style.*	**£6.20**	Widely available	(B)
CASABLANCA CHARDONNAY 1995 Casablanca	*Lemon/grapefruit nose with soft mellow fruit on palate with a long lingering finish.*	**£6.20**	Widely available	(S)
UNDURRAGA CHARDONNAY RESERVA 1995 Maipo Valley	*Full-blown oak and citrus nose, with a buttery, ripe fruit palate. Long and persistent.*	**£6.20**	AV MWW DBY HOU AMA	(G)
CALITERRA RESERVA CHARDONNAY 1995 Maipo Valley	*Soft vanilla oak on the nose, a youthful fresh citrus taste. Lively finish.*	**£6.30**	FUL WR BI D CVR DBY BU TH	(B)
CASABLANCA VALLEY SANTA ISABEL ESTATE CHARDONNAY/SAUVIGNON 1995, VIÑA CASABLANCA Casablanca	*Pleasant, ripe tropical fruit and well-integrated oak achieving a mature balance and finesse.*	**£6.30**	TH EP BTH MOR HVW	(B)
ERRAZURIZ ESTATES CHARDONNAY RESERVE 1995 Casablanca	*Aroma of ripe tropical fruit, well balanced with subtle oak and a lasting rich fruit finish.*	**£6.80**	TO OD CEB DBY WMK FEN	(S)
SANTA CAROLINA GRAN RESERVA CHARDONNAY 1995 Maipo Valley	*Small clean delicate oak nose. Lychee and passion fruit combine well to produce a lovely palate.*	**£7.50**	TH ECA G&M HOU BU WR WR	(S)
MONTES ALPHA CHARDONNAY 1995, DISCOVER WINES LTDA Curico	*Stylish wine with concentrated apple/grapefruit aromas mellowed by an intense buttery tropical fruit palate.*	**£8.30**	Widely available	(S)

Santa Carolina Chardonnay Reserva De Familia 1995 Maipo Valley	*Quite aggressive stalky nose, intensely ripe palate, weighty but classy style. Drive and power on finish.*	**£9.20**	OD ECA	**B**

URUGUAY • RED

Sainsbury's Merlot/Tannat 1995, Establecimiento Juanico Juanico	*Rich, soft orangey fruits highlight a clean, juicy, simple style. Well balanced and full flavoured.*	**£3.80**	JS	**B**

SPAIN

WITH INCREASING INTERNATIONAL COMPETITION and consumer knowledge, Spain has realised the need for variety, reliability and quality. Top-class and original wines are now beginning to emerge at competitive prices, as the deeply-entrenched conservative attitudes to wine making give way to fresh new ideas. The superb Nekeas Chardonnay 1995 from Navarra is a great example.

RED

DON DARIAS TINTO NV, BODEGAS VITORIANAS Northern Spain	*Still a bit young and harsh, with aggressive tannins, but has the potential to develop well.*	**£3.40**	Widely available	B
SANTA CATALINA TEMPRANILLO/GARNACHA 1995, VINÍCOLA DE CASTILLA La Mancha	*Full of cloves and spices, this wine is laden with ripe fruits and velvety, vanilla aromas.*	**£3.50**	TO	B
MALT HOUSE VINTNERS VALDEPEÑAS RESERVA 1989, BODEGAS FÉLIX SOLÍS Valdepenas	*Plenty of fruit here to balance a tight, closely-knit structure which should evolve well.*	**£3.70**	MHV	B
ASDA RIOJA 1992, FIUSA ARNEDO LA RIOJA Rioja	*Wonderful fruit and spice giving powerful aromas and a complex palate. A real bargain.*	**£3.80**	A	B
PALACIO DE LÉON 1992, VIÑOS DE LÉON Castillo Léon	*Well-made wine with a complex nose and sweet, spicy fruit on the palate.*	**£3.90**	FDL WCR A&A BU WR TH	S

SPAIN • RED				
TERRA ALTA BUSH VINES GARNACHA 1995, TARRACO ALIMENTOS Terra Alta	*Bright ruby-red colour, soft cherry nose. On the palate well made, if slightly commercial.*	£4.00	A	(B)
VIÑA MATER ROVIRA RESERVA 1989, PEDRO ROVIRA Tarragona	*Showing some age, this has old oak aromas; clovey and complex.*	£4.00	VER	(B)
COSECHA RIOJA VIÑA BAROJA SIN CRIANZA 1995, BODEGAS HEREDAD DE BAROJA Rioja	*Deep blackcurrant robe, masses of fruit and good grip from well-structured mature tannins.*	£4.00	MOR	(B)
SEÑORÍO DE GUADIANEJA TEMPRANILLO RESERVA 1992, VINÍCOLA DE CASTILLA La Mancha	*Typical style - strong oak and lots of warm vanilla tones. Gorgeous on a cold autumn day.*	£4.00	MHW	(B)
ST. MICHAEL PEÑASCAL CASTILLA Y LEON NV, HIJOS DE ANTONIO BARCELÓ Ribero del Duero	*Delicate ruby-red colour, very perfumed nose, chewy palate with young tannins; masses of oak.*	£4.00	M&S	(S)
DRAGÓN TEMPRANILLO 1994, BODEGAS BERBERANA Rioja	*Aromas of summer berries and cinnamon together with soft, smooth tannins giving a smooth, lasting finish.*	£4.10	FUL KWI DBY SMF CWS	(B)
LAS CAMPAS CRIANZA 1992, VINÍCOLA NAVARRA Navarra	*Ruby-red wine with an almost porty, stewed fruit character; good acidity, long finish.*	£4.50	HOU SCA OD GI WMK WCR MFS	(B)
OROBIO RIOJA RESERVA 1990, BODEGAS ARTADI Rioja	*Subdued nose but plenty of soft fruit. An easy to drink wine and not too overpowering.*	£4.50	JS OD	(B)

Name	Description	Price		
SAINSBURY'S DAMAR DE TORO 1994, FARINA Toro	*Herbaceous nose with a good balance of tannins and ripe berry fruits; lightly astringent finish.*	£4.50	JS	(B)
CARTA DE PLATA CVC NV, BODEGAS BERBERANA Rioja	*Despite a vegetal, rather stalky nose this is a quaffable wine showing plenty of fruit.*	£4.60	U VIL OD DBY COK A&A CWS	(B)
BERBERANA OAK AGED RIOJA 1994 Rioja	*Sweet berry fruit aromas are balanced with fine tannins; surprisingly approachable and drinking now.*	£4.80	BOO SAF VIL	(B)
ZAGARRON TINTO JOVEN 1995, NUESTRA SEÑORA DE MANJAVACAS MOTA DEL CUERVO La Mancha	*Light red in colour, jammy nose. Quite simple but very approachable. A great food wine.*	£5.00	STB RWL	(B)
CÁNCHALES VINO NUEVO ELABORACIÓN PROPIA 1995, BODEGAS RIOJANAS Rioja	*Lovely and rich, showing wine making at its best. A good starting point to Rioja.*	£5.00	STB RWL	(B)
VIÑA VALORIA RIOJA 1995 Rioja	*Intense cherry-purple hue with ripe, fresh berry fruits on the palate; still showing young tannins.*	£5.00	THP	(B)
TESCO SPANISH MERLOT RESERVA 1991, RAIMAT Costers del Segre	*Intense savoury nose with aromas of new oak, crushed brambley fruits and well-knit tannins.*	£5.00	TO	(S)
ARTADI TINTO 1995 Rioja	*Young fresh colour, with delicate spices on the nose, well-integrated fruit and mature oak.*	£5.20	CNW OD CNL	(B)

SPAIN • RED				
PALACIO DE LA VEGA TEMPRANILLO 1994 Navarra	*Mid-ruby colour, hints of purple, youthful summer berries and spice; nicely balanced fruit flavours.*	£5.30	Widely available	**B**
GUELBENZU JARDIN 1995, BODEGAS GUELBENZU Navarra	*Full of plummy fruits, this wine is still showing some tightly-knit tannins yet to mature.*	£5.50	Widely available	**B**
MARQUÉS DE VELILLA TINTO JOVEN 1995, GRANDES BODEGAS Ribera Del Duero	*Ripe plummy nose with just a touch of Cabernet on the palate; tannins slightly astringent.*	£5.50	PTR BTH MOR MFS	**B**
TESCO VIÑA MARA RIOJA RESERVA 1988, BERBERANA Rioja	*Mature nose of slightly stewed fruit; good acidity, long and well-made with an elegant finish.*	£5.50	TO	**B**
AGRAMONT TINTO CRIANZA 1992, BODEGAS PRÍNCIPE DE VIANA Navarra	*Garnet red with aromas of stewed summer fruits; lovely warm-mouth feel and excellent balance.*	£5.50	Widely available	**S**
EL COTO TINTO CRIANZA 1993, EL COTO DE RIOJA Rioja	*Pale aged colour, vanilla oak nose and classic style; well balanced, stylish with a long finish.*	£5.60	CKB D GGW NRW A&A AMA	**B**
MARQUÉS DE GRIÑON RIOJA 1994 Rioja	*A big powerful wine. Great depth of fruit with plenty of tannin content.*	£5.60	Widely available	**S**
VIÑA ALCORTA CAMPO VIEJO CRIANZA 1993 Rioja	*Delicate ruby robe, abundant summer fruits, soft tannins and ready to drink now.*	£5.70	Widely available	**B**

Wine	Tasting Notes	Price	Stockists	
MURUVE CRIANZA 1991, BODEGAS FRUTOS VILLAR Toro	*Plenty of fruit but young, firm tannins need time to soften.*	£5.80	COC PST VLW CPW SEL DBY L&S	B
CORTESIA RIOJA RESERVA 1990, BODEGAS FUENTORO Rioja	*Mature savoury fruit, good balance and sweet tannins with an attractive figgy, creamy finish.*	£5.90	MHV	B
PALACIO DE LA VEGA MERLOT CRIANZA 1993 Navarra	*Light purple, leafy notes with mint and cassis on the nose; a wine for future drinking.*	£5.90	PEA CDE CEN CAP WTR OD CAX RAV	B
HERENCIA LASANTA CRIANZA 1992 Rioja	*Garnet red with a cherry and cassis nose; lively on the palate – slightly herbaceous tones.*	£6.00	MOR	B
BANDA AZUL 1993, PATERNINA Rioja	*Plenty of summer fruits on the nose; well-structured wine which is starting to soften.*	£6.00	VHW MTL A&A	B
CONDE DE VALDEMAR RIOJA 1993, MARTINEZ BUJANDA Rioja	*Bursting with crushed raspberries and youthful aromas, this wine has excellent tannic balance.*	£6.20	Widely available	S
ARTADI VIÑAS DE GAIN CRIANZA 1993 Rioja	*Brick red rim belies the youthful summer fruit on the palate, with a glorious spicy finish.*	£6.40	CNW OD CNL	B
GUELBENZU 1994 Navarra	*Deep ruby with purple tones; masses of berry fruit, hints of spice and dry tannins.*	£6.40	Widely available	B

	SPAIN • RED			
RAIMAT TEMPRANILLO 1991 Costers del Segre	*Lovely damson flavours, slightly hot alcoholic feel on the palate; chunky meaty finish with a great length.*	£6.40	Widely available	**B**
ENATE TINTO CRIANZA 1993, CRIANZAS DEL ALTO ARAGON Somontano	*Black cherries in abundance, with very fine tannins giving a lovely smooth wine.*	£6.50	Widely available	**B**
VEGA CUBILLAS CRIANZA 1991, BODEGAS SEÑORÍO DE NAVA Ribera del Duero	*A great wine from Spain. Delicious, elegant and fruity. A must for Spanish fans.*	£6.50	BKW WSO WCR	**B**
RAIMAT CABERNET SAUVIGNON 1991 Lerida	*Powerful deep colour, well structured wine with good backbone and an elegant finish.*	£6.50	Widely available	**B**
SOMERFIELD SEÑORÍO DE AGOS RIOJA RESERVA 1989, MARQUÉS DEL PUERTO Rioja	*Jammy fruit and creamy oak. A good bargain to start with for an introduction to Rioja.*	£6.50	SMF	**B**
CAMPO VIEJO RESERVA 1990, BODEGAS & BEBIDAS Rioja	*Browning rim and gamey nose, light but composed mature Spanish style; classical but uncomplicated wine.*	£6.60	Widely available	**B**
PINOT NOIR VIÑAS DEL VERO 1991, COMPAÑÍA VITIVINÍCOLA ARAGONESA Somontano	*Light, young red colour; pleasant youthful nose, lovely soft fruit with firm tannins.*	£6.60	Widely available	**B**
VALDUERO RIBERA DEL DUERO 1992 Ribero del Duero	*Vibrant ruby red with purple hints; lovely black cherries on the palate and good grip.*	£6.80	J&B DBY VLW L&S BU WR TH	**B**

BALBÁS TRADICIÓN 1994 Ribeira del Duero	*Peppery character and lots of sweet vanilla oak and spicy notes; full-bodied and warming.*	£7.00	MWW	(B)
SEÑORÍO DE NAVA RESERVA 1989 Ribero del Duero	*A big, chunky wine with heaps of flavour. Try this for a change.*	£7.00	FUL AMA	(B)
BARÓN DE LEY RESERVA 1991 Ribero del Duero	*Gamey nose with creamy, vanilla oak and sweet blackcurrants on the palate. This is brilliant with food.*	£7.10	A BV CLA BU WR TH CWS	(S)
MATARROMERA RIBERA DEL DUERO 1994, VIÑEDOS Y BODEGAS Ribera del Duero	*Wonderfully flavoursome, bursting with summer fruits; easy-drinking wine to warm up any winter evening.*	£7.30	LNR BWC	(B)
BARÓN DE LEY RIOJA RESERVA 1991 Rioja	*Hugh mouthful of delicious, sweet jammy fruits. Very approachable now but will keep.*	£7.30	CLA HVW BU WR TH	(B)
FAUSTINO V TINTO RESERVA 1991 Rioja	*Delicate and elegant wine; well-defined with attractive berry fruits and a soft finish.*	£7.50	Widely available	(B)
HEREDERAS DEL MARQUÉS DE RISCAL RESERVA 1991 Rioja	*Traditional, somewhat oxidized, style; spicy, warm fruit palate with meaty tannins and a lingering finish.*	£7.90	Widely available	(B)
MARQUÉS DE GRIÑÓN DOMINIO DE VALDEPUSA SYRAH 1993 Toledo	*A solid, rich and chocolatey modern-style wine. Peppery and spicy with soft tannins.*	£8.00	TO	(B)

VIÑAS DEL VERO MERLOT/ CABERNET SAUVIGNON RESERVA 1991, COMPAÑÍA VITIVINÍCOLA ARAGONESA Somontano	*Big, bright, youthful raspberry nose, packed with ripe fruit; an easy-drinking style.*	£8.20	TP RTW DWS DBY PIM	**B**
OCHOA RESERVA 1987 Navarra	*Fudgey nose, fruity and jammy; nice length if a little dry – especially good with food.*	£8.30	Widely available	**B**
PALACIO DE LA VEGA CABERNET SAUVIGNON RESERVA 1992 Navarra	*Aromas of stewed fruit, redcurrants and rose-hips; the palate shows wonderful soft tannins and length.*	£8.30	Widely available	**G**
MARQUÉS DE GRIÑÓN DOMINIO DE VALDEPUSA SYRAH 1993 Toledo	*An intense deep-coloured wine packed with fruit and well-knit tannins; perfectly poised to age.*	£9.00	FUL TO	**G**
MARQUÉS DE GRIÑÓN DOMINIO DE VALDEPUSA CABERNET SAUVIGNON 1993 Toledo	*Rich purple robe, brambley fruits. This wine is still adolescent and will develop well.*	£9.30	FUL DBY MHW BU WR	**B**
CAMPO VIEJO RIOJA GRAN RESERVA 1985 Rioja	*Bright ruby-garnet colour; lots of new, sweet coconut oak on the nose; soft tobacco flavours.*	£9.50	Widely available	**B**
ANIMA MASCARÓ CABERNET SAUVIGNON 1988, ANTONIO MASCARÓ Penedés	*Traditional-style Rioja; ripe, fruity nose with plenty of structure. Masses of vanilla and oak.*	£9.60	FSW TP	**B**
PAGO DE CARRAOVEJAS 1994 Ribera del Duero	*Very dense colour, with a gamey nose, plummy fruits and well-balanced tannins. This wine should age impressively.*	£9.70	Widely available	**G**

Viña Ardanza Reserva 1989, La Rioja Alta Rioja	*Considerable age in the colour but tannins still quite harsh; plenty of fruit though.*	£10.30	Widely available	S
Guelbenzu Evo 1992 Navarra	*Slightly closed on the nose but fresh summer fruits underneath; a bit severe now, needs time.*	£10.50	Widely available	B
Paternina Gran Reserva 1987 Rioja	*A classic example of an ageing Rioja that keeps getting better. You should not resist this one.*	£10.50	VHW A&A	B
Conde de Valdemar Gran Reserva 1986, Martínez Bujanda Rioja	*Classic Rioja and ready to drink; delicate, soft vanilla aromas with a smooth, dry finish.*	£10.70	JN CHF DBY FTH VEX	B
Conde de la Salceda Gran Reserva 1987, Viña Salceda Rioja	*A huge mouthfilling wine of great flavour and elegance giving a lasting length.*	£11.00	SHJ BLS WON WIC TAN	B
Martínez Bujanda Garnacha Reserva 1990 Rioja	*Tawny in colour with a raisiny nose which shows some maturity, but still plenty of redcurrant fruit in evidence.*	£11.20	HVW MTL VEX BU	F
Conde de Valdemar Rioja Gran Reserva 1989, Martínez Bujanda Rioja	*Ripe, fleshy nose with plenty of depth; good berry fruit and excellent, long, stylish finish.*	£11.20	PAV HVW MTL VEX BU WR TH	D
Contino Rioja Reserva 1989 Rioja	*Chocolate mint creams with figs on the nose; big, blockbusting middle-palate and lovely finish.*	£11.50	VWC MOR DWS THP RBS SOB L&S	D

SPAIN • WHITE				
Martínez Bujanda Rioja Reserva 1989 Rioja	*Old-style Spanish wine with deep mahogany colour and slightly volatile nose. This is ready to drink now.*	£12.60	CHF BD MTL VEX BU	(B)
Viña Real Rioja Gran Reserva 1986, Compañía Vinícola del Norte de España Rioja	*A stylish wine that is at its peak. This has an excellent balance of fruit and tannin.*	£13.00	Widely available	(S)
Viña Valoria Gran Reserva 1985 Rioja	*Delicately pale in colour; an elegant duchess of a wine with lots of fruit and grip.*	£14.30	THP	(B)
Gran Reserva 904 1985, La Rioja Alta Rioja	*An elegant Grande Dame; spicy nose full of berries. This is finely balanced with an impressive finish.*	£16.60	Widely available	(S)
Barón de Chirel Reserva 1988, Marqués de Riscal Rioja	*Brick-red hues and mature soft tannins. Ready to drink now.*	£29.00	MFS	(B)

WHITE

Viña Malea Viura 1995, Coop. Antonio Abad Manchuela	*Clean, ripe, unoaked style with herbaceous nose and short, balanced palate leading to a dry finish.*	£3.30	HWM SAF	(B)
Santara Chardonnay 1995, Hugh Ryman/Bodega Concavins Tarragona	*Wonderful, rich Spanish Chardonnay. This is an excellent example of a well-made, balanced wine.*	£4.00	JS RYW	(B)

SPAIN • SPARKLING

PALACIO DE BORNOS RUEDA 1995, BODEGAS DE CRIANZA CASTILLA LA VIEJA Rueda	*A fine, fresh grapefruit nose; soft and well-balanced with plenty of zingy flavour.*	**£4.70**	THP RAV	**B**
AGRAMONT BLANCO NAVARRA VIURA/ CHARDONNAY 1995, BODEGAS PRÍNCIPE DE VIANA Navarra	*An attractive sweet lime nose; a balanced zesty lemon palate rounded with pleasant creaminess and vanilla.*	**£4.90**	OD SCA SAF VLW W L&S	**B**
NEKEAS CHARDONNAY BARREL FERMENTED 1994, NEKEAS Navarra	*A beautiful complex Chardonnay with ripe fruit aromas and a flavour to hit you between the eyes.*	**£6.10**	AK BAL OD NY TRO	**G**
ARTADI VIÑAS DE GAIN BLANCO RESERVA 1994, COSECHEROS ALAVESES Rioja	*Smooth and well-balanced with an orange nose; pleasantly sweet fruit, oak and a clean finish.*	**£7.00**	DOD	**B**
LAGAR DE CERVERA RÍAS BAIXAS ALBARIÑO 1995, LAGAR DE FORNELOS Rías Baixas	*Clean, lemony fruit and soft, creamy, oak flavours. This is a crisp and flavoursome wine.*	**£8.40**	TAN RBS SEL CPW RD L&W L&S WR	**B**

SPARKLING

ST. MICHAEL CAVA BRUT NV, SEVISA Cava	*Soft, savoury nose with yeast; good mousse, firm dry lemon and gooseberry palate. Well-balanced.*	**£5.00**	M&S	**B**
TESCO CAVA BRUT TRADITIONAL NV, SANT SADURNÍ D'ANOIA Cava	*Complex pineapple and goat's cheese nose; deep, balanced green apple and lemon palate. Dry finish.*	**£5.00**	TO	**S**

MONTSERRAT CAVA SELECCIÓN ESPECIAL NV, CONUISA SANT SADURNI D'ANOIA Cava	*Ripe, toasty nose and zesty palate with mature fruit and a citric acidity on the finish.*	**£7.40**	BD	**B**
SELFRIDGES VINTAGE CAVA 1993, SEVISA Cava	*Clear and bright, small fading bubbles; long, clean-as-a-whistle palate of luscious fruit.*	**£8.00**	SEL	**S**

FORTIFIED

TESCO SUPERIOR OLOROSO SECO, BODEGAS SÁNCHEZ ROMATE HERMANOS Jerez	*Wonderful initial suggestions of almonds and Christmas cake. Creamy with a firm, dry finish.*	**£3.40**	TO	**B**
SOMERFIELD MUSCATEL DE VALENCIA NV, VICENTE GANDIA Valencia	*Fresh Seville orange fruit, ripe pineapples and peaches combine with smooth honey and refreshing zesty acidity.*	**£3.40**	SMF	**S**
SÁNCHEZ ROMATE OLOROSO SECO SUPERIOR NV Jerez	*Nutty aromas lead to dry, well-balanced fruit. Firm palate with good structure and fresh finish.*	**£3.50**	VWC VW	**B**
TESCO SUPERIOR MANZANILLA, BODEGAS SÁNCHEZ ROMATE HERMANOS Jerez	*Pale yellow with aroma of salty almonds. Crisp and fresh with good balance and acidity.*	**£4.00**	HOU TO	**B**
CABRERA MANZANILLA DRY NV, D G GORDON Jerez	*Hint of nuts giving tremendous freshness. Initial impact softens to firm but delicate finish.*	**£4.00**	HOU MTL POR MHW WRT	**S**

Name	Description	Price		
SÁNCHEZ ROMATE PEDRO XIMÉNEZ SUPERIOR NV Jerez	*Treacle brown. Sweet, dried fruit with hints of liquorice. Unusual, rich and intense.*	£4.00	VWC VW	(S)
SOMERFIELD FINO SHERRY NV, LUIS CABALLERO Jerez	*Green gold with a sweet, rich nose. Nutty, citric fruit undertones with spice and salt.*	£4.20	SMF	(B)
SOMERFIELD MANZANILLA NV, ESPINOSA DE LOS MONTEROS Jerez	*Fresh and lively on the nose. Initially soft, developing to a firm finish with good balance.*	£4.20	SMF	(B)
CASTILLO DE LIRIA MOSCATEL NV, VICENTE GRANDIA Valencia	*Fresh orange fruit. Quite ripe and powerful but with refreshing acidity to balance. Honeyed finish.*	£4.30	FUL WIN W KWI CRS CBW WMK TAN	(B)
SÁNCHEZ ROMATE PALO CORTADO NV Jerez	*Nutty nose with vanilla and cream flooding the palate. Great toasted nut finish.*	£4.50	VW	(S)
TESCO FINEST SOLERA AMONTILLADO SHERRY, BODEGAS SÁNCHEZ ROMATE HERMANOS Jerez	*Very elegant lighter style. Raisins and fruit with aroma of toasted nuts. Soft, balanced finish.*	£5.00	TO	(B)
DOUBLE CENTURY ORIGINAL, DOMECQ Jerez	*Wonderful walnut on the nose. Complex but well-structured this is mellow and clean.*	£5.10	Widely available	(B)
PANDO SUPERIOR FINO DRY SHERRY NV, BODEGAS WILLIAMS & HUMBERT Jerez	*Pale green with a big, nutty nose. Excellent balance and length from strong fruit and saltiness.*	£5.50	BRW	(S)

Wine	Description	Price	Stockist	
TANNERS MARISCAL MANZANILLA FINEST LIGHT SHERRY NV, VINICOLA HIDALGO Jerez	*Delightful fresh, nutty manzanilla. Crisp and dry with a wonderful full, balanced finish.*	£6.20	TAN	(S)
ALEGRIA MANZANILLA NV, PEREZ MEGIA Jerez	*A very pale sherry with plenty of fresh fruit and character. Dry and well-balanced.*	£6.80	DBY AMA	(B)
FORTNUM & MASON AMONTILLADO SHERRY MEDIUM DRY NV, EMILIO LUSTAL Jerez	*Elegant and rich. Aromas of sultanas, roasted nuts and soft spice. Great sherry.*	£6.80	F&M	(S)
ALFONSO OLOROSO SECO SHERRY, GONZÁLEZ BYASS Jerez	*Full of ripe, fresh fruit and dry, nutty spice. Hints of oak and heaps of flavour.*	£7.10	OD DBY MTL VLW MM	(S)
TÍO PEPE FINO MUY SECO SHERRY, GONZÁLEZ BYASS Jerez	*Pale white gold. Sweet, light aromas lead to nuts and exceptional dryness. Teasingly complex.*	£7.10	Widely available	(S)
TANNERS VFO SANLUCAR AMONTILLADO NV, VINÍCOLA HILDAGO Jerez	*Light amber with hints of raisin and nut on the nose. This is dry with wonderful balance.*	£7.20	TAN	(B)
DOM RAMOS VERY DRY MANZANILLA NV Jerez	*Aromas of biscuits and salty almonds. Big, firm, fresh flavour with a crisp, delicate finish.*	£7.20	U AMA	(S)
MÁLAGA VIRGEN NV, LOPEZ HERMANOS Malaga	*Rich, mature style packed full of dried figs and sweet raisins. Lively acidity adds balance.*	£7.80	BAL FSW WFL PTR SEL WAW MFS	(B)

DON ZOILO OLOROSO, LUIS PAÉZ	*Bright and complex nose leading to dry almonds and cream. Great balance, elegant power.*	£8.40	VIL RTW AMA BU WR TH	**S**
EMILIO LUSTAU SOLERA RESERVA Jerez	*Rich marmalade and peachy fruit combined with a gentle, nutty character. Soft, woody finish.*	£8.60	RVA GDS DWS VLW ADN	**B**
VINO DULCE DE MOSCATEL GRAN RESERVA 1995, BODEGAS OCHOA Navarra	*Apples baked with sultanas and sweet raisins. Gentle caramelised sweetness; rich with a lingering finish.*	£9.40	TPW ES K&B JAV TP RTW DWS L&S	**B**
LUSTAU OLD EAST INDIA SHERRY Jerez	*Sweet marmalade and nut flavours balanced by crisp acidity. Rich and smooth with tremendous length.*	£9.60	Widely available	**S**
HARVEYS PALO CORTADO NV Jerez	*Aromas of baked raisins and caramel. Sweet with a surprisingly creamy softness through the long finish.*	£10.00	FEN ADD	**G**
HARVEYS FINE OLD AMONTILLADO NV Jerez	*Golden brown. Leafy nose with a peppery finish that lingers. Lively and fresh.*	£10.10	TP FEN ADD AMA	**B**
HARVEYS RICH OLD OLOROSO NV Jerez	*Deep amber colour. Toffee nose, hints of caramel and walnut with firm flavour and strong finish.*	£10.20	TP FEN MM ADD AMA	**S**
DOS CORTADO RARE OLD DRY OLOROSO NV, BODEGAS WILLIAMS & HUMBERT Jerez	*Expansive aromas of spices, Christmas and freshly-cracked nuts. Rich yet dry and a very long finish.*	£10.40	CHF SEL DBY MM AMA	**G**

SPAIN • FORTIFIED				
NOE PEDRO XIMÉNEZ, GONZÁLEZ BYASS Jerez	*Wonderful aroma of fruitcake and warm raisins. Lusciously covers the mouth and makes it water.*	**£19.60**	OD VLW AMA	(S)
APÓSTOLES OLOROSO VIEJO, GONZÁLEZ BYASS Jerez	*Brown gold with hints of warm sultanas and Christmas cake. Rich, nutty, lingering finish.*	**£20.40**	Widely available	(S)
MATUSALEM OLOROSO, GONZÁLEZ BYASS Jerez	*Savoury, tangy and intense nose. Sweet, rich and raisiny with a terrific, lingering length.*	**£20.70**	Widely available	(G)

OTHER COUNTRIES

THIS YEAR'S INTERNATIONAL WINE CHALLENGE saw a shake-up in this particular group. Out go last year's little-known winners, Morocco and Luxembourg, but the Lebanon makes a welcome return. Greece has performed well, doubling the number of its winners since last year. All these wines make a wonderful change from the average bottle on the merchant's shelf.

GREECE

DOMAINE HATZIMICHALIS CABERNET SAUVIGNON 1994 Atalante Valley	*Charred wood with cherry fruits; upfront berries. Simple, fresh tannins with hints of mint.*	**£8.50**	GWC	**B**
STROFILIA RED 1992, MALTEZOS-LAMPSIDIS STROFILIA SA Anavissos	*Complex, strawberry-and-vanilla bouquet precedes a woody palate and firm, balanced tannins. Good length.*	**£8.50**	GWC	**B**
CHATEAU CARRAS 1992, DOMAINE CARRAS Hallkidiki	*Excellent deep-purple/ ruby colour and unusual coconut and liquorice aromas pervade. Should develop well.*	**£8.80**	PF NEI SEL DBY POR GWC AMW	**S**
SATIRIKON 1989, DIMITRIS ANASTASSIOU Patras	*Garnet-red colouring and beautiful plummy, vanilla aromas. Creamy, straw-berry flavours – attractive and well-balanced.*	**£9.50**	GWC	**B**
DOMAINE HATZIMICHALIS CAVA RED 1992, Atalante Valley	*Sweet strawberry and ripe berries combine to produce a developed, complex aroma. Intense, fruity palate.*	**£12.00**	GWC	**B**

DOMAINE HATZIMICHALIS MERLOT 1994 Atalante Valley	*Sweet, ripe, cassis fruit. Firm, lean, liquorice style. A hint of coriander on the fruit flavours.*	**£15.00**	GWC	**B**

LEBANON

CHATEAU MUSAR 1989 Bekaa Valley	*Mature with rich aromas. Leafy fruit flavours, oak and warming tannins give a long finish.*	**£8.80**	Widely available	**B**

Tempus Amabilis Vin de Pays d'Oc 1994, Sica du Haut Pays d'Oc	£2.70	B
Gatsberg Cabernet Sauvignon 1994, Egervin	£2.80	B
Kwik Save Montepulciano d'Abruzzo 1995, Gruppo Italiano Vini	£3.00	B
Entre Rios Chilean Red NV, Vinos de Chile	£3.00	B
Bodega Escoritivela Mendoza Red 1995	£3.00	B
Safeway Sicilian Red 1995, Calatrasi	£3.00	B
Asda California Red NV, Arius Cellars	£3.00	S
Alta Mesa 1994, São Mamede Coop	£3.20	B
Safeway Falua Vinho Regional Ribatejo 1995, Falua Sociede de Vinhos	£3.20	S
Vino de Chile NV, Xpovin	£3.30	B
Lazio Rosso Casale del Giglio 1995	£3.40	B
Bulgarian Merlot/Gamay 1993, Vinprom Russe	£3.40	B
Don Darias Tinto NV, Bodegas Vitorianas	£3.40	B
Valea Mieilui Vineyards Special Reserve Pinot Noir 1990, Ceptura	£3.50	B
Santa Catalina Tempranillo/Garnache 1995, Vinícola de Castilla	£3.50	B
Somerfield California Dry Red NV, Sebastiani Vineyards	£3.50	B
Co-op Côtes de Ventoux NV, Louis Mousset	£3.60	B
Villa Mantinera Montepulciano di Molise 1994, Vini Cliterina	£3.60	B
Puglian Red 'The Country Collection' 1995, Cantele	£3.60	B
Malt House Vintners Valdepeñas Reserva 1989, Bodegas Felix Solis	£3.70	B
Ridgemount Bay Shiraz/Cabernet 1995, Angoves	£3.70	B
Somerfield Grilli di Villa Thalia 1993, Calatrasi	£3.70	S
Cono Sur Cabernet Sauvignon 1994, Viña Cono Sur	£3.80	B
La Agricola Cabernet Sauvignon 1995	£3.80	B
Etchart Tinto 1994, Arnaldo Etchart	£3.80	B
Meia Encosta Dão Red 1994, Sociede dos Vinhos Borges	£3.80	B
Sainsbury's Merlot/Tannat 1995, Establecimiento Juanico	£3.80	B
Asda Rioja 1992, Fiusa Arnedo La Rioja	£3.80	B
Las Colinas Cabernet Sauvignon 1994, Viña Tocornal	£3.90	B
"Les Capitelles" 1995, Les Vignerons des Trois Terroirs	£3.90	B
Nanya Estate Malbec/Ruby Cabernet 1995, Angoves	£3.90	S
Domaine Boyar Suhindol Cabernet Sauvignon Special Reserve 1990, Lovico Suhindol	£3.90	S
Palacio de León 1992, Viños De León	£3.90	S
Andes Peaks Cabernet Sauvignon 1994, St Emiliana	£4.00	B
Vila Regia 1993, Sogrape	£4.00	B
Torrevento Castel del Monte Rosso 1993, Azienda Agricola Torrevento	£4.00	B

Fitou Préstige de Paziols 1993, Cave de Paziols	£4.00	B
Fitou Millésime 1994, Producteurs du Mont Tauch	£4.00	B
Principato Merlot/Cabernet 1994, Ca'Vit	£4.00	B
Domaine Commanderie St Jean 1995, Château de Grezan	£4.00	S
Balbi Vineyard Malbec 1995, Allied Domecq Argentina	£4.00	B
Terra Alta Bush Vines Garnacha 1995, Tarraco Aliments	£4.00	B
Viña Mater Rovira Reserva 1989, Pedro Rovira	£4.00	B
Taburno Rosso 1994, Cantina Taburno	£4.00	B
Bodegas Lurton Malbec 1995, Jacques Lurton	£4.00	B
Oak Village Vintage Cabernet Sauvignon 1994, Vinfruco	£4.00	B
Domaine Boyar Lambol Special Reserve Cabernet Sauvignon 1990, Vinis Lambol	£4.00	S
Cosecha Rioja Viña Baroja Sin Crianza 1995, Bodegas Heredad de Baroja	£4.00	B
Merlot Piave 1995, Ricordi Ca' Vendramin Group	£4.00	B
Marienberg Cottage Classic Cabernet Sauvignon/Mourvèdre 1994, Marienberg Wine Company.	£4.00	B
Safeway Fitou 1994, Les Chais Beaucairos	£4.00	B
Safeway Casa di Giovanni Red 1994, Calatrasi	£4.00	B
H G Brown Shiraz/Ruby Cabernet Bin 60 1995, BRL Hardy Wine Company	£4.00	B
St. Michael Peñascal Castilla y Leon NV, Hijos de Antonio Barceló	£4.00	S
Señorío de Guadianeja Tempranillo Reserva 1992, Vinícola de Castilla	£4.00	B
Tesco Australian Shiraz/Cabernet Sauvignon NV, BRL Hardy Wine Company	£4.00	S
Vacqueyras Vieux Clocher 1993, Arnoux et Fils	£4.00	B
Dragón Tempranillo 1994, Bodegas Berberana	£4.10	B
Syrah "Le Midi" Vin de Pays d'Oc 1995, Les Vignerons des Trois Terroirs	£4.20	B
Orlando RF Ruby Cabernet/Shiraz 1995	£4.20	B
Co-op Australian Cabernet Sauvignon 1993, Angoves	£4.30	B
Merlot Trentino Brione 1995, Concilio	£4.30	B
Gabriel Meffre Oak Aged Côtes du Rhône 1995	£4.30	B
Sangiovese San Crispino Riva 1993, Cantine Ronco	£4.40	B
La Serre Merlot 1995	£4.40	B
Santa Carolina Merlot/ Cabernet Sauvignon 1995, Viña Santa Carolina	£4.40	S
Domaine La Tour Boisée Rouge 1994, Marie-Claude & Jean-Louis Poudou	£4.50	B
Simonsvlei Wynkelder Reserve Pinotage 1995	£4.50	B
Cape Afrika Pinotage 1993	£4.50	B
Canepa Merlot 1994, José Canepa	£4.50	B

as Campanas Crianza 1992, Vinícola Navarra	£4.50	B
Domaine de Picheral 1995, GAEC de Picheral	£4.50	B
Cape View Merlot 1995, Kym Milne at Botellary Co-op	£4.50	B
V' De Violet 1995, Emily Faussie	£4.50	B
addle Mountain Grenache 1994, Stimson Lane	£4.50	S
Orobio Rioja Reserva 1990, Bodegas Artadi	£4.50	B
anta Carolina Cabernet/Merlot 1995, Viña Santa Carolina	£4.50	B
ainsbury's Damar de Toro 1994, Fariña	£4.50	B
osé de Sousa Reguengos de Monsaraz 1992, José Maria da Fonseca Succs	£4.50	S
hâteau St Louis la Perdrix Costières de Nîmes 1993	£4.50	S
omerfield Australian Cabernet/Shiraz 1991, Penfolds (Southcorp)	£4.50	B
istalba Estate Syrah 1995, Casa Nieto Senetiner	£4.60	B
rimitivo del Salento Vino da Tavola 1994, Azienda Vinicola Cantele	£4.60	S
indemans Cawarra Shiraz/Cabernet 1995	£4.60	B
arta de Plata CVC NV, Bodegas Berberana	£4.60	B
alpolicella Classico Il Maso 1994, Casa Vinicola Zonin	£4.60	B
ellier du Bondavin Costières de Nîmes 1994	£4.60	B
ontepulciano d'Abruzzo Barone Cornacchia 1993, Azienda Agricola Baron Colnacchia	£4.60	S
arbera d'Asti Bricco Zanone 1994, Terra Vadino	£4.70	B
owlands Brook Shiraz/Cabernet 1994, Penfolds (Southcorp)	£4.70	B
almeras Estate Oak Aged Cabernet Sauvignon 1994, Viña Santa Emiliana	£4.70	B
imara Cabernet Sauvignon/Merlot 1994, Montana Wines	£4.70	B
iperouse Vin de Pays d'Oc 1995, Val d'Orbieu & Penfolds	£4.70	B
asqua Valpolicella Vigneti Casterna 1993, Pasqua	£4.80	B
omaine de La Baume Philippe de Baudin Merlot 1994, BRL Hardy Wine Company	£4.80	B
anepa Cabernet Sauvignon 1995, José Canepa	£4.80	B
hâteau La Commanderie de Queyret 1994, Claude Comin	£4.80	B
erberana Oak Aged Rioja 1994	£4.80	B
omaine de la Présidente Côtes de Rhône Villages 1995	£4.90	B
ardy's Nottage Hill Cabernet Sauvignon/Shiraz 1994, BRL Hardy Wine Company	£4.90	B
os Lenvège Futs de Chêne Cuvée a L'Ancienne 1992, Jacques Blais	£4.90	B
omaine de Thélin Syrah 1992	£4.90	B
edwood Trail Cabernet Sauvignon 1993, Sterling Vineyards	£4.90	S
ter Lehmann Vine Vale Shiraz 1994	£4.90	B
eorges Duboeuf Domaine des Moulins 1995	£5.00	B

Montepulciano d'Abruzzo Jorio 1993, Umani Ronchi	£5.00	B
South Bay Vineyards Zinfandel, California Direct	£5.00	S
Ruitervlei Estate Wine Cinsault 1995	£5.00	S
Côtes du Rhône Maitre de Chais 1995, Monbousquet Monbousquet	£5.00	B
Vignobles des Vallées Perdues Coteaux du Languedoc Montpeyroux 1995, Gabriel Meffre	£5.00	B
La Chasse du Pape Reserve 1994, Gabriel Meffre	£5.00	B
Château de Lage 1994, J Calvet	£5.00	B
Château Saint Auriol Corbières Lagrasse 1993	£5.00	B
Domaine de Fontbertière Cuvée Franck - Edward 1994	£5.00	B
Château Marmorières la Clape 1993	£5.00	B
Quinta da Lamelas 1995, Quinta da Rosa Vinhos	£5.00	S
Winelands Shiraz/Cabernet Sauvignon 1995, Kym Milne	£5.00	G
Rawson's Retreat Bin 35 Cabernet/Shiraz 1994, Penfolds (Southcorp)	£5.00	B
Zagarrón Tinto Joven 1995, Nustra Señora de Manjavacas Mota del Cuervo	£5.00	B
Canchales Vino Nuevo Elaboración Propia 1995, Bodegas Riojanas	£5.00	B
La Cotte Grand Rouge 1995, Co-op Franschhoek Vineyards	£5.00	B
Yvecourt Premium 1993, Yvon Mau	£5.00	B
Viña Valoria Rioja 1995, Bodegas Viña Valoria	£5.00	B
Breakaway Grenache Shiraz 1994, Stratmer Vineyards	£5.00	B
Château Léon Première Côtes de Bordeaux 1993, Phillippe Pieraerts	£5.00	B
St. Michael Malbec Oak Cask Reserve 1992, Bodegas Trapiche	£5.00	B
Bright Brothers Douro 1995	£5.00	G
Fiuza Cabernet Sauvignon 1994, Fuiza & Bright	£5.00	G
Tesco Spanish Merlot Reserva 1991, Raimat	£5.00	S
Crozes Hermitage Celliers de Nobles 1993, Celliers de Noblens	£5.00	G
Somerfield Oak Aged Claret NV, Peter Sichel	£5.00	B
Somerfield Médoc NV, Les Chais du Pré La Reine	£5.00	P
Montagne Noire 1995, Les Producteurs Réunis Foncalieu	£5.00	B
Château Saint James 1993, Christophe Guelio	£5.00	B
La Palma Cabernet /Merlot Reserva 1995, Viña La Rosa	£5.00	S
Fiuza Cabernet Sauvignon 1994, Fiuza & Bright	£5.00	S

Bianco del Lazio Gabbia d'Oro Vino da Tavola 1995, Cantina Gadoro	£2.70	B
Asda Muscadet Baud 1995, Baud	£3.00	B
Domaine Boyar Bulgarian Country White NV, Vinex Slaviantzi	£3.00	B
Sainsbury's do Campo White 1995, J P Vinhos	£3.00	B
Domaine Boyar Targovischte Chardonnay 1995	£3.20	B
Spar Muscat St. Jean de Minervois NV, Val d'Orbieu	£3.20	B
Vin de Pays du Jardin de la France Sauvignon Blanc 1995, Domaine Baud	£3.30	B
Viña Malea Viura 1995, Coop Antonio Abad	£3.30	B
Filipetti Extra Dry NV	£3.30	B
Santa Carolina White 1995	£3.40	B
Somerfield Moscatel de Valencia NV, Vicente Gandía	£3.40	S
Malt House Vintners Muscadet Sèvre et Maine Debreuil 1995, Edgard Debreuil	£3.60	B
Paarl Heights Colombard 1995, Boland Wynkelder	£3.60	B
Chenin Jardin de la France Ackerman 1995	£3.60	B
Winter Hill Semillon/Chardonnay 1995, Foncalieu	£3.70	B
Segesta Sicilian White 1995, Firriato	£3.70	B
Dalwood Medium Dry White 1995, Southcorp Wines	£3.70	B
Ridgemount Bay Colombard/Chardonnay 1995, Angoves	£3.70	B
Soave Classico Corte Olivi 1995, Cantine Lenotti	£3.80	B
Sauvignon Blanc Chevalier de Rodilan 1995	£3.80	B
Malt House Vintners Australian Semillon NV, Redello Wines	£3.90	B
Tesco Orvieto Classico Abboccato NV, Barbi	£3.90	S
Bidoli Sauvignon Blanc 1995	£4.00	S
Forest Flower Fruity Dry White 1995, Maison Vin	£4.00	B
Co-op English Table Wine 1993, Three Choirs Vineyards	£4.00	B
Celliers du Prieuré Muscadet de Sèvre et Maine Sur Lie 1995	£4.00	B
Andes Peak Sauvignon Blanc des Peak 1995, Santa Emiliana	£4.00	B
Kings Canyon Chardonnay 1995, Arciero Winery/Hugh Ryman	£4.00	B
Langenbach Solo 1995, Hermann Kendermann Weinkellerei	£4.00	B
Chevalier de Rodilan Chardonnay 1995	£4.00	S
Tesco New Zealand Dry White NV, Maison Vin Tesco	£4.00	S
Santa Inés Sauvignon Blanc 1996	£4.00	B
Viña Carta Vieja Sauvignon Blanc 1996	£4.00	B
Welmoed Winery Sauvignon Blanc 1995	£4.00	B
Valley Vineyards Stanlake 1994, Thames Valley Vineyard	£4.00	B
Château de Bel Air l'Esperance Mauregard 1995, Yvon Mau	£4.00	B
Santara Chardonnay 1995, Bodega Hugh Ryman/Concavins	£4.00	B
Domaine de la Tuilerie Chardonnay 1995, Hugh Ryman	£4.00	B
Nutbourne Vineyard Sussex Reserve 1995, Nutbourne Manor	£4.00	B
Cantina Tollo Bianco NV	£4.00	B

Safeway Bordeux Blanc (Sec) Oak Aged 1995, Caves Union Prodiffin Ian Derrouat	£4.00	B
Monty's Hill Victoria Chardonnay/Colombard 1995	£4.00	B
St. Michael Casa Leona Chardonnay 1995, Viña Peumo	£4.00	B
Erben Kabinett 1994, Franz Wilheim Langguth Erben	£4.00	B
Tesco Domaine Saubagnere 1994, Grassa	£4.00	B
Andes Peaks Casablanca Chardonnay 1995, Vina St Emiliana	£4.10	S
Long Mountain Chardonnay 1995	£4.20	B
Muscat St Jean de Minervois Petit Grains, Les Vignerons de Septimanie	£4.20	B
Kirchheimer Schwarzerde Beerenauslese NV, Zimmermann Graeff	£4.30	S
Hardy's Stamps of Australia Semillon/Chardonnay 1995, BRL Hardy Wine Company	£4.30	B
Timara Dry White 1995, Montana Wines	£4.30	B
Castillo de Liria Moscatel NV, Vicente Gandía Plá	£4.30	B
Somerfield Gewürztraminer Halbtrocken 1993, Coop Rietburg	£4.30	B
Château la Perriere 1995, Francois Fargueyret	£4.30	B
Le Trulle Chardonnay del Salento 1994, Azienda Vinicola Cantele Kym Milne	£4.40	B
KWV Chenin Blanc 1995	£4.40	B
Santa Carolina Chardonnay 1995	£4.40	B
Caliterra Chardonnay 1995	£4.50	B
Domaine La Baume Philippe de Baudin Sauvignon Blanc 1995, BRL Hardy Wine Company	£4.50	S
Rowan Brook Oak Aged Chilean Chardonnay Reserve 1995, José Canepa y Cia	£4.50	B
Château de la Botiniere Muscadet de Sèvre et Maine Sur Lie 1995, Jean Beauquin	£4.50	B
Penfolds Val d'Orbieu Laperouse 1995, Penfolds (Southcorp)	£4.50	B
Schloss Lieserer Schlossberg Riesling Spätlese 1989, Schloss Lieser	£4.50	B
Malt House Vintners Pinot Grigio 1995, Bidoli	£4.60	B
KWV Sauvignon Blanc 1995	£4.60	B
Bruisyard St Peter Medium Dry 1994	£4.60	B
Bruisyard St Peter Medium Sweet 1994	£4.60	B
Longridge Bay View Chenin Blanc 1995	£4.70	B
Chilean Chardonnay 1995, V M Limited	£4.70	B
Fairview Chenin Blanc 1995, Charles Back	£4.70	B
Palacio de Bornos Rueda 1995, Bodegas de Crianza Castilla la Vieja	£4.70	B
Waterside White 1995, Graham Beck Wines	£4.70	B
Domaine Bassac Sauvignon 1995, Louis Dechon	£4.70	B
Angove's Chardonnay Classic Reserve 1995, Angoves	£4.70	B

Bidoli Pinot Grigio Ca Pradai 1995	£4.80	B
Philippe de Baudin Chardonnay 1994,		
BRL Hardy Domaine la Baume	£4.80	B
La Baume Chais Baumière Chardonnay 1994,		
BRL Hardy Wine Company	£4.80	B
Vigneto Caramia Chardonnay del Salento 1995, Cantele	£4.80	S
Nobilo White Cloud 1995, House of Nobilo	£4.80	B
West Peak Sauvignon Blanc 1995, Nooitgedacht Cellars	£4.90	B
Etchart Chardonnay 1995, Arrnaldo Etchart	£4.90	B
August Sebastiani Chadonnay 1994	£4.90	B
Carr Taylor Schönburger Dry NV	£4.90	B
Domaine de Rivoyre Barrel Fermented Chardonnay 1994,		
Hugh Ryman	£4.90	B
Agramont Blanco Navarra Viura Chardonnay 1995,		
Bodegas Príncipe de Viana	£4.90	B
Chardonnay Ranch Series 1995, H Suter	£5.00	S
Cartlidge & Browne Chardonnay 1995	£5.00	S
Galet Vineyards Sauvignon Blanc 1995, Gabriel Meffre	£5.00	B
Monchhof Erdener Treppchen Riesling 1991, Robert Eymael	£5.00	B
Tollana Oak Matured Chardonnay 1993	£5.00	B
Greco di Puglia 1995, A.Cantele & Kym Milne	£5.00	B
Copperidge Chardonnay NV, Ernest & Julio Gallo	£5.00	B
La Cotte Chenin Blanc 1995, CO-OP Franschhoek Vineyards	£5.00	B
Tenterden Estate Dry NV,	£5.00	B
Chapel Hill Barrique Fermented Chardonnay 1994,		
Balatonboglar Winery	£5.00	B
Kings Canyon Black Label Chardonnay 1995,		
Hugh Ryman/Arciero Winery	£5.00	B
Domaine du Fief Guerin Muscadet Sur Lie 1995	£5.00	B
Castillo de Molina Sauvignon Blanc 1995, Viña San Pedro	£5.00	B
Lavis Chardonnay 1995, Lavis	£5.00	B
Domaine de la Jalousie Cuvée Bois 1993, Yves Grassa	£5.00	B
Domaine de la Jalousie Late Harvest 1993, Yves Grassa	£5.00	B
Aschratt Hochemier Hölle Riesling Kabinett 1995,		
GRH Rat Aschratt	£5.00	B
Shawsgate Müller Thurgau/Seyval Blanc Medium Dry 1993	£5.00	B
Laroche Grand Cuvée Chardonnay, 1995	£5.00	S
Montagne Noire Chardonnay 1995, Les Producteurs		
Réunis Foncalieu	£5.00	B

Oldacres Sauvignon Spritzer NV, Oldacres & Three Choirs Vineyard	£2.00	B
St. Michael Cava Brut NV, Sevisa	£5.00	B
Tesco Cava Brut Traditional NV, Sant Sadurní d'Anoia	£5.00	S
Deinhard Yello Chardonnay/Riesling NV	£5.90	S
Seaview Brut NV, Seaview Wines	£6.00	B
Chapel Down Century Extra Dry NV, Chapel Wines	£6.50	B
Clairette de Die NV, Cave Cooperative de Die	£6.70	B
Cuveé Krone Borealis Brut 1992, Twee Jonge Gezellen	£7.00	B
St. Michael Bluff Hill New Zealand Brut Sparkling NV, Montana Wines	£7.00	B
Graham Beck Madeba Brut NV, Madeba	£7.30	G
Montserrat Cava Selección Especial NV, Conuisa Sant Sadurní d'Anoia	£7.40	B
Seaview Pinot Noir/Chardonnay 1993, Seaview Wines	£7.90	S
Hardy's Sparkling NV, BRL Hardy Wine Company	£8.00	E
Redbank Cuvée Emily Brut NV	£8.00	B
Charles Duret Blanc de Blanc Chardonnay NV	£8.00	P
Selfridges Vintage Cava 1993, Sevisa	£8.00	S
Domaine de Lamoure Crémant de Limoux 1992, Domaine Martinolles	£8.50	E
Cuvée Two Sparkling Cabernet Sauvignon NV, Yalumba	£8.50	S
Cuvée One Pinot Noir/Chardonnay NV, Yalumba	£8.70	E
Seppelt Sparkling Shiraz 1992, B Seppelt & Sons Ltd	£8.80	S
Bouvet-Ladubay Saumur Rubis Rouge NV	£9.10	E
Bouvet-Ladubay Trésor Brut NV	£10.00	E

CHAMPAGNE £15 AND UNDER

Champagne Richard Lourmel Brut NV, Centre Vinicole de la Champagne	£9.00	B
Champagne Laytons Brut NV, F. Bonnet	£11.50	B
Tesco Champagne Blanc de Noirs Brut NV, J C International	£11.80	B
Asda Champagne Brut NV, Centre Vinicole de la Champagne	£12.00	B
Champagne Brossault NV, Ferdinand Bonnet	£12.70	B
Champagne André Simon Rosé NV, Co-op de Bethon	£14.00	S
Waitrose Champagne Blanc de Blancs NV, F Bonnet	£14.00	S
Champagne H. Blin Cuvée Tradition Brut NV	£14.00	B
Champagne F Bonnet Brut Heritage NV	£14.00	B
Champagne Brossault NV, Ferdinand Bonnet	£14.10	B
Champagne Le Mesnil Blanc de Bancs Brut NV, L'Union des Propriétaires Récoltants	£14.20	B
Champagne Louis Boyier & Cie Brut NV, El Vino	£14.90	B
Champagne le Brun de Neuville Blanc de Blancs Brut NV	£15.00	S
Champagne Ariston Brut NV	£15.00	S
Champagne de Nauroy Black Label Brut NV	£15.00	B
Champagne Princesse de France Grande Réserve Brut NV, Ferdinand Bonnet	£15.00	S
Champagne Albert Etienne Vintage Brut 1990, Marne & Champagne Diffusion	£15.00	B
Champagne Patrick Arnould Grand Cru Réserve NV	£15.00	S
Prince William Champagne Rosé NV, Henri Mandois	£15.00	B
Champagne de Nauroy Cuvée Speciale Millennium NV	£15.00	S

Every wine in this guide has at least one stockist code beside its entry, identifying where the wine can be sourced. The list below translates the code into the company name, with a telephone number for you to make enquiries direct.

Where the stockists are stated as WIDELY AVAILABLE there are more than 10 outlets who stock this wine. In these cases you should be able to find your wine in most good wine retailers.

Every effort has been made to list all the stockists with their relevant wines. Should you encounter any problems with finding a wine listed in this guide, then please write to: The International WINE Challenge, Publishing House, 652 Victoria Road, South Ruislip, Middlesex, HA4 0SX.

3D	3-D Wines	01205 820745
A	Asda	0113 2435435
A&A	A & A Wines	01483 274666
A&N	Army & Navy	0171 8341234
ABB	Abbey Cellars	01460 62546
ABY	Anthony Byrne Fine Wines	01487 814555
ACH	Andrew Chapman	01235 550707
AD	Andrew Darwin	01544 230534
ADD	Allied Domecq Spirits & Wine	0117 9785216
ADN	Adnams	01502 727222
AK	Arriba Kettle	01386 833024
ALD	Allders International	01703 644599
ALE	Alexander Wines	0141 8820039
ALI	Alivini Company Ltd	0181 8802525
ALL	Alliance Wine Company Ltd	01505 506060
ALZ	Allez Vins!	01423 771868
AMA	Amathus	0181 8863787
AMW	Amey's Wines	01787 377144
AP	Arthur Purchase	01243 783144
AR	Arthur Rackham	01932 351585
AS	André Simon	0171 3885080
AUC	Australian Wine Centre	01753 594925
AUS	Australian Estates	01438 820955
AV	Averys of Bristol	01275 811100
AWS	Albion Wine Shippers	0171 2420873
B&B	Bottle & Basket	0181 3417018
BAB	Bablake Wines	01203 228272
BAK	Barkham Manor Vineyard	01825 722103
BAL	Ballantynes of Cowbridge	01446 774840
BBR	Berry Bros & Rudd Ltd	0171 3969600
BBU	Bruce Burlington	01268 562224
BBV	Breaky Bottom Vineyard	01273 476427
BC	Booker C & C	01933 440404
BCL	Best Cellars	01364 652546
BD	Bordeaux Direct	0118 9481718
BEC	Beaconsfield Wine Cellars	01494 675545
BEL	Bentalls	0181 5461001
BEN	Bennetts	01386 840392
BES	Bestway C & C	0181 4531234
BH	B H Wines	01228 576711
BI	Bibendum Wine Ltd	0171 7225577
BKT	Bucktrout	01481 724444

BKW	Berkeley Wines (Cheshire)	01925 444555
BLN	G Belloni & Company	0171 7048812
BLS	Balls Bros	0171 7396466
BLV	Bacchus Les Vignobles	0171 4044640
BNK	Bottleneck (Broadstairs)	01843 861095
BOD	Bodegas Direct	01243 773474
BOL	Bacchus of Olney	01234 711140
BOO	Booths of Stockport	0161 4323309
BRB	Brown Bros	01628 776446
BRP	Brompton Wines	0171 5842060
BRU	Bruisyard Vineyard	01728 638281
BSD	Boisdale Wines	0171 7300548
BTH	Booths of Preston	01772 251701
BU	Bottoms Up	01707 328244
BUD	Budgens	0181 4229511
BUT	The Butlers Wine Cellar	01273 698724
BUY	Buy the Case	01622 672622
BWC	Berkmann Winecellars	0171 6094711
BWI	Bute Wines	0171 3610061
C&B	Corney & Barrow	0171 2514051
C&H	Cairns & Hickey	0113 2673746
CAP	Cape Province Wines	01784 451860
CAR	C A Rookes	01789 297777
CAT	Cantino Augusto	0171 2423246
CAX	Cason Tower	0181 7584500
CC	Chiswick Cellars	0181 9947989
CDE	Cote d'Or	0181 9980144
CDO	Chapel Down	01580 763033
CEB	Croque-en-Bouche	01684 565612
CEL	Cellar 5	01925 444555
CEN	Centurion Vintners	01453 763223
CES	Cellar Select Limited/Winefinds	01225 852711
CF	Perfect Partners	01580 712633
CFT	The Clifton Cellars	0117 9730287
CHF	Chippendale Fine Wines	01943 850633
CHH	Chas Hennings	01798 872485
CHL	Chateau Lascombes	01283 512777
CHV	Champagne de Venoge	0171 2338717
CKB	Cockburn & Campbell	0181 8757008
CLA	Classic Wines and Spirits Ltd	01244 288444
CM	Chateau Musar UK Ltd	0181 9418311
CMI	Charles Mitchell Wines Ltd	0161 7751626
CNL	Connolly's	0121 2369269
COC	Corks of Cotham	0117 9731620
COK	Corkscrew Wines	01228 43033
COR	Corn Road Vintners	01669 20240
COT	Cotswold Wine Company	01242 678880
CPW	Christopher Piper Wines	01404 814139
CRM	Craven's Wine Merchants	0171 7230252
CRS	Cooperative Retail Services	0161 8328152
CT	Montrachet Wine Merchants	01372 728330
CTH	Charterhouse Wine Co	01775 630680
CTL	Continental Wine & Food	01484 538333
CTV	Carr Taylor Vineyards	01424 752501
CVR	Celtic Vintner	01633 430055
CVY	Chanctonbury Vineyard	01903 892721
CWI	Case of Wine	01558 650671
CWL	Charles Wells	01234 272766
CWS	Co-op	0161 8275925
CWW	Classic Wine Warehouses	01244 288444
D	Davisons	0181 6813222
DAV	Dartmouth Vintners	01803 832602
DB	Davis Browning	0171 4081438
DBO	Domaine Boyar	0171 5393707
DBS	Denbies Wine Estate	01306 876616
DBY	D Byrne & Co	01200 23152
DIO	Dionysus	0181 8742739
DIR	Direct Wine Shipments	01232 238700
DVY	Davy & Co Ltd	0171 4079670
DWS	Freixnet (DWS) Limited	01707 265532

E&J	E & J Gallo	01895 813444
EBA	Ben Ellis Wines	01737 842160
ECA	Edward Cavendish & Sons	
		01794 516102
ELV	El Vino	0171 3535384
ENO	Enotria Winecellars	0181 9614411
EOR	Ellis of Richmond	0181 9434033
EP	Eldridge Pope	01305 251251
ES	Edward Sheldon	01608 661409
ETD	Eastenders	00 33 21345333
ETV	Eton Vintners	01753 790188
EUR	Europa	0181 8451255
EVI	Evingtons	0116 2542702
EWC	English Wine Centre	01323 870164
F&M	Fortnum & Mason	0171 7348040
FDL	Findlater Mackie Todd	0181 5430966
FEN	Fenwick	0191 2325100
FNZ	Fine Wines of New Zealand	
		0171 4820093
FRN	Frenmart	01384 892941
FS	Francis Stickney Agencies	0181 2019096
FSW	Frank Stainton Wines	01539 731886
FTH	Forth Wine	01577 863668
FUL	Fuller's	0181 9962000
G&G	Godwin & Godwin	01225 337081
G&M	Gordon & Macphail	01343 545111
GAR	Garland Wine Cellar	01372 275247
GC	Graingers Ltd.	0114 2730235
GDS	Garrards Wine Merchants	
		01900 823592
GGW	The Great Gaddesden Wine Co Ltd	
		01582 840002
GHL	George Hill of Loughborough	
		01509 21277
GI	Grape Ideas	01865 722137
GLY	Gallery Wines	01504 48762
GNW	Great Northern Wine Co	0113 2461200
GON	Gauntleys	0115 9417973
GRI	Griersons	0181 4518880
GRO	Grog Blossom	0171 7947808

GRT	Great Western Wine	01225 446009
GS	Gerald Seel	01925 819695
GSH	Grape Shop (London)	0171 9243638
GWC	Greek Wine Centre	01743 364636
GWI	General Wine Company	01428 722201
GWW	George Ward Wines	01737 44599
H&D	Hicks & Don	01258 456040
H&H	Hector & Honorez	01480 411599
HAE	Halewood Vintners	0151 4808800
HAL	Hall & Batson	01603 415115
HAM	Hampden Wine Co	01844 201641
HAR	Harrods	0171 7301234
HAW	The Hantone Wine Company	
		0171 9785920
HAY	Hayward Bros	0171 2370576
HBJ	Heyman Barwell Jones	01473 232322
HCK	Pierre Henck Wines	01902 751022
HD	Hollywood & Donnelly	01232 799335
HHC	Haynes Hanson & Clarke	0171 2590102
HN	Harvey Nichols	0171 2355000
HOL	Holland Park Wine Co	0171 2219614
HOT	House of Townend	01482 326891
HOU	Hoults Wine Merchants	01484 510700
HV	Harveys of Bristol	0117 9275000
HVW	Helen Verdcourt	01628 25577
IIW	Hedley Wright	01279 506512
HWL	Howells of Bristol	01454 294085
HWM	Harvest Wine Group	0118 9344290
HWW	High Weald Winery	01622 850637
IRV	Irvine Robertson	0131 5533521
ISW	Isis Wines	01628 771199
IT	Italvini	01494 680857
IVY	Ivy Wines	01243 377883
J&B	Justerini & Brooks	0171 4938721
JAG	J A Glass	01592 651850
JAK	James Aitken & Son	01382 221197
JAR	John Armit Wines	0171 7276846
JAV	John Arkell Vintners	01193 823026
JBR	J B Reynier	0171 4810415
JCB	J C Broadbent	01534 23356

JCK	J C Karn	01242 513265	
JEH	J E Hogg	0131 5564025	
JFR	John Frazier	0121 7043415	
JHL	J H Logan	0131 6672855	
JMC	James E McCabe	01762 333102	
JN	James Nicholson Wine Merchant		
		01396 830091	
JOB	Jeroboams	0171 8235623	
JS	J Sainsbury Plc	0171 9217664	
JSS	John Stephenson & Sons	01282 698827	
JUS	Just-in-Case	01489 892969	
K&B	King & Barnes Ltd	01403 270470	
KWI	Kwik Save Stores Ltd	01745 887111	
L&S	Laymont & Shaw Ltd	01872 70545	
L&W	Lay & Wheeler Ltd	01206 764446	
LAU	Lauriston Wines	01372 459270	
LAY	Laytons Wine Merchants Ltd		
		0171 3884567	
LCC	Landmark Cash and Carry		
		0181 8635511	
LEA	Lea & Sandeman	0171 3764767	
LNR	Le Nez Rouge	0171 6094711	
LOH	Larners of Holt	01263 712323	
LTW	Littlewoods Organisation	0151 2352222	
LU	Luigi's Deli	0171 3527739	
LUC	Luckins Wines	01371 872839	
LV	La Vigneronne	0171 5896113	
LWE	London Wine Emporium	0171 5871302	
LWL	London Wine Ltd	0171 5871302	
M&S	Marks & Spencer	0171 2683855	
M&V	Morris & Verdin	0171 3578866	
MAR	Marco's Wines	0181 8714944	
MD	Michael Druitt Agencies	0171 4039191	
MFS	Martinez Fine Wines	01943 603241	
MFW	Marcus Fyfe Wines	01546 603646	
MGN	Michael Morgan	0171 4073466	
MHV	Malt House Vintners	01933 371032	
MHW	Mill Hill Wines	01482 29443	
MIS	Mistral Wines	0171 2625437	
MK	McKinley Vintners	0171 9287300	
MM	Michael Menzel Wines	0114 268557	
MON	Mondial Wines	0181 3353455	
MOR	Moreno Wine Importers	0171 2860678	
MRF	Mark Reynier Fine Wines	0171 9785601	
MRN	Morrison Supermarkets	01274 494166	
MRS	Morrisons	01924 870000	
MTC	Manningtree Wine Cellar	01206 395095	
MTL	Mitchells Wine Merchants	0114 2745587	
MTR	Montrachet	0171 9281990	
MVN	Merchant Vintners	01482 329443	
MWW	Majestic Wine Warehouses		
		01923 816999	
MYS	Mayor Sworder	0171 7350385	
NAD	Nadder Wine Co	01722 325418	
NBV	Nutbourne Vineyard	0171 6573800	
NEI	R & I Neish	01779 472721	
NET	Nethergate Wines	01787 277244	
NG	The South African Wine Centre		
		0171 2241994	
NI	The Nobody Inn	01647 252395	
NIC	Nicolas U.K. LTD	0171 4369338	
NRM	Norman's Limited	01772 51701	
NRW	Noble Rot Wine Warehouse		
		01527 575606	
NSV	Northbrook Springs Vineyard		
		01489 892659	
NUM	Vinum	01234 343202	
NUR	Nurdin & Peacock	0181 9711638	
NY	Noel Young Wines	01223 844744	
OD	Oddbins	0181 9444400	
OSW	Old School Wines	01886 821613	
P	Parfrements	01203 503646	
P&R	Peckham & Rye	0141 3344312	
PAL	Pallant Wines	01903 882288	
PAT	Patriarche UK Ltd	0171 3814016	
PAV	Pavilion Wine & Co	0171 6288224	
PEA	Peake Wine Assocs	0171 7335657	
PEY	Phillip Eyres Wine Merchant		
		01494 433823	
PF	Percy Fox	01279 626801	

PHI	Philglas & Swiggot	0171 9244494
PHP	Phil Parrish	01377 252373
PIM	Pimlico Dozen	0171 8343647
PLA	Playford Ros Ltd	01845 526777
PLE	Peter Lehmann Wines (UK) Limited	01227 731353
PON	Le Pont de la Tour	0171 4032403
POR	Portland Wine Company (Manchester)	0161 9628752
PRG	Paragon Vintners	0171 8871800
PST	Penistone Court Wine Cellars	01226 766037
PTR	Peter Green	0131 2295925
PV	Prestige Vintners	01264 335586
PWW	Peter Watts Wines	01376 561130
PWY	Peter Wylie Fine Wines	01884 7555
QR	Quellyn Roberts Wine Merchants	01244 310455
R	R S Wines	0117 9631780
RAC	Rackham's Dept Store	0121 2363333
RAE	Raeburn Fine Wine & Foods	0131 3431159
RAV	Ravensbourne Wine	0181 6929655
RBS	Roberson Wine Merchants	0171 3712121
RD	Reid Wines	01761 452645
REM	Remy & Associates	01753 752600
RES	La Reserve	0171 5892020
REW	La Reserva Wines	0171 9785601
RIC	Richard Granger	0191 2815000
RID	Ridgeway Wines	01227 265015
ROB	T M Robertson	0131 2294522
ROD	Rodney Densem	01270 623665
ROS	Rosemount Estate Wines	01483 211466
RTW	The Rose Tree Wine Company	01242 583732
RVA	Randalls (Jersey)	01534 873541
RW	Richards Walford	01780 460451
RWL	Richmonde Wines Ltd	01562 822777
RYW	Rystone Wines	01455 559389

S&D	Saltmarsh & Druce	01993 703721
SAC	Le Sac a Vin	0171 3816930
SAF	Safeway Stores plc	0181 7562248
SAN	Sandiway Wine Co	01606 882101
SAS	Sherston St. Albans Wine Company	01727 858841
SCA	Scatchard	0151 2366468
SEA	Seagram UK Limited	0171 2001801
SEB	Sebastopol Wines	01235 850471
SEL	Selfridges	0171 3183730
SHA	Shawsgate Vineyard	01728 723232
SHG	Wine Shop on the Green	01437 766864
SHJ	S H Jones	01295 251179
SIP	Peter A Sichel	01580 715341
SKW	Stokes Fine Wines Ltd (London)	0171 5829265
SLM	Salamis Wine Merchants	0171 6091133
SMF	Somerfield	0117 9357357
SNO	Snowdonia Wine Warehouse	01492 870567
SNW	Sandiway Company	01606 882101
SOB	Stones of Belgravia	0171 2351612
SOM	Sommelier Wine Co	01481 721677
SPR	Spar Landmark Ltd	0181 8635511
SSM	Stewarts Supermarkets	01232 704434
ST	Styria Wine	0181 2960770
STB	Stokes Bros (Folkestone)	01303 252178
STW	Stewarts Wine Barrels	01232 704434
SV	Smedley Vintners	01462 768214
SWS	Stratford's Wine Shippers	01628 810606
T&W	T & W Wines	01842 765646
TAN	Tanners of Shrewsbury	01743 232007
TCW	T C Wines	0151 9313390
TDS	Thresher Drink Stores	01707 328244
TEL	Teltscher Bros Limited	01703 312000
TH	Thresher	01707 328244
THP	Thos Peatling	01284 755948
THR	Throwley Vineyard	01795 890276
THV	Thwaites Vintners	01254 54431

TLC	Tony Lamont Consulting/ Valdivieso UK	01494 678971
TO	Tesco	01992 632222
TOU	Toucan Wines	01232 790909
TP	Terry Platt Wines	01492 592971
TPA	Thomas Panton	01666 503088
TPW	Topsham Wines	01392 874501
TRO	Trout Wines	01264 781472
TRV	Transit Vin Limited	0181 6746344
TV	Tenterden Vineyard	01580 763033
TVV	Thames Valley Vineyard	01734 340176
TW	Thames Wine Sellers	0171 9288253
TWB	The Wine Bank	01892 891122
U	Unwins	01322 294469
UNC	Uncorked	0171 6385998
V&C	Valvona & Crolla	0131 5566066
VAU	Vaux Breweries	0191 5676277
VDV	Vin du Van Wine Merchants	01233 83727
VER	Vinceremos Wines	0113 257545
VEX	Vinexports	01886 812510
VHW	Victor Hugo Wines	01534 32225
VIL	Village Wines	01322 558772
VLW	Villeneuve Wines	01721 722500
VNO	Vinoceros	01209 314711
VR	Vintage Roots	01734 401222
VW	Victoria Wine	01483 715066
VWC	Victoria Wine Cellars	01483 715066
W	Waitrose	01344 424680
WAC	Waters of Coventry Ltd	01926 887416
WAV	Waverley Vintners	01738 629621
WAW	Waterloo Wine Co	0171 4037967
WCR	Wine Cellar (Greenalls)	01925 444555
WDI	Wine Direct Limited	01932 820490
WEP	Welshpool Wine Company	01938 553243
WER	Wine Cellar (Douglas)	01624 611793
WES	Wessex Wines	01308 427177
WF	Wine Finds	01584 875582
WFB	Mildara Blass (UK) Ltd	0181 9474312
WGW	Woodgate Wines	01229 85637
WH	Wine House	0181 6696661
WIC	Jolly's Drinks	01237 473292
WIL	Willoughby's of Manchester	0161 8346850
WIM	Wimbledon Wine Cellar	0181 5409979
WIN	The Winery	0171 2866475
WKV	Wyken Vineyard	01359 251173
WMK	Winemark	01232 746274
WNC	Winchcombe Wines	01242 604313
WNS	Winos	0161 6529396
WOC	Whitesides of Clitheroe	01200 22281
WOI	Wines of Interest	01473 215752
WON	Weavers of Nottingham	0115 9580922
WOW	Weavers of Westhorpe	01283 820285
WR	Wine Rack	01707 328244
WRT	Winerite	0113 2837654
WRW	Wright Wine Co	01756 700886
WSC	The Wine Schoppen	0114 2553301
WSG	Walter Siegel	01256 701101
WSO	Wine Society IEC	01438 741177
WST	Western Wines	01746 789411
WTL	Whittalls Wines	01922 36161
WTR	Wine Treasury	0171 7939999
WTS	T B Watson (Dumfries)	01387 720505
WWG	Wingara Wine Group	0181 5428101
WWI	Woodhouse Wines	01258 452141
WWT	Whitebridge Wines	01785 817229
YAP	Yapp Bros	01747 860423
YOB	Young & Co	0181 8757007

INDEX

INDEX

INDEX

INDEX

INDEX

INDEX

INDEX

ACKNOWLEDGEMENTS

Putting this guide together was not entirely dissimilar to the task of extracting a pearl from an oyster without the aid of scuba gear. Despite the immense amount of work that goes in, the end result is relatively small – though beautiful – and there is a very definite time limit. We would like to thank the team behind this book for their hard work, time, effort and dedication, and hope that some of them are able to resume a normal social life soon. By name they are;

• **for their proof reading** – Mark Manson of The Australian Wine Club, Luciana Lynch, Donald Mason of Wines from Spain, Luciann Flynn of Catherine Scott PR, Jordanis Petridis of the Greek Wine Centre, Margaret Harvey MW of Fine Wines of New Zealand, Victoria Williams of Wines of Chile, Justin Howard-Sneyd, Chris Hardy of Majestic Wine and Susy Atkins.

• **from the International WINE Challenge** – to the whole team for pulling together under immense pressure and particularly to the computer-tappers and hand-writing decipherers – hopefully the experience has not put them off wine for life. We are also grateful for the help, advice and support of all the tasters who participated in the Challenge, unfortunately too numerous to name here.

• **from WINE magazine** – Marcin Miller, Robert Joseph, Charles Metcalfe, Damian Riley-Smith, Paul Flint, Richard Davies, Alan Scott, Rebecca Hopkins and Sarah Chapple.

• **for subbing and database management** – Jamie Ambrose, Mary Lewens, Anthony Evans-Pughe, Peter Makin of Makin Rochard and particular thanks to Tor Brook and Manny Lewin for working so hard, so long.

Finally, special thanks to **editor** Chris Mitchell and **designer** Frances Kiernan for their dedication, energy and sheer hard work – and for smiling when many would have cried.

HOW YOU CAN HELP US

If you have any ideas about how we can improve the format of the
WINE Magazine Pocket Wine Buyer's Guide then please write to us at
652 Victoria Road, South Ruislip, Middlesex, HA4 0SX.

The type of subjects we would particularly like to hear about are:
• **Do you prefer to have countries sub-divided by region or grape variety?**
• **Do you find the £5 and Under guides useful?**
• **Would food and wine pairing suggestions be useful?**
• **How else might you like to see the wines sorted or divided?**
• **What other information regarding wines and stockists would be of interest?**
• **Would you prefer the Guide to be ring-bound or loose leafed?**